THE NARROW ROAD

Finding Christ in an Uncertain World

Jolene McCall

The Narrow Road
Finding Christ in an Uncertain World
Finding Christ in an Uncertain World
Copyright © 2020 by Hori-Son Press

All rights reserved. No portion of this book may be reproduced, stored in a retrieval system, or transmitted in any form or by any means electronic, mechanical photocopy, recording, or any other except for brief quotations in printed reviews, without the prior permission of the Publisher or Copyright Owner.

Cover Design by Lynn H. Pellerin
Cover Photo by Kristin Hawkins

ISBN 978-1-938186-07-3

SAN 920-251X

Throughout this book, the name satan has deliberately not been capitalized. To capitalize a name would be proper grammar, and it also shows respect to that person. Since, I have no respect for satan or any demonic force of that nature, I choose to be grammatically incorrect and refrain from capitalizing his name.

"Scripture taken from the NEW AMERICAN STANDARD BIBLE®, Copyright © 1960, 1962, 1963, 1971, 1972, 1973, 1975, 1977, 1995 by The Lockman Foundation. Used by permission."

Scripture taken from the HOLY BIBLE, NEW INTERNATIONAL VERSION®. Copyright © 1973, 1978, 1984 Biblical. Used by permission of Zondervan. All rights reserved.

"Scripture taken from the New King James Version. Copyright © 1982 by Thomas Nelson, Inc. Used by permission. All rights reserved."

"Scripture quotations taken from the Amplified® Bible, Copyright © 1954, 1958, 1962, 1964, 1965, 1987 by The Lockman Foundation. Used by permission." (www.Lockman.org)

"Scripture quotations marked (ESV) are from The Holy Bible, English Standard Version® (ESV®), copyright © 2001 by Crossway, a publishing ministry of Good News Publishers. Used by permission. All rights reserved."

Scripture quotations from THE MESSAGE. Copyright © by Eugene H. Peterson 1993, 1994, 1995, 1996, 2000, 2001, 2002. Used by permission of NavPress. All rights reserved. Represented by Tyndale House Publishers, Inc.

Scripture quotations are taken from the Holy Bible, New Living Translation, copyright ©1996, 2004, 2007, 2013, 2015 by Tyndale House Foundation. Used by permission of Tyndale House Publishers, Inc., Carol Stream, Illinois 60188. All rights reserved.

Scriptures marked HCSB are taken from the HOLMAN CHRISTIAN STANDARD BIBLE (HCSB): Scripture taken from the HOLMAN CHRISTIAN STANDARD BIBLE, copyright© 1999, 2000, 2002, 2003 by Holman Bible Publishers, Nashville Tennessee. All rights reserved.

Public domain Bibles may be used freely, without restriction and without prior permission. The following Bibles in the English section of BibleGateway.com are in the public domain and can be used freely without restriction or prior permission from us or anyone else:

King James Version (Crown copyright/Public Domain in the United States)

American Standard Version (No copyright information is available)

New Life Version (No copyright information is available)

Weymouth New Testament Scripture quotations marked Weymouth are from the Weymouth New Testament, Richard Francis Weymouth, 1912. Public domain in the United States.

ACKNOWLEDGEMENTS

To my Heavenly Father,

I pray these words within this book do not fall on deaf ears but that those who have ears can hear! Often times, we read but we only see what is at the very surface. It shall never be about reading but about how one reads. How sad for the soul that cannot fathom the depths of the Word of God. It is poetry to our ears and opens our soul through our eyes when we are able to gain the perspective of those fortunate disciples who were the first to witness the marvelous words and works of our Lord and Savior, Jesus Christ.

Lord, these are not just words on a sheet of paper which mean absolutely nothing to the soul, but they bring life when we are willing to allow Your Spirit a glimpse within our own soul to awaken us from eternal damnation.

Your Words and Your Life have become the meaning to my existence, for without You and Your unconditional love, where would I be? This world has become a place of mere existence as the inhabitants busy themselves about acquiring what pleasures and luxuries to form a creature that has no depth only a mere body with a dark soul. Your Words bring all to a place of awareness when we dare to look deep within where we are able to feel your presence, not from a fleshly perspective but from faith that coincides with the heart that has known You—the Creator of all things. For it is within You that we find that which is good rather than evil. Within each of us are desires and that we should pray diligently for our desires to be the very existence of You—our Shepherd.

Keep me close as you speak to the depths of my heart that I continue on the pathway You designed specifically for me. An unknown pathway, as I trust you day to day for your mercy and grace upon my life and those that you lead across my path where I would from within the depths of my heart share You always!

Dedication

This book is dedicated to my son-in-law, Kevin Hawkins. We often hear of negative relationships between the mother-in-law and son-in-law. I'm so very thankful that my relationship with my son-in-law is not distasteful but rather quite informative, as we have spent many times sharing in the things which God has enlightened within our lives.

My son-in-law is the man of God which is the watchman over my daughter and my beautiful grandchildren. He may not have always been the man of God that he is today, as most of us have fallen short many times in our own lives. However, I am proud to acknowledge him as a great man of God, a wonderful husband to my daughter and magnificent father to my grandchildren.

I have witnessed him as a broken man from the loss of his mother way too soon, but I have also watched as God transformed him into the man his mother would have been so proud of today. I am fortunate as his mother-in-law to witness his worth. Even though, I never had the privilege to know his mother, I already know how great a mother she was because it is seen within the son she and her husband raised.

I thank you Lord for him and pray always that your hands will be upon his life, as he leads his family through the good times and that they remain close through the hard times. I thank you Lord that he is a rock and that you build your church upon his name and that the gates of hades will never bring his family down.

I pray for your Love Father to engulf him always that he is there for his wife first and foremost and then for his children—teaching them Your ways and training them to be strong and confident in Your Truth, Oh Lord, as he always loves them through You. Your love Lord, which is perfect love, casts out all fear!

Table of Contents

Acknowledgement i
Dedication iii
Introduction vii
1 The Journey 1
2 The Wilderness Road 11
3 The Voice Less Followed 23
4 The Voice of Evil 39
5 Visionary Leaders 61
6 The Con-Artist 81
7 Gatekeepers 113
8 Two Pathways ~ Two Choices 137
9 Cold ~ Lukewarm ~ Hot 173
10 Storing Treasures on Earth 209
11 The Crooked Road 223
12 Crossing Over 263
13 Living Outside of Christ 273
14 Let His Church Arise 305
15 The Reflection of Your Life 343
Conclusion 355
References 359

INTRODUCTION

Let those who have eyes to see, see what You see Lord; let those who have ears to hear, hear Your voice Lord.

Matthew 13:15 (ESV) For this people's heart has grown dull, and with their ears they can barely hear, and their eyes they have closed, lest they should see with their eyes and hear with their ears and understand with their heart and turn, and I would heal them.

As we draw closer to Him, He will draw closer to us. Have you ever prayed, *"Lord, let me see what others are not seeing; let me know you to a degree that others do not perceive; let me know Truth today like there is no tomorrow."* If you are not praying something similar to this, I would encourage you to do so. Hopefully, you have chosen to read this book because you have felt that there is something missing in what we call the church today. Hopefully, your desires have become more to really know truth instead of settling for a watered-down message that is seen on many street corners in America, within the buildings that we call church. Hopefully, you have come to a place where you are really asking, seeking, and knocking. If so, I pray that this book not only answers questions you have had but also leads you to continue searching for truth through the Word of God.

Christianity should never become stale, and we should never become complacent where we put up our tent and camp out throughout the duration of this life we are given. We should continually be stirred up in a way that we *"go,"* as Jesus tells us—into this world to bring clarity and truth to the *"many"* in hopes that some shall be saved from the wide road which is traveled heavily by those who have been blinded.

This book was the result of years of stepping out from religion and seeking God to a level based on the belief that there had to be more to what we call Christianity today. I knew God and heard His voice for years and years, but the more I studied the more I realized that what the church looks like today did not line up with Scriptures. I wanted more and hungered for more which led me to seek and pray to my God for truth.

CHAPTER ONE
THE JOURNEY

I remember a time many years ago where I had felt that God had poured so much revelation in me. I felt as though I was so blessed that He had opened my eyes to the things He wanted me to see. I thought all was good and that I was exactly where I was supposed to be with God, and I was. I was where I was supposed to be then. I was blessed that He had given me so much revelation but what I didn't realize was that this was only a season. What I didn't realize was that I wasn't to remain at that place!

If you have ever gone on a road trip, you know that part of the adventure is not remaining in one place. Several years ago, my granddaughter and I went on one such journey. I wanted to take her back to experience my memories as a child. Therefore, we traveled to the places I grew up, as well as those special places I had experienced many times myself as a child and on into adolescence. Our road trip began in one state and continued into three other states. Of those states we explored, two of them were where I spent most of my years growing up. We visited with people I had known most of my life. We went kayaking down rivers and hiking through woods. We swam in rivers, lakes, and creeks. We jet-skied, explored caves, climbed up and down mountain sides, stayed in cabins tucked back into the woods, and went horse-back riding through the mountains and crossing rivers.

One evening, we went to watch the Passion Play performance while sitting on the side of a mountain at dusk in the northern part of Arkansas. We traveled through the wilderness by train to see towns that no longer existed, and we ziplined over the mountain side. My purpose for this journey was to be able to impart to my granddaughter many of the glorious things God created in this world which allows His people to experience

His existence in all things. In this life that we live daily, we get so caught up doing the routine things day by day that we fail to recognize just how great our God really is. Jesus said to His Father, *"They fail to recognize You."*

John 16:3 (WNT) And they will do these things because they have failed to <u>recognize</u> the Father and to discover who I am.

Most translations of the Bible use the word *"known"* instead of *"recognize"*. However, to know and recognize have the same meaning but when I had come across this translation years ago, I was able to gain a different perspective as I thought about this world and how He designed the world for man's pleasures. I'm not talking about what man has created but about the natural wonders and the beauty of our world. It is in this that we have failed to know the Father or even recognize Him.

As I have traveled countless roads with My Savior, He has shown me so many simple things in this world that have actually helped me to grow stronger as a Christian and more aware of the true meaning of His Word. God designed this world for man with all its wonders and with each generation, we continue to step further and further away from His goodness. We continue to step further and further away from Truth.

Going back to those places I explored as a child, I was able to teach my granddaughter that there was so much more to Christianity. I was able to allow her to have a hands-on experience to show her many of the awesome things which God created for man's pleasure. Living a city-life as parents, we are so caught up in getting ahead that we do not realize our children are growing up to find their pleasures in the things which man created. Children are programmed to this technology era and many times never are shown that there is a big world out there to explore with glorious things created for man's enjoyment. Fast forward several years, you can still ask my granddaughter of all the places she has gone, which was her favorite and she would tell you the road trip.

In a time, years ago where things were very simple, children experienced God's creation. In those days, families came together as one, serving one God. You did not see churches on every street corner so that you could choose how you wanted to serve God. There was one church and one God and there was one belief. What I mean by one belief is that whatever small church existed within the small communities, they believed in Jesus Christ and believed in the Word of God. Today, we have so many choices and with those choices, we have forgotten the journey. We get involved in a particular denomination and are programmed to believe as they believe, all the while we pitch up a tent and begin to camp out in whatever ministry we have become accustomed. We spend years in that same place until the day we meet our Savior. What I mean is that we get so comfortable in a certain church or denomination with the same group of people that become our church family, that our journey with God stops. God never meant for us to remain until the day we die in that one place going through the same motions of serving Him. Let me say, it is not necessarily about going to that same group of people or that same building, it is more about pitching up a tent and your walk with your Savior becomes stagnant. Dependent upon what God has called you to do, your walk with Him will never be one that sits on a church pew week after week producing zero fruit in your life. We are all called to be disciples and as disciples, there will be fruit which is the fruit of the Spirit evident in our lives.

Many years ago, there normally was just one church in each town, but it was a different era. Years ago, prior to the Industrial Era, the only way to travel was to either walk or go by horse and boats. However, there was no need to go explore other denominations because it was not about the building as it is today. Years ago, Christianity was taught in the home. Parents taught their children the Word of God, but they also taught them by example how to walk the life as a Christian. Godly principles began in the homes whereas the church building was a place for all that believed to come together to draw strength in order to continue the walk as true Christians. In those days, it was never about making money to live extravagant but to make money to provide the simple things for your family. It was about sharing with your neighbor when times were hard. It was about all Christian families to include the one pastor in the town to work together in raising the children within that town up in the ways of the Lord. In those days they understood the term, *"It takes a village to raise a child."* Children knew that the whole village or town was in-tuned to all the happenings in their surroundings. It wasn't classified as being *"nosy"* because the small towns knew that they needed each other for survival. It was about being neighborly and caring about each other to include everyone. The small-town mentality was about instilling godly-principles in their children. It was about teaching them the simple things of life and not about striving for riches; whereas today, life in America for most people has evolved to choices. I'm not saying that all people in those days were Christians because we know that isn't true, but in those days, godly principles were taught and God was not excluded from public places. He was in the schools and the town hall meetings, as well as in the homes. People prayed because they understood that they needed God in their lives, and they strived to walk by faith to believe that their crops produced an abundance that would carry them through the winter months. They turned to Him during sickness for healing because there weren't hospitals and medicine like we have today. Yes, people died just like they do today, but this did not turn people away from God because He was their only hope to survive.

I had a great-aunt who used to tell me the story of when she was born. She lived to be close to 90 years old and was an amazing woman. She was born in the early 1900s prior to electricity being brought into most of the homes in America. It was in 1882 that Edison helped form the Edison Electric Illuminating Company of New York which brought electric light to parts of Manhattan but progress was very slow, and most Americans still used gas light and candles for another 50 years. By 1925, only half of all homes in the United States had electric power. My aunt's family were very poor, and she was also born prior to the advancement of medical science. At birth, she weighed less than 4 lbs. They had called the doctor in that town who was there to assist with delivery in their home. It was unheard of in those days for such a small premature baby to live, so the doctor told the family to call for the pastor because the baby would not live. Her grandmother picked up the baby and said, *"As long as there is breath in this child, there is hope."* Her grandmother took her and put her in a basket and hung it on the side of their cooking stove which was wood-burning. She hung it there as an incubator to keep her warm and kept fire going continually. She was too small to suck the breast, so around the clock the grandmother took a cloth and soaked it in milk to put on her lips to get substance within her. My aunt had several brothers and sisters in her day, but she was the oldest sibling; however, she outlived every single one of her brothers and sisters.

As we continue to advance in this era, our choices continue to grow. We can pick and choose what religion we desire to follow based on many things, and the majority choose those religions based on wealth. The majority would never set foot in a small church that had very little to offer. We want the best of everything from buying a home to cars, clothes to all the new advanced technology, and even the church we choose to follow. We want vibrant churches so that we can proudly tell others that we are members of *"such and such"* church. We want the church with the coffee shops and fabulous entertainment from the pulpit to include music and all the latest technology which has made serving God more delightful. We want to feel that by giving our tithe, we are doing all that Jesus commanded us to do. After all, many churches use part of the tithe to send to other countries to help the poor, as well as providing funds for different programs within their own community. Yes, Jesus we have done our part! We can continue to serve God by simply attending our church service on a weekly basis or if we are not able to attend weekly, that is quite alright as well because we are still giving our money to do what Jesus called us to do, right?

As I said, the majority would never even explore the small church because it is not appealing, even though, there may be a small church out there that is trying to teach the people Truth instead of false teachings. However, the multitudes are more attracted to what looks good on the outside, and they never stop to consider what is being taught on the inside. Isn't that true on most aspects of life today? Are we not more concerned with how "we" even look on the outside and pay little mind to what we look like on the inside to God? By living this way, we even create the kind of god that fits into our schedule in order to make our life easier in this world. We strive so hard to try and make life easy but what we have failed to see is that we have made life harder because our desires continue to be for more of this world. Life is hard enough as it is, but we make it even harder as we strive to acquire and pay for all the modern inventions such as nice cars and the newest technology gadgets and then on top of that, we want big homes, extravagant vacations, and even plastic surgery to look better and/or try to stay young. All of these things put so much financial pressure on this generation where our lifestyles have become accustomed to working long hours, taking on two jobs, or continually striving for more education in order to bring home more money. Our society has become all about striving to bring in more and more and more in order to acquire more and more and more. Those who do not have the education may have a trade in a field where they are a plumber, electrician, etc., but these normally put in long hard hours as well. Then you have those that still want the things others have—with no means to acquire those things which cause many to go down the road that leads to theft and dishonesty. All of these lifestyles have produced one thing and that is sacrifice. We sacrifice the way we live because of the desires to have more. These sacrifices come at a price. Depending on your choices in this life, your sacrifice will affect your time or your decisions, but both of these will affect relationships.

In this age, we are programmed to go to college in order that we can make good money to live well. It's not the message about going to college but the message of living well. We consider that living well consists of making enough money in order that we can buy the good things in this life. Most in college today, desire to get a degree where they can make a good living in order that they can have the nice cars, big homes, money in the bank, etc. I'm not saying that these things are bad, but when our values are more for the things in this world instead of the Word of God, we have sacrificed God in order to have the finer things in this world. Let me clarify, years ago God was first to those who were Christians. In those days, their spiritual life was important as were their children. When we sacrifice those things in order to place our values for the finer things in this world above our spiritual life, it is at a cost. It costs us our relationships. It costs us a real relationship with our Creator, with our children, family, friends, and people in general! We sacrifice really knowing the true God in order to have the world and all it has to offer today!

The road trip that my granddaughter and I went on was also a time for me to reflect on my own childhood and a time to reflect on my life as a young adult when I first met Jesus. On this trip, I was able to visit with a few people who were mentors to me in my twenties at a time when I became a Christian. They were huge influences in my life at that time, and today, they are still traveling that narrow road which leads to heaven. On this road trip, God sent others across my path that I was able to witness to and I was able to experience nature on a different level, overcoming many fears that I may have had. This road trip served its purpose but coming home from this trip, I was able to see that God ultimately had a specific journey for my life that would continue to play out over the years to come. We all have a specific journey which will lead us through different plains, plateaus, over mountains, through rivers and lakes, streams and creeks, valleys and canyons. On your journey you will experience new horizons and you will gain a new perspective of God's specific plan for your life.

To begin your journey with Jesus Christ, it will take you stepping out of your comfort zone and saying, *"Yes Lord, I surrender all to you, send me for I will go."* Be prepared because when you step out to be faithful to our Lord, you can expect your journey to take you through bad times as well as good times. You may suffer loses in the bad times, but you will also gain great things in the good times. Jesus warned us that if they hated Him, they would hate us; if they persecuted Him, they would persecute us. He warned us that this journey would be hard traveled, there would be hard times.

John 16:33 (ESV) "I have said these things to you, that in me you may have peace. In the world you will have tribulation. But take heart; I have overcome the world."

Matthew 10:16, 22 (ESV) "Behold, I am sending you out as sheep in the midst of wolves, so be wise as serpents and innocent as doves. ^{22}And you will be hated by all for my name's sake. But the one who endures to the end will be saved."

2 Timothy 3:12 (ESV) Indeed, all who desire to live a godly life in Christ Jesus will be persecuted.

Our journey in this life will never ever be about trying to please God, in order that our gain will be to have the riches and desires of this world. God does not reward us with the riches of this world. I'm not saying that in this world He will not bless you with wealth but don't count on it. Wealth in this world is not something we should ever desire. When we desire earthly things, our heart is not right with God. Material things are not what truly brings happiness and it never will. Besides, if you will remember the rich young ruler that approached Jesus with a question, he was unable to walk away from his earthly possessions.

Mark 10:21-23 (ESV) And Jesus, looking at him, loved him, and said to him, "You lack one thing: go, sell all that you have and give to the poor, and you will have treasure in heaven; and come, follow me." 22Disheartened by the saying, he went away sorrowful, for he had great possessions. 23And Jesus looked around and said to his disciples, "How difficult it will be for those who have wealth to enter the kingdom of God!"

Let me first say that this was not about selling everything he had, this was about the heart. Jesus knew that this man had great wealth and that wealth stood in the way of him being able to let go of the world and become a follower of Christ. Most Americans have too much! I heard for years the Lord telling me to simplify my life. I can't tell you how many times I have cleared out my life from material possessions and just given the stuff away. I have taken great loss and do not regret any of it one bit; however, it continues to be a process as this world is full of desires. Each day is a new day with the Lord and each day may be a day that He speaks to us to let go of something we are holding onto that is in the way of serving Him. In order for me to draw closer to my Lord, I cannot have stuff cluttering up my life. I am no different than anyone else, as He continues to deal with me to stop accumulating things. God knows our heart, and He knows when there are things in the way that keep us from drawing close to Him. This was why Jesus told the rich young ruler to sell all because He already knew that the man's possessions had become his idols. God will NOT share those who are His with anything of this world. Material wealth has a way of keeping us bound and conformed to this world. We are no different than the rich young ruler, when the request is too hard, do we not compromise? Compromising is nothing more than conforming to this world, being like the world.

Myself, I had to come to a place where I had to examine my heart on what I really wanted in this life. Having material wealth is very tempting. I came to a place where I said to God, *"If having wealth will change who I am inside, Lord, please never let me have that wealth."* Can you pray that prayer to God and really mean it? Far too often, we are actually praying for material things. Can you honestly look at your life and say, *"Lord, if I never have anything more, it has all been good enough!"*

CHAPTER TWO
THE WILDERNESS ROAD

As God led me on this new journey, I began to think a lot about the wilderness and a lot about the early pioneers. When God gets a hold of you and begins to open your eyes to certain elements in His Word, get prepared because it will lead you into the unknown. That was how this journey began some time ago and deep within there was this yearning to search for a much deeper meaning to this life and the life after. I became very dissatisfied with what Christianity looked like in most American churches today, and there was this burning inside to step out and look for something unknown. I was not sure what lay on the other side, but I was prepared to walk away from everything and everyone if need be to find what He was trying to show me. When you get to that place where you cry out to God, as you realize that the fundamentals you have been taught by man do not line up with the knowledge you have gained as you study His Word, be prepared because He will send you into the wilderness just as He did John the Baptist.

As we know, John the Baptist went out into the wilderness to prepare for the coming of Jesus Christ. People came from all over to see this man who basically left all behind to go and live in a desolate place. In fact, Jesus said at one point to a crowd, what did you go to see?

Matthew 11:7-10 (ESV) As they went away, Jesus began to speak to the crowds concerning John: "What did you go out into the wilderness to see? A reed shaken by the wind? [8]What then did you go out to see? A man dressed in soft clothing? Behold, those who wear soft clothing are in king's houses. [9]What then did you go out to see? A prophet? Yes, I tell you, and more than a prophet. [10]This is he of whom it is written,

'Behold, I send my messenger before your face, who will prepare your way before you.'"

John the Baptist was a pioneer which is one who is unafraid to go into places others will not venture. Only few will go into those wilderness places and even fewer will remain. As I studied about pioneers, I could easily see how my life had always been one like a pioneer, as I was always willing to explore and travel into areas which others were unwilling to go. In fact, in high school I was able to talk most friends into doing things others would have been scared to do, but I always just plowed ahead. Again, when I was 21, I decided to leave from my hometown where I was raised and where I had grown up. It was on the spur of the moment that I made the decision to leave and within one week, I was on the road traveling across country with my 2-year old daughter. I left all behind other than what would fit in my car. It was a crazy unprepared journey, but one that shaped my character for the good.

Looking back at my life today, I realize that I was called to be so much more. In this life many times, we settle for where we are and remain there until we die. We become complacent and begin looking at Christianity as what we hear week after week from the pulpit, and we never experience the kind of relationship with God that those we read about in the Bible encountered. Having a pioneer mentality, you will naturally begin exploring and that my friend is a good thing. We were never meant to serve our Savior by attending a service week after week and doing nothing more. Being a pioneer does not necessarily mean that you pick up roots and travel from city to city, but it could mean that dependent on your own personal calling. However, being a disciple of Jesus Christ will take you into the unknown and a willing spirit that says, *"Lord, send me for I will go."*

In my journey, I began researching the wilderness. The wilderness refers to a place where there is nothing! There is no entertainment and nothing to distract you. Remember, even Jesus once He had been baptized by John, went into the wilderness for forty days and forty nights. *(Matthew 4:1-11)*

In that place, there is nothing! Even though, there are no earthly distractions as we know them, there will always be two choices in that desert place. You will hear the voice of satan and the voice of the Holy Spirit. Once Jesus was baptized, the Holy Spirit descended upon Him and led Him into the wilderness. Jesus' choices were to either listen to satan or to God. We too have those same choices every single day, but we live in the midst of all the distractions which have been created by man-kind. Those very distractions are surrounding us every single day, every place we go. People surround us, and every single person has their own beliefs and opinions. We listen to our friends, family, church people, pastors, priests, television, radio, social media, etc. All these distractions keep us far from the wilderness and far from being able to step back and really listen to what God may be trying to reveal to us.

John went away for a purpose and Jesus also had a purpose. If you consider yourself a Christian, you too have a purpose but many times, you are unable to see what God is trying to do in your life because you cannot hear His voice.

Let's explore exactly what the wilderness looks like. To define wilderness, it would be referring to a region that was uninhabited or undisturbed by human activity; not affected by human activity; an empty pathless area; a naturally developed life community; wild and uncultivated state where few would live; a barren or desolate place. For those few in the wilderness that would choose to journey, their voice may be crying out in that desolate place, but their pleas would be unheard to those which were gathered together with the multitudes in places inhabited by people, such as the church building. Those who find that narrow pathway, they continually cry out to those who cannot see nor hear. Their cries go unheard. As those who are surrounded by distractions, they do not hear that voice in the wilderness crying out. Those in the wilderness no longer have influence within the cities and communities, and they would no longer be recognized or known.

John the Baptist was one who stepped forth unafraid and laid everything down to prepare the way for Jesus Christ by going into an unknown region. People came from all around to witness this person who seemed to be strange to leave all behind to go live in a place where there was nothing. Today, people are no different. They may go to witness this strange type of person, but they do not go because they desire to walk away and follow in the footsteps of those who have chosen to leave all behind. John lived in the day and time of the Pharisees and all those who considered themselves religious leaders. However, John walked away from what appeared to be the real religion of that day to become what would very soon be known to all as the real church. John was preparing the way for Jesus Christ, and the church's mission is the same as we are to prepare for the second coming of Jesus Christ. We are to step forth, even when we have no idea what lay ahead. If God is calling us to prepare for Jesus' return, it will take the *"John the Baptists"* of this world to step out unafraid of what lay ahead and venture into those barren places.

In America, if you were to really examine what we call the church today, you would see that our churches look nothing like those first churches which Jesus began in His day. You do not see members of the church willing to say, *"God, send me for I will go."* You may hear people say, *"God, send me but not into a desolate place."* Yes, we will prepare for Jesus' return as long as the journey that God lays ahead of us does not require any sacrifice on our part.

Let's go a little further to expand on those definitions mentioned on wilderness. If we desire to be the *"John the Baptists"* of this generation, we must understand exactly what that looks like. Referring to the wilderness, the word uninhabited means there are few. Perhaps that is why the

Word of God tells us that the many will stand before God one day as He tells them, *"I never knew you"* and likewise, He will welcome the few into heaven. I get tired of hearing the Christian community say that the Word of God did not mean that literally. Well yes, literally maybe it does not mean 2 or 3, but I do believe that the majority of those who claim to be Christians will never see heaven. Why would we want to listen to a mere man or woman instead of God when it has to do with our own personal salvation. If I am wrong, then maybe you will see heaven; however, if I am right, you won't. Would it not be better for our walk to look more like those who really followed Jesus instead of those in this world today that claim to be following in His footsteps, yet their walk looks nothing like the walk of the disciples in Jesus' day? (*Matthew 7:21-23*)

The wilderness is a place undisturbed by human activity. Think about that. There was no activity created by humans for any type of entertainment or socializing. This would include football, movie theaters, concerts, social events, etc. This would be the place where most who claim to be Christians would shut this book and decide that I am some rambling *"Jesus freak."* That is perfectly alright because there were many in Jesus' day who felt like His disciples were freaks as well. Even behind Christopher Columbus' back, there were many who claimed he was some rambling person who was crazy.[1] It is amazing how our History books show little to no account of those who were great among us, yet they gave the credit to God. Go to a library and read it yourself if you do not believe me, the reference is in the back of this book. However, those who have a voice crying in the wilderness know that only few will listen, are you one of the few? Those few are unafraid of what lies ahead. Those few are willing to sacrifice for the sake of their salvation and that of their loved ones. This is life or death; this is not a message that is meant to bring comfort food to your flesh. On the contrary, this is a message that may require you to let go of this world completely but in the end, you will be one that stands before our Creator as He welcomes you into the Gates of Heaven.

The wilderness is a naturally developed life community because it was naturally created by God, and it is life not death. We should acknowledge that which God created. What do we naturally see in the wilderness? We see mountains, lakes, rivers, trees, canyons, plains, etc. God gave us a glorious world with everything man needed to thrive. With all of the world's beauty, over the years man has gradually walked away from that which was naturally created to live a life that was created by man—artificial. Most even prefer entertainment within the cities over enjoying time together with family and friends outside of city life.

A wild uncultivated state where few would live refers to a place that has not been corrupted by man. A place where man has not brought in his concepts, inventions, etc. At this place is where most would never venture because it does not feel safe, it feels unsure. I often have thought about what would happen in the event our grid system went down in America. It would put us back somewhere in time prior to electricity, in a day where people actually knew how to live off the land. However, today people have no idea how to survive without man's inventions. We trust in those things which were created by man and those things are what make us feel safe. To clarify, as I have done in other books, God did not create everything. God created the heavens and earth, the sun and moon, people, animals and all of creation and all the natural wonders that we see, but much of what we see outside of the wilderness was made by man. Man used the natural things God created to invent and make the things we depend on daily. Once God created everything noted in Genesis, He stated, *"It is good."* However, I doubt that God looks down from heaven on the nightclubs and says, *"It is good."* This is only one example, but I think you get my point! Therefore, it is safe to say that man feels safe and has faith based on that which was made by man.

Yes, I do believe that much of what man has made was inspired by God, and I also know that much of what has been created in this technology era was done so for a reason. All of the technology will play its part in ushering in the anti-christ, which will ultimately bring this world to an end, as we know it today because Jesus will also return for His true Church and defeat satan and all evils. However, even though the technology of this age has a purpose, at what cost is it to those who claim to be Christians? It is at a huge cost when those who claim to be Christians spend countless hours entertaining themselves with all the newest inventions that there is little time to seek God much less find Him. We should venture out into the wilderness and spend time minus our phones, computers, and all of our luxuries just once to really seek a God that gave so much for those who would dare to let go of the comforts of this world to find Him.

Another meaning of the wilderness is that it is not affected by human activities. Prior to discovering America, it was a barren place. Even the Indians lived in the wilderness but they chose to live off the land as it was, without changing the landscape with inventions. As I said, the inventions were necessary for the return of Jesus Christ, but the point is when the multitudes came to America, they brought civilization. Once man moves into a land, it becomes affected by human activity and is no longer considered the wilderness. This can also refer to the church. Jesus created the church to be different than this world. He tells us that we are not to be conformed to this world.

Proverbs 1:15 (ESV) My son, do not walk in the way with them; hold back your foot from their paths.

Romans 12:2 (ESV) Do not be conformed to this world, but be transformed by the renewal of your mind, that by testing you may discern what is the will of God, what is good and acceptable and perfect.

The first church was not conformed to this world. The first church was different than the world. The people stood out to be different. He tells us that we are not of this world only in this world; he tells us that if they hated Him, they will hate us. He warns us that the road we will travel as His church will be a hard road that we will have much heartache.

John 15:19 (ESV) If you were of this world, the world would love you as its own; but because you are not of the world, but I chose you out of the world, therefore the world hates you.

John 16:33 (ESV) I have said these things to you, that in me you may have peace. In the world you will have tribulation. But take heart; I have overcome the world."

However, like everything else, when man got a hold of the church, it became civilized. It became like this world. We can look at the first church in Acts in which Jesus began and then look at the state of the church today and see that they are no longer one and the same.

The wilderness is a barren and desolate place. There may be times when we wind up in a wilderness place in the natural, but most will not remain there because we have a hard time of going it alone. When I made the decision to walk away from the modern church in America, I found myself alone in the wilderness. There were many times that I wanted to go back and agree with the church because I did not want to go it alone. However, I cried out to God many times because I felt as though I was the one wrong and everyone else was right, even though it was not what was in the Bible. Thankfully, God sent others across my path many times that were my confirmation that what I was seeing was God. I made a choice to hang in there all alone for a good 6 months because I trusted the voice I was hearing and stood by faith waiting on Him to lead me on the pathway that was my specific calling. I can tell you today, even though I am not totally alone, it has never been a crowded place and the multitudes are not striving to find the wilderness.

It was in the wilderness that I have heard His voice many times and continue to do so. When you are surrounded by the multitudes, it is hard to hear God as He speaks with that still quiet voice. However, as John the Baptist was the voice crying out in the wilderness, when you make that choice to go it alone, you too will hear that voice speak to you and reveal many hidden secrets. Revelation will pour into you as you seek Him, and you will find Him. Not too long ago, my son-in-law wrote a blog where he made a statement that is so true. *"Christians and those who are non-Christians, weigh in on Biblical matters without ever picking up the Bible and reading it cover to cover."*[2] Remember, God still speaks today but the distractions can far outweigh His voice if we are not striving to seek Him in those intimate times alone.

Going further into defining what life looks like in the wilderness for the few that would dare step out of the modern churches to be the voices crying in those desolate places, we first see that they are but few. There have been many times that God has led me to others who have made the choice to go it alone which has been comforting to know they are out there. In fact, there are even churches out there that are living and preaching truth, but they are the very few. When those who have stepped out trying to share truth with those who are living a *"so-called"* Christian life based on what they have been taught by man, their voices are ignored. When you step out to that desolate place because your eyes and ears have been opened to truth, you will see that the multitudes whom believe they are following truth, will not listen. You will see that in the wilderness place, your voice is of no influence to the multitudes as it may have been when you were within their congregations. As Jesus said, *"You will leave all behind to follow Him."* At first, it is hard when you lose that group of close friends but once you develop that intimate relationship with Jesus, there is nothing more that you need. Are you willing to lose everything, would be the question?

To travel the narrow road, which will be discussed in detail throughout this book, will be a road that only few will choose to try and find. Most people do not really want to follow Jesus.

It is no different than when Jesus walked this earth. Even when they rejected Him, it was because He was not the god they were looking for. They did not want to follow the true God that required them to give up their life as it was.

Isaiah 53:3 (ESV) He was despised and rejected by men, a man of sorrows and acquainted with grief; and as one from whom men hide their faces he was despised, and we esteemed him not.

Luke 10:16 (ESV) "The one who hears you hears me, and the one who rejects you rejects me, and the one who rejects me rejects him who sent me."

On the narrow road, there will be times of great storms but know that we were never called to stay in a storm. We are only to embrace the storm for a time and season. Everything has a time and season and as God's children, we are privileged to be part of this world and part of His puzzle for our lives. Often times, I share that we can look at this world as one huge puzzle. It is God's puzzle, but we all have our own little puzzle as well. All those storms in this life we go through, God is merely trying to mold our own little puzzle to fit into His larger puzzle. Ultimately, we are part of His plan for creation, and His plan for the end times. When we get our puzzles lined up with His, we become part of preparing the way for the second coming of Jesus Christ. We take joy in the suffering knowing that the sun does shine every morning.

James 1:2-4 (ESV) Count it all joy, my brothers, when you meet trials of various kinds, ³for you know that the testing of your faith produces steadfastness. ⁴And let steadfastness have its full effect, that you may be perfect and complete, lacking in nothing.

Psalm 30:3-6 (ESV) O LORD, you have brought up my soul from Sheol; you restored me to life from among those who go down to the pit. ⁴Sing praises to the LORD, O you his saints, and give thanks to his holy name. ⁵For his anger is but for a moment, and his favor is for a lifetime. Weeping may tarry for the night, but joy comes in the morning. ⁶As for me, I said in my prosperity, "I shall never be moved."

CHAPTER THREE
THE VOICE LESS FOLLOWED

John 10:27(NKJV) My sheep hear my voice, and they follow me.

Have you ever asked yourself whose voice you are really following? Jesus tells us that if we are His sheep, we will follow His voice. I doubt that most people even consider the voice they are following. In fact, statistics show that those who claim to be Christians seldom even read the Word of God. There are all kinds of surveys which have been done in America, and the findings are all relatively the same. I chose to go with two of those because of different conclusions. LifeWay's findings showed that over half of Americans have read little or none of the Bible. Most have rarely even picked up the Bible, and even among worship attendees, less than half of those read the Bible daily. Most American's amount of knowledge they have of the Bible was by hearing it through someone else reading it. This survey shows that 10% have never read the Bible at all. It shows 13% claim they have only read a few sentences of the Bible, 30% have read several passages or stories, 15% have read half of the Bible, 12% have almost read all of it, 11% have read all of it once, and 9% have read the Bible more than once.[1] The other findings, were written in a blog through Juicy Ecumenism, Institute on Religion & Democracy, where the author found among those who claim they do read the Bible, 22% read a few passages each day, 30% look up passages on a need-to-know basis, 19% reread their favorite passages, 17% flip open the Bible and read random passages, 27% read passages recommended by others, 16% look up passages to help others.[2]

From my own experience, <u>most dedicated Christians</u> who are devoted to a particular church, listen intently to that pastor and strive to follow by his methods or teachings. The sad part is that much of what is being taught from the pulpits today is not even accurate with Scriptures. The majority of pastors today teach out of context or they even teach their own beliefs and philosophies based on what they have learned from all those who have influenced their lives from day one, including other ministers over the years. Anyone can teach a small section of Scripture without mentioning what was said prior or after and do a pretty good sermon on what they want those listening to believe. Unfortunately, most pastors who teach by that method are merely using this as a means of control in order to keep their congregations at hand, all the while growing churches to mega proportions. Teaching out of context distorts the actual meaning behind the message more often than not, where those listening that seldom read the Word of God themselves, have gained their knowledge based on false teachings. The mega-type churches, take a massive amount of time and effort to present such a spectacular, <u>secular</u> performance with the sound, lighting, and dance presentations within their sanctuaries, no wonder that their leaders teach out of context. Anyone can teach out of context and do not need the assistance of the Holy Spirit. These churches are filled with goats and goats are easy to keep in the flock as long as someone is making them feel important and/or entertaining them. Many of the churches today are even filled with the same kind of entertainment as the world. This movement has allowed the world to define the church. In order for a church to grow in massive numbers, pastors have to cross the line where they are no longer a church of God but a church of man. Their teachings have gained congregations that are full of goats even though there may be sheep among them, eventually those sheep will NOT remain if they are truly striving to seek and find God one on one. Goats love to be leaders over something and these mega-type churches must have massive amounts of leaders to carry out the performance's week after week.

We hear far too often, that God's grace covers our sin and believe that we can be joined with others who all claim to be believers, covered by His grace for our weaknesses and sin. We are quick to speak of God's grace, but are we stewards of that grace?

1 Peter 4:1-11(ESV) Since therefore <u>Christ suffered in the flesh, arm yourselves with the same way of thinking, for whoever has suffered in the flesh has ceased from sin</u>, ²so as to live for the rest of the time in the flesh <u>no longer for human passions but for the will of God</u>. ³For the time that is past suffices for doing what the Gentiles want to so, living in sensuality, passions, drunkenness, orgies, drinking parties, and lawless idolatry. ⁴<u>With respect to this they are surprised when you do not join them in the same flood of debauchery, and they malign you</u>; ⁵but they will give account to him who is ready to judge the living and the dead. ⁶For this is why the gospel was preached even to those who are dead, that <u>though judged in the flesh the way people are, they might live in the spirit the way God does.</u> ⁷The end of all things is at hand; therefore, be self-controlled and sober-minded for the sake of your prayers. ⁸Above all, keep loving one another earnestly, since love covers a multitude of sins. ⁹Show hospitality to one another without grumbling. ¹⁰<u>As each has received a gift, use it to serve one another, as good stewards of God's varied grace:</u> ¹¹whoever speaks, as one who speaks oracles of God; whoever serves, as one who serves by the strength that God supplies – <u>in order that in everything God may be glorified through Jesus Christ</u>. To him belong glory and dominion forever and ever. Amen.

There is a lot to say about the above Scripture, but I am just going to touch on a few items at this time because there will be much teaching throughout this book on this day and time that we live in which is full of deception. First, to answer the question prior, are we stewards of God's grace? I know we hear a lot about stewardship in the means of giving money or tithes, but that is not what is being spoken of here. When we carry out God's plan as His chosen people, we are being good stewards of what we have whether that is in money, time, gifts, or talents. A steward is someone who manages or looks after another's property. As a steward for God, it has to do with His grace. When we walk by God's Spirit, not by the flesh, we are given the grace needed to be stewards of that which He has given to us. God gives to those who ask but only to those who ask with the right heart. When our heart is right with God, our purpose on this earth will line up with His purpose. We will then have His grace in the way of talents, gifts, finances and/or anything else that we need to carry out His plan, not our plan. Notice, it says that whatever gift we receive, we will use it to serve one another – not to be served! Man can never do this in themselves because their flesh gets in the way. Most churches today operate in the flesh and not in the spirit. As fleshly beings, we are also always looking for God in a movement or by feelings. *"I felt the Lord's presence in that church!"* Not so, God is not a God who operates in the flesh but in the spirit. The new age movement in our churches today have captured the attention of the masses because people always want a sign or they want to be able to *"feel"* the presence of God.

Matthew 16:4 (ESV) "An evil and adulterous generation seeks for a sign, but no sign will be given to it except the sign of Jonah." So, he left them and departed.

Jesus used the metaphor of Jonah because he was referring to the 3 days that Jonah was in the belly of the whale, and the final sign to come would be His resurrection on the 3rd day after the crucifixion. However, it is clear to see that man has not changed because we still seek for those signs. The majority would never even set foot in a church today if that church could not give them some kind of sign that Jesus was real, and that His presence was felt in that church. Yet, remember that Jesus said in John that blessed are those who have not seen and yet have believed. *(John 20:29)*

The presence of God has nothing to do with physical feelings, but it has everything to do with faith. The majority today follow certain ministries or movements where God's presence is perceived to be based on natural feelings, not by faith in His Word. God is NOT just here at a particular church but He is omnipresent, which means He is everywhere and at all times. We come to know Him intimately, one on one, and it will be our faith that knows He is always there. David, in Psalm 139, gives a pretty awesome description of who God is and where He is. I have listed a few of David's insights, but this Scripture would be a great place to get a better image of who God really is by reading all of Psalm 139.

Psalm 139 (ESV)

- (2) You know when I sit down and when I rise up; you discern my thoughts from afar.
- (7) Where shall I go from your Spirit? Or where shall I flee from your presence?
- (8) If I ascend to heaven, you are there! If I make my bed in Sheol, you are there!
- (13) For you formed my inward parts; you knitted me together in my mother's womb.
- (23) Search me, O God, and know my heart! Try me and know my thoughts!
- (24) And see if there be any grievous way in me, and lead me in the way everlasting!

We do not become a particular denomination or go to a particular church to find God. If that is what we are doing, we do not have a clue who God is. We come to know Him through faith only because the sign that He is real and He is God was the crucifixion and the resurrection of Jesus Christ. That is our sign and most people will not follow a sign when they have no evidence. Our evidence is in the Word of God, and it is by faith that we believe every single thing written in His Word. This is why blessed be those who have NOT seen but yet believe because great is their faith. If we have to attend a particular church that puts on a performance in order that we *"feel"* something in the natural sense, we do not need faith to believe. God is not a feeling, like I have said, He is a spiritual being and operates in the spirit not in the flesh.

To clarify, God is everywhere. God is not in one place more than another based on human efforts to set the right scene or stage to satisfy Him where He manifests His approvals based on our inferior works in the production of man's methods of magnificent performances to please Him.

It's quite evident why we are told in His Word that our thoughts and ways are not His because there are but few churches today that have really experienced His grace to understand how we are nothing without really knowing Him. *(Isaiah 55:8)* As Scripture teaches, it takes a people who come to the end of themselves in order to see and know His presence.

Proverbs 3:5-6 (ESV) Trust in the LORD with all your heart, and do not lean on your own understanding. ⁶In all your ways acknowledge him, and he will make straight your paths.

It is clear to see based on the statistics of how seldom people read the Word of God, that they really do not know Him and have no faith. They only know a god that has been created by man through the wisdom of man, in order that men are increased and glorified. It is through His Word that we acquire faith. You cannot have faith unless you seek Him in which few do. As we are told, the Word of God is alive, it comes alive to those who read it. It is not about doing a daily devotion; it is about having that desire from within to find Him. You seek and you find but the problem is that people do not have time in their lives to really seek for the real God, and therefore, they will never find Him.

Hebrews 4:12 (ESV) For the word of God is living and active, sharper than any two-edged sword, piercing to the division of soul and of spirit, of joints and marrow, and discerning the thoughts and intentions of the heart.

These are powerful words. His Word comes alive inside of us. It is sharp enough that it divides our soul from our spirit in order that we can be saved. We are all sinful; His Word discerns our thoughts and our intentions of our heart. Without His Word, man is deceived and is evil. Without His Word dividing us, we are NOT saved. Without spending time in His Word, the only life we have living inside of us is worldly and we live as the world, but as we absorb those very words in the Bible, they begin to live in our heart and we begin to change where our heart is NOT deceived because His Word discerns the hearts intentions. This is huge, your heart deceives you if you are following the world and its methods of religion and not spending time in the Word of God. We already know by statistics that the majority are following a heart that is deceitful because few really read and study His Word. As we do study to really know Him, we understand that God is more concerned with the redemption of man through His Son and then with the relationship that grows as we grow to know Him. Our relationship only happens as we truly let go of any obstacles that stand in the way of uniting our spirit with His— any obstacle that stands in the way of spending time in His Word which brings life.

Hebrews 12:1-2 (ESV) Therefore, since we are surrounded by so great a cloud of witnesses, let us also lay aside every weight, and sin which clings so closely, and let us run with endurance the race that is set before us, ²looking to Jesus, the founder and perfecter of our faith, who for the joy that was set before him endured the cross, despising the shame, and is seated at the right hand of the throne of God.

You cannot feel His presence through your flesh but only through your spirit, as your heart becomes one with Him. We are told in His Word, that we become one with Him. He is not speaking about the multitudes that do not even have time in their life to truly find Him. It takes much effort and much time on our part to encounter Jesus Christ, and it will only be the few that truly do find Him.

1 Corinthians 6:17 (NKJV) But he who is joined to the Lord is one spirit with Him.

Those who believe they know Him by a feeling, their heart has deceived them. We are warned that our own heart will deceive us.

Jeremiah 17:9 (NKJV) The heart is deceitful above all things, and desperately wicked; Who can know it?

The world will tell you to trust your heart, but man's heart is deceitful. However, we see in the book of Proverbs, which is the book of wisdom that we are to trust in the Lord only with our heart.

Proverbs 3:5-7 (ESV) Trust in the LORD with all your heart, and do not lean on your own understanding. ⁶In all your ways acknowledge him, and he will make straight your paths. ⁷Be not wise in your own eyes; fear the LORD, and turn away from evil.

In knowing that we are NOT deceived, our heart must be changed by His Word as I have said, where we come to know He lives in us by faith and our desires will also line up with His desires. Mere words mean nothing to God when your actions and desires are no different than the world that we live in. True Christians will be different. Their lives will be different, their desires will be different, and their time will be spent differently than those in this world.

As for natural signs of His presence, we are told that the hour is here when true worshipers will worship in spirit and truth.

John 4:23 (ESV) But the hour is coming, and is now here, when the true worshipers will worship the Father in spirit and truth, for the Father is seeking such people to worship him.

Notice that it does not say those that worship in the flesh but in the spirit. We cannot worship in the spirit if we are living as the world lives. We cannot live in the spirit without His Word, which is Truth, living inside of us. In order to have truth, you must seek Him. If you do not seek, you will never find Him, and you do not know Him. We are told in His Word, that He doesn't know those either who are not truly His. *(Matthew 7:21-23)*

Jesus tells us in John that He is the bread of life. Without Him and without faith in believing He is who He said He is in Scripture, you will perish.

John 6:35-40 (ESV) Jesus said to them, "I am the bread of life; whoever comes to me shall not hunger, and <u>whoever believes in me</u> shall never thirst. ³⁶But I said to you that you have seen me and yet do not believe. ³⁷All that the Father gives me will come to me, and whoever comes to me I will never cast out. ³⁸For I have come from heaven, not to do my own will but the will of him who sent me. ³⁹And this is the will of him who sent me, that I should lose nothing of all that he has given me, but raise it up on the last day. ⁴⁰For this is the will of my Father, that everyone who looks on the Son and believes in him should have eternal life, and I will raise him up on the last day."

To make one fast note here, Jesus said this is for those who BELIEVE in Him. This is a heart issue and we have already determined that our heart is deceitful. How many times in this world have people thrown the word *"love"* around but it really meant nothing? Just because someone tells you they love you does not mean they really do. If we can say to another person, *"I love you,"* and walk out that door to climb in the bed with someone else instead of that person we are married to, the word love is meaningless. Love shows action and the word believe also shows action. People who claim to be Christians will all say they believe in Jesus, but if their actions based on His Word do not portray the life of Christ, that word means nothing to Jesus. How can we say we believe and never pick up the Word of God or if we do, it is seldom? We have no problem turning on our televisions daily and spending hours on our computers and cell phones but little to no time to spend in the Word of God to KNOW Him. You cannot believe in something that you do not know!

Living for that *"feeling"* of God's presence is sensual, it appeals to our senses which are all part of the flesh and not to our spirit. Above all, God gets the glory through Jesus Christ but in our modern-day churches, they are consumed with gaining the recognition, popularity, and glory. You will quickly hear those who are followers of the modern-day churches say, *"The presence of God is felt through this pastor or their services, etc."* This merely gives glory to that particular man or movement not to God. As sensual people, we are always looking for God through our senses even though the Bible teaches that we find God through His Word alone!

Psalm 19:7-11(ESV) The law of the LORD is perfect, reviving the soul; the testimony of the LORD is sure, making wise the simple; ^{8}the precepts of the LORD are right, rejoicing the heart; the commandment of the LORD is pure, enlightening the eyes; ^{9}the fear of the LORD is clean, enduring forever; the rules of the LORD are true, and righteous altogether. ^{10}More to be desired are they than gold, even much fine gold; sweeter also than honey and drippings of the honeycomb. ^{11}Moreover, by them is your servant warned; in keeping them there is great reward.

Psalm 119:160 (ESV) The <u>sum</u> of your word is truth, and every one of your righteous rules endures forever.

A quick note is the word *"sum."* The sum of something is when you add everything up. It is the sum of His Word that is truth, meaning that every single word written in the Bible all added together makes truth. We cannot pick and choose what Scriptures we want to follow and what ones we do not. Of course, it is a growing process as you spend time with Him in His Word that you continually grow in truth but NOT by following a particular denomination or a particular man or woman.

We know that God speaks through His Word, but He also speaks with that small quiet voice that the majority never hear because of the distractions in this world, which I have touched on this subject and will continue to emphasize this throughout this book.

I would also like to emphasize that I am not saying that you will never feel His presence, but when you feel His presence, it is going to be because you spent time seeking Him alone and you did not need a new-movement church that has all the right music, sound systems, talented dancers, etc. that conjured up a god for you to feel. God is NOT a genie in the bottle that when we rub it the right way, we feel His presence. Besides, God is looking for a people who desire to seek Him diligently through His Word. In seeking Him alone, you will find Him, and it will be because His Words come alive within your spirit. We are all spiritual beings and our spirits can connect with His spirit but only if we truly seek Him to know Him not because we desire a god to fix our lives. It is His Word, the Word of God that is alive and dwells within us but it does not dwell within most people who claim to be Christians because they seldom seek Him. He cannot and will not abide within the lives of those who are fake Christians. He knows His sheep because they know Him and know His voice and choose to follow His voice not a man-made conjured up modern-day church service. It is merely a spectacle to bring glory to man's methods to create a god, and it is no different than when Moses went to the top of Mt. Sinai in order to spend time with God. Moses returned only to see the creation of a man-made god that the people chose to follow because it appealed to their senses just as the churches today have gone way out into left field.

If you go back to the statistics that I gave on the percentages of how many really seek God, it is clear to see that most people are not really looking for the real God. Just like in the desert for 40 days, they did not want the real God, they wanted to make their own god that gave them sensual pleasures just like the modern-day churches do today. They want a god that allows them to live their sensual lives breaking all kinds of commandments as they choose. They want to believe that the god they serve will surely not send them to hell, but they better read the Scriptures because only few will make it to heaven.

I touched on debauchery, which merely means excessive indulgence in sensual pleasures. Debauchery is for those who seek for self-indulgence and pleasure. It actually surprises these new modern-day movements why all the churches do not have eyes to see and ears to hear what they are feeling. They feel that they are the only ones that are really hearing from God because they *"feel"* His presence. What these churches are actually doing is speaking spitefully and critical of those who do not agree with their sensual means of growing their churches to mega proportions. You can be reading this and claim that I am doing the same thing; however, darkness always comes to the light and darkness will be exposed. I have no problem naming darkness when I see it for what it is because God's Word is the ultimate guide on what is right and what is wrong. I myself continue to give my own experiences of being in such churches, even as a leader and what goes on behind the scenes. These churches are money makers where the head leaders are gaining fortune and fame. These movements are being led by false teachers and prophets in which we are warned about in the Word of God, and there will be further discussion throughout this book on that topic.

The Scripture back on page 25, 1 Peter 4, in which I underlined several areas, also speaks of suffering in the flesh as Christ suffered in the flesh. Our heaven is NOT on this earth and neither will our blessings be on this earth. We live out these lives for Jesus Christ, solely. It is not for our pleasures. We are NOT to live for human passions but for God's will for our lives. I promise you, His will for your life will be all about Jesus Christ not about you. The modern-day churches are full of debauchery which as I have said, is merely sensual pleasures. If we feel a certain way during worship, we assume that this is the presence of God where He is pleased with offering up our worship to Him. However, those feelings that are present are through our flesh, they are not feelings of living in the spirit as we are required. There is only one way to know God and that is through faith. We experience faith which is knowledge in knowing Him. We can only know Him through His Word, not through man's methods that they have construed in order to bring a false perception of a god that does not exist. The new church movements are not Biblical.

Hebrews 11:1 (NKJV) Now faith is the substance of things hoped for, the evidence of things not seen.

Romans 10:17 (NKJV) So then faith comes by hearing, and hearing by the word of God.

God is omnipresent, and we come to know Him NOT through a particular song or a particular denomination in which man produces. God is already right there, but when we use those methods thinking that we are conjuring up God for that moment, that is incorrect thinking, and whatever god you think you are following, it is NOT Biblical. Yes, there are many songs out there that minister to our spirit which helps us to realize that He is right there, but it was not the song that brought Him there; He was already there. satan can corrupt our methods and enjoys doing so, where we believe that those feelings are conjuring up the one true God, but far too often, you are conjuring up the wrong spirit instead of God Himself.

He is not a feeling and He is not an emotion; He is God! Are we stewards of His grace or are we merely going through man's methods to conjure up a god that we don't even know? Are our methods to bring forth this god in order that our prayers are answered the way we want them answered? Are our prayers for things of this world and for the pleasures of this world?

It is and never will be about how much time a man or woman of God spends preparing a message to share with others but how much time they spent in the presence of God that will determine their walk with the Lord. If there is NOT time spent, there is NO truth. Think about it this way, based on the surveys we covered, there are few that really spend anytime seeking and studying the Scriptures. Only God's Word is Truth.

1 John 3:18 (NKJV) My little children, let us not love in word or tongue, but in deed and in truth.

John 1:17 (NKJV) For the law was given through Moses, but grace and truth came through Jesus Christ.

Psalm 25:5 (NKJV) Lead me in Your truth and teach me, For You are the God of my salvation; On You I wait all the day.

Psalm 145:18 (NKJV) The LORD is near to all who call upon Him, To all who call on Him in truth.

You cannot pour out truth if truth is NOT inside of you. Whatever you spend your time weekly doing, that is what you are full of. Your desires, your rituals, your beliefs, all of these things are based on what is on the inside of you. If you have very little Jesus inside of you, it will not come forth. What we are full of is what will come forth out of our mouth because what is in our heart comes out of our mouth. This goes for those who are ministers of the Word of God, as well as those who claim to be Christians. If you are not pouring Him inside of your heart, then He is NOT there!

Matthew 15:8-9, 18 (ESV) "This people honors me with their lips, but their heart is far from me; ⁹in vain do they worship me, teaching as doctrines the commandments of men." ¹⁸But what comes out of the mouth proceeds from the heart, and this defiles a person.

The words within the Bible are life to those who find them and once you truly find that life, you will also know what voice to follow!

CHAPTER FOUR
THE VOICE OF EVIL

As I have said, I was a leader in a large church myself many years ago. I was able to see the politics behind the scenes that the people will never see. I even learned that there are websites out there where you can actually buy your sermon. Look it up, it is not difficult to find and there are many to choose from. The church I frequented many years ago, as a leader, we were given insight into this if we ever needed to purchase a sermon ourselves. Many pastors today take advantage of someone else doing the work for them and the congregation has no idea that their pastor did NOT hear from God! It is not surprising to me to hear about these things, since I have witnessed firsthand many *"behind the scene"* practices that the congregation is unaware.

To go a bit deeper, the mega-type churches became very popular during the church growth movement that took root in the 70s. There are many articles written on this topic as well as documentaries, in which I have focused on a few that I have given credit to and references at the back of this book. I urge everyone to spend time on this topic which is very Biblical for these end times, as there will be multitudes led astray by these movements from lack of knowledge. It is imperative, as God's people, to be wise to the craftiness of man's wickedness and extremely important in these times to study the Scriptures ourselves, in order to know the Truth and then to impart these Truths to our children and every single person that the Holy Spirit sends across our paths.

I will begin with a brief history on Peter Drucker. Drucker was born in Vienna, he moved to America in the 30s and became a professor and public intellectual. He was a key player in the corruption of the modern-day church movement called the seeker-sensitive church movement which falls under the name, Church Growth. This movement began in the 50s independently by pastor Robert Schuler and seminary professor Donald McGavran. The movement's focus was on identifying sociological factors that attract or repel people from the churches and to promote the knowledge of these factors. It was in the 80s that Drucker came on the scene and chose 3 Evangelical leaders Rick Warren, Bill Hybels, and Bob Buford. He mentored them in the application of his management theories to church government. These men used his marketing strategies and his secular wisdom to increase church growth.[1]

Drucker had witnessed the rise of Nazism and communism and had concluded that the Western societies were fundamentally sick, and he dedicated his life to finding a means of social renewal. In his findings, he created what has become the modern theory of management out of a belief that corporations could spearhead social renewal by providing man with the community he needs. He eventually came to the conclusion that the megachurch was the key to influencing society for the better.[2]

Drucker, not being a Christian at all, took his knowledge in the 80s in order to mentor those 3 men who have all become leaders of megachurches today. These megachurches have used the marketing tools and wisdom of man in order to build their empires, not the wisdom of God. We fail to see that it is only through seeking and walking with Our Creator will we fulfill His purpose, not man's purpose on this earth. I will touch on many of these topics, as it is extremely important that we know whose voice we are following. It will NEVER be about following man's voice or wisdom but following the voice of the Holy Spirit and God's wisdom.

Drucker, an unbeliever of the Bible, used his findings to play a major role in the corruption of the modern-day churches in America and other parts of the world today. Drucker's agenda never lined up with God's agenda. Through man's wisdom, the Church Growth Movement has become an outlet for people to come and be seduced by this world. These movements are being led by false prophets, as I will show through Scripture.

Rick Warren's name began to emerge in the 90s. Today, Warren, pastor of the 6th largest church in the U.S. and author of *The Purpose Driven Life, The Purpose Driven Church,* among others, was also named one of the top 15 world leaders who mattered most by Times Magazine. Warren went on to build *The Purpose Driven Network*, which is a global alliance of pastors trained to be purpose driven churches in 162 countries. Items that are worth noting are that this church growth movement has swept our country, as well as other countries and continues to grow. This movement is a new reformation within the church where those following this method have chosen to build a ministry based on what people want instead of these ministries being Biblically based. They omit the gospel teachings where they give the people what they want instead of what they need. Their methods are based on the philosophies of man's business model, in order to reach a huge majority of people. Yet, the Bible tells us that there are only the few that will go to heaven while Jesus will tell the majority, *"I never knew you!"*

Luke 13:23-24 (ESV) And someone said to him, "Lord, will those who are saved be few?" And he said to them, 24"Strive to enter through the narrow door. For many, I tell you, will seek to enter and will not be able.

Warren, along with many others who have stepped out to build their empires, have chosen to select bits and pieces of the Scriptures to fit into their own propaganda. However, what they select does not convict people of their sin nor lead them to the cross to be forgiven. These celebrity pastors, desire to be praised by man and to be glorified which is quite the opposite of what John the Baptist taught.

John 3:27-28,30 (ESV) John answered, "A person cannot receive even one thing unless it is given him from heaven.

²⁸You yourselves bear me witness, that I said, 'I am not the Christ, but I have been sent before him.' ³⁰He (Christ) must increase, but I must decrease.'"

The Bible clearly laid out roles for a range of church leadership instead of a celebrity pastor as the sole leader. (Ephesians 4:11-12) A celebrity pastor is not even a church office in the Bible. Why are these pastors referred to as celebrities? Well the word celebrity is defined as someone who is well known, popular among many, a household name, a star. When people in a certain city refer to a certain church that has gained a great reputation with the many, as *"pastor so and so's church,"* that pastor has just been increased as Jesus was decreased.

There are many church leaders today that are redefining the word pastor. According to the Word of God, a pastor is a shepherd, and a shepherd is to watch over God's flock. They are to be willing to serve God's people not for gain nor for fame.

1 Peter 5:1-2 (ESV) So I exhort the elders among you, as a fellow elder and a witness of the sufferings of Christ, as well as a partaker in the glory that is going to be revealed: ²shepherd the flock of God that is among you, exercising oversight, not under compulsion, but willingly, as God would have you; not for shameful gain, but eagerly.

These megachurches are redefining the true Biblical teachings in order to bring in the masses and control the manner in the way people do church. In doing so, they have been successful in growing massive churches, as they have absolute authority over these man-made organizations which bring in millions of dollars annually. I would have to say that is pursuing dishonest gain, as they are exempt from paying taxes and even though they use some of the funds for good, these celebrity pastors live like kings, while Jesus lived quite the opposite.

Matthew 21:5 (NKJV) "Tell the daughter of Zion, 'Behold, your king is coming to you, Lowly, and sitting on a donkey, A colt, the foal of a donkey.'"

Matthew 23:10-12 (ESV) Nor are you to be called instructors, for you have one Instructor, the Messiah. [11]The greatest among you will be your servant. [12]For those who exalt themselves will be humbled, and those who humble themselves will be exalted.

Rick Warren, pastor of Saddleback Church, has stated that the primary role should be changed of the pastor from minister to leader. When asked if we should stop talking about pastors as shepherds, Andy Stanley, founder of North Point Ministries as well as senior pastor of many other churches, responded, *"Absolutely, that word needs to go away, it was culturally relevant in the time of Jesus but it's not culturally relevant anymore."*[2]

Deuteronomy 12:32 (NKJV) "Whatever I command you, be careful to observe it; you shall not add to it nor take away from it.

Revelation 22:18-19 (ESV) I warn everyone who hears the words of the prophesy of this book: if anyone adds to them, God will add to him the plagues in this book, [19]and if anyone takes away from the words of the book of this prophesy, God will take away his share in the tree of life and in the holy city, which are described in this book.

As leaders of these megachurches, they cast visions to their congregations who follow their lead because they are taught that only their leader has a direct line to God and any who do not want to follow their vision can either leave or pretty much stay in their place and not cause waves to their teachings.[2]

As these leaders cast their vision to their congregations, they claim these visions are from God directly to that leader on how that ministry should evolve and the people must follow that man as he is the visionary. Elevation Church claims they are united under the visionary, Steven Furtick, their leader. One of their videos states that they are united under one vision; Elevation is built on the vision that God gave to pastor Steven and they will aggressively defend their unity and that vision. Also noted on their website, they state that they serve a lead pastor who seeks and hears from God[2], even though the role of a pastor is to serve the people not the other way around.

Matthew 20:26b-28 (ESV) "But whoever would be great among you must be your servant, 27and whoever would be first among you must be your slave, 28even as the Son of Man came not to be served but to serve, and to give his life as a ransom for many."

John 13:12-17 (ESV) When he had washed their feet and put on his outer garments and resumed his place, he said to them, "Do you understand what I have done to you? 13You call me Teacher and Lord, and you are right, for so I am. 14If I then, your Lord and Teacher, have washed your feet, you also ought to wash one another's feet. 15For I have given you an example, that you also should do just as I have done to you. 16<u>Truly, truly</u>, I say to you, a servant is not greater than his master, nor is a messenger greater than the one who sent him. 17If you know these things, blessed are you if you do them.

Jesus was saying that He is the Lord and the ultimate Teacher and there is none greater than He that has walked among us, and if He being the greatest and willing to wash our feet and serve us, we are to do likewise. Those messengers, the ones who are truly sent by God, recognize that they are NOT God and NOT to be exalted because they will never be greater than the One who sent them! One more thing to note, when you see the word "truly," which is "verily" in the King James Version, in the Greek it is *"amen."* When we say amen after praying, it stands for completeness or being finished, having the last word. There are times when we hear a message that is really making a stance, and we will say *"AMEN."* We do this because we are in agreement that what was just said was very important to be in agreement with. This word in the Greek is used by Jesus because we are to know that He is saying something that is of utmost importance, and we should not only be paying attention but also be in agreement to do what He is saying.

The Crossing Church in Elk River, MN, also claim that they are united under one vision and will also aggressively defend the vision that God gave to their leader, Eric Dykstra. They claim in a video that they do not want to go against God, in their own words and I quote, *"Not saying that Eric is God, but that Eric is the visionary that hears from God and to go against that would be going against God."* They will do church the way that Eric wants to do church based on his visions, as he is their visionary and hears from God. If any oppose the vision, they are opposing God![2] All these practices are unbiblical, as there is nothing in the Word of God about vision casting except when it is spoken of as false and misleading.

Lamentations 2:14 (ESV) Your prophets have seen for you false and deceptive visions; they have not exposed your iniquity to restore your fortunes, but have seen for you oracles that are false and misleading.

As stated above, these visionaries would be prophets if they claim they hear from God but they are false and misleading because their messages are not spoken to expose sin or iniquities as stated above. To make this clearer, these visionary's visions are being given spiritually but not by the right spirit according to Scripture, they have seen oracles which is prophesy given by a priest or leader acting as a medium where they receive the prophesy from false gods. This is not a new practice, as it has always been a battle between good and evil and will continue until the return of Jesus Christ for His true church.

Bill Hybels, founder and former senior pastor of Willow Creek Community Church in South Barrington, Illinois, has had conversations with those in his church who do not agree with the vision. His way of handing that situation, is to simply ask those not in agreement, *"Must you leave the church?"* Or basically, can they remain at the church and not sin?[2] In other words, he is making the statement that he is right and they are wrong, and if they cannot agree with him, they are in sin. Many of these pastors believe that there are many stubborn people in the church that do not agree with the vision and these people will have to die off just as they did in the desert in Biblical days.

Andy Stanley, in an article that I have referenced in the back of this book, claims there are 3 components that will be included in vision casting.[3] I am sure that Stanley would not give me permission to quote his methods, but I assure you that the methods are those created by the world and not found in the Bible. I encourage those reading this to pull up his article and read it for themselves. The problem with all these pastors is they have redefined the Biblical teachings of Jesus Christ. It is no longer about following what the Word of God says but about following a mere man.

Pastor Mark Driscoll, founder and visionary of Mars Hill Church in Seattle, used an illustration of a *"bus,"* where he stated that there was a pile of dead bodies behind the Mars Hill bus, and by God's grace, it would be a mountain by the time they were done, stating that you either get on the bus or you get run over by the bus because the bus was not going to stop. To Driscoll, there are a few kinds of people, those who get in the way of the bus and get runover, those who want to take turns driving the bus because they want to go somewhere else and they get thrown off, those who just sit on the bus and shut-up, and as long as they cause no waves, they just let them ride along, even though they do nothing to serve or help. Then there are those who are helpers and serve his vision.[2] I found it strange that he used a bus for his illustration, I guess he never read the book by C.S. Lewis, *The*

Great Divorce, or perhaps he did. In Lewis' book, those who were either in hell or purgatory, had a choice to get on the bus which took them to the foothills of heaven; however, it was not heaven, only the foothills. In the foothills, they were all like ghost. Even though it was beautiful, they were all in great pain to walk on the grass or touch anything because everything was solid except for their transparent bodies. This was their last chance to get it right but as normal, the majority chose to get back on the bus and return to hell. There was too much effort on their part to continue the long journey from the foothills to heaven just as we also see in John Bunyan's book, *The Pilgrim's Progress*. Those who choose to be persecuted as Jesus was will be the only ones that make it through the foothills of pain and suffering all the way to that narrow gate which leads to heaven. However, it's a bit too late for Driscoll, as his visions came to an end in 2014, as shady things began to be uncovered of his character and honesty. I suppose Driscoll could be considered one of those dead bodies behind the Mars Hill bus, after all. You can read about the *"Rise and Fall of Mars Hill Church"* from my reference at the end of this book."[4] Perhaps Driscoll, along with the others who <u>rode</u> in the bus will one day realize they need to hear from the true God and make things right where they will make it to heaven.

This will not be the last we hear of the rise and fall of a megachurch. According to the Word of God which is seldom preached in its entirety in the megachurches today, these churches will all fall that have chosen to teach contrary to the Word of God.

Ezekiel 13:9 (ESV) My hand will be against the prophets who see false visions and who give lying divinations. They shall not be in the council of my people, nor be enrolled in the register of the house of Israel, nor shall they enter the land of Israel. And you shall know that I am the Lord God.

Jeremiah 23:16 (ESV) Thus says the LORD of hosts: "Do not listen to the words of the prophets who prophesy to you, filling you with vain hopes. They speak visions of their own minds, not from the mouth of the LORD.

Church for the Unbelievers

To bring truth to light, these mega-type churches visions are all about the unchurched which is also unbiblical. Warren, in growing the Saddleback church, walked the neighborhoods to survey why people did not attend church, in order to create a church for the unchurched. These mega-type churches are very adamant about their congregations knowing that the church they are growing is not about those who know Jesus Christ, but they are about those who are the unchurched or the unsaved. The church according to Scripture is the body of Christ, it is NOT a building. As believers, we are His church and we are instructed to be joined with other believers.

Colossians 1:18 (ESV) And he is the head of the body, the church. He is the beginning, the firstborn from the dead, that in everything he might be preeminent.

Ephesians 4:15 (NKJV) but, speaking the truth in love, we may grow up in all things into Him who is the head – Christ.

If you study the 7 churches in Revelation, it is easy to see the state of the churches today. Whereas, it is evident that unbelievers have NO place in fellowship with believers. We can bring the gospel of Jesus Christ to the lost which is what we all should be doing if we truly belong to Christ, then we go forth sharing the true message of salvation to those who cross our paths, but unbelievers have NO place in fellowship with believers. As the church is made up of believers only, the true church is not a building but rather those who are in communion with Jesus Christ. The word church in the Greek is *ekklesia* which is translated to mean *"called-out ones, religious congregation, community of members on earth or saints in heaven or both."* Those who belong to Jesus Christ are called out as His disciples. There is nothing in Scripture about unbelievers being joined with those who have been called, but the Bible is clear that Jesus calls those who are His and they follow. The Bible is clear that the church refers to those who are believers.

John 10:3-5 (NKJV) To him the doorkeeper opens, and the sheep hear his voice; and he calls his own sheep by name and leads them out. ⁴And when he brings out his own sheep, he goes before them; and the sheep follow him, for they know his voice. ⁵Yet they will by no means follow a stranger, but will flee from him, for they do not know the voice of strangers."

Romans 1:5-6 (NKJV) Through Him we have received grace and apostleship for obedience to the faith among all nations for His name, ⁶among whom you also are the called of Jesus Christ.

Romans 8:28-30 (NKJV) And we know that all things work together for good to those who love God, to those who are the called according to His purpose. ²⁹For whom He foreknew, He also predestined to be conformed to the image of His Son, that He might be the firstborn among many brethren. ³⁰Moreover whom He predestined, these He also called; whom He called, these He also justified, these He also glorified.

We are not to be following the lead of a visionary who sets forth <u>his</u> vision. We are all to be following the ONE voice which is that of the Holy Spirit. My sheep hear My voice, Jesus did not say that His people will know Him by His visionaries that He gives all authority to. Being under compulsion as stated earlier and again below in 1 Peter 5, means following a leader who pushes and drives us to follow under his command. This is none other than following someone who has conned those to listen to him which will be discussed further in chapter six.

1 Peter 5:2-3 (ESV) ²shepherd the flock of God that is among you, exercising oversight, not under <u>compulsion</u>, but willingly, as God would have you; not for shameful gain, but eagerly; ³not <u>domineering</u> over those in your charge, but being examples to the flock.

John 10:27 (NKJV) My sheep hear My voice, and I know them, and they follow Me.

The Bible clearly teaches us that in those days, there will be many false prophets arise. *(Matthew 24:11)* The Bible also teaches us that there is NO need we be taught by MAN because our teacher is the Holy Spirit. *(1 John 2:27)* No one can get into heaven, not even those visionaries unless they are hearing the voice of the Holy Spirit. Overseers of the flock of God will be men who are humbled and you do not see humility among those leading the huge flocks, but you see the desires to bring in the multitudes in order that they gain more of this world.

Titus 1:7-9 (ESV) For an overseer, as God's steward, must be above reproach. He must not be arrogant or quick-tempered or a drunkard or violent or greedy for gain, ⁸but hospitable, a lover of good, self-controlled, upright, holy, and disciplined. ⁹He must hold firm to the trustworthy word as taught, so that he may be able to give instruction in sound doctrine and also to rebuke those who contradict it.

Wolves in Sheep Clothing

We are warned in Scripture regarding these times and those who will come forth as wolves in sheep clothing. To come in sheep clothing merely means that they will come to deceive, as they will present themselves as a true sheep of God. From the outwardly, they will seem as a true sheep but inwardly, they are wolves.

When I was on the streets ministering weekly to those who were homeless, during one of my teachings, I passed around a stuffed toy sheep for all to examine. My question to those that day was, *"Does this look like a sheep?"* Well, yes outwardly it did look like a sheep. I then said, *"If I were to tell you that this was a wolf, would you believe me?"* The answer to that is NO! It looked like a sheep on the outside in every way. There would be NO way I could convince anyone that it was a wolf because WE look on the outside, but God sees on the inside! Hear my voice as I say this, YOU WILL BE DECIEVED IF YOU DO NOT HEAR THE VOICE OF THE HOLY SPIRIT! You cannot follow God if you do not hear His voice. If you are following anything other than His voice, you will be led astray! We hear His voice by coming to know Him and you cannot come to know Him if you are NOT reading and studying the Word of God entirely in your quiet time alone with Him.

Acts 20:29-30 (ESV) I know that after my departure fierce wolves will come in among you, not sparing the flock; ^{30}and from among your own selves will arise men speaking twisted things, to draw away the disciples after them.

The church growth model as I have said, is unbiblical. This movement was designed to bring in the masses as their goal is all about numerical growth. They stand up boldly to proclaim that preaching should be judged by the numerical results, meaning that a good preacher brings in the numbers. I suppose Jesus would not have been judged rightly since the multitudes came, but He was unable to keep them. Jesus did NOT have a huge following. When the multitudes came, it was for the miracles and then they walked away. The multitudes came for the food and then they walked away.

As a former leader of a large church, I taught on it being all about the numbers because we were taught that your fruit was based on numbers. These teachings bothered me in my spirit, even before I knew the truth because it did not feel like God.

I battled with this inside especially when the pastor looked at our fruit based on the numbers each leader was bringing forth. If you were not bringing in the numbers as a leader, you evidently were not spiritual enough. The other problem I had was in their methods to bring in the numbers and keep them. I'm not going to go into deep detail on my own experience, I just want to add that following our Lord and Savior has nothing to do with numbers. Christianity is not measured by numbers but by your individual walk and relationship with your Creator. It is easy to go back to the Scriptures and know that the only fruit in the Bible is the fruit of the Holy Spirit. The picture looks more like this, when you spend time with your Creator by seeking Him through His Word, you will grow in truth. As you grow in truth dependent upon how much time and effort you give to knowing Him, your life will change beginning on the inside and it will spill out on the outside. When we continue filling our lives with this world, that is what will be seen on the outside, but when we fill our lives with Him, you will be able to see Him on the outside. Never measure the worth of someone based on what their words claim but measure them by what you see on the outside. Yes, you <u>can</u> tell a book by the cover, Jesus never said that you can't. The Bible clearly tells us that you can tell a person's heart by their actions.

Proverbs 27:19 (NKJV) As in water face reflects face, So a man's heart reveals the man.

Matthew 15:18 (NKJV) But those things which proceed out of the mouth come from the heart, and they defile a man.

To emphasize this, your fruit is measured by your actions and when you are walking with His Spirit, you will do the things He has called you to do. In this, there will be abundant fruit that follows you and this is not about people. It is about you sharing truth, but we are not called to save people only to share truth with them and then that person is saved only when they step out to seek Jesus Christ themselves. This is the problem with the megachurches today; they bring in the masses and they teach them their own philosophies and never encourage them to study and read for themselves. A true man or woman of God will only lead someone to the Cross but from that point, it is dependent upon that person for their own salvation. How can these megachurches even teach people about salvation when they omit the teachings of the Crucifixion and repentance? You cannot be saved without the knowledge of the true Word of God in its entirety with nothing being left out.

In these churches, any who would challenge the leadership by the Word of God are not welcome. Warren teaches that many churches do not grow because they have people within their congregations that will basically not change to follow the church growth movement and in those cases, that church may not be able to grow until they die off or leave. I have shared this briefly, but Warren uses the Scriptures that teach on Moses leading God's people into the desert and that God allowed them to spend 40 years until most of them had died. However, Warren is claiming that the problem is with those who do not want to follow the pastor or leader by following their vision for church, as these leaders claim that God has evidently given them the gift on how to do church. The other problem here is that the Bible shows all how to do church. What most of the churches today look like is not what the church looked like in Biblical days, and this newer movement goes against the teachings of Jesus Christ. Let me just say, it is not hard to google any of these pastors, as there are many of them who are in videos, documentaries, etc. They enjoy being highlighted on their beliefs. I have just given a few references, but there are many out there as well as the books they write in which they make millions. You can browse through their books and find numerous beliefs that are not Biblical. If you are in one of these churches, try to show those leaders what true Biblical teachings are and you will see how fast they will come against you. Warren along with others in this movement, choose not to teach on sin, repentance, the cross/crucifixion, and they do not teach on Bible prophesy. In fact, many of these movements teach an anti-doctrinal message and discourage any study of Bible prophesy. There are some who claim that Bible prophesy is a diversion from the devil, even though, 1/3 of the Bible is prophesy. Their focus is all about fulfilling their mission not studying nor teaching prophesy.

2 Tim 4:2-5 (ESV) preach the word; be ready in season and out of season; reprove, rebuke, and exhort, with complete patience and teaching. ³For the time is coming when people will not endure sound teaching, but having itching ears they will accumulate for themselves <u>teachers to suit their own passions</u>, ⁴and will turn away from listening to the truth and wander off into myths. ⁵As for you, always be sober-minded, endure suffering, do the work of an evangelist, fulfill your ministry.

These were Paul's words. If we are truly seeking Jesus Christ, we will find Him. We will NOT find Him in a man but one on one. Your relationship with Jesus will lead you on a pathway that will look like the same pathway as the disciples who walked with Jesus. We are to be ready in season and out of season, and we cannot be ready for what He has called us to if we are NOT seeking Him and seeking Truth! As we pour into His Word, He will pour into us.

There will be suffering while here on earth and we will be persecuted, if we are doing the work that He called us to and if we are striving to fulfill our own personal ministry. We all have a ministry and it begins with truly knowing Jesus not knowing the pastor. However, we see by the above Scripture that there are going to be people who seek for those teachers who give them a god that fits into their own lives. This is why the megachurches grow in abundance of people because the majority of people want a god that makes them feel good about themselves and a god that allows them to continue living in their sins.

The methods of the megachurches on salvation contradict Biblical teachings. Warren's method is to simply pray, *"Jesus,*

I believe in you and receive you!" Warren, in his books and on stage, will stand up and recite this method of salvation and then say, *"If you meant that prayer, congratulations, welcome to the family of God!"* There is no mention of repentance to sin at all and no mention of faith in Christ.

Matthew 7:21 (ESV) I Never Knew You 21 "Not everyone who says to me, 'Lord, Lord,' will enter the kingdom of heaven, but the one who does the will of my Father who is in heaven.

Luke 13:3 (NKJV) I tell you, no; but unless you repent, you will all likewise perish.

Ephesians 2:8 (NKJV) For by grace you have been saved through faith, and that not of yourselves; it is the gift of God.

Probably, the most quoted Scripture is John 3:16, which states that all who believe in Him will have eternal life. However, we cannot just focus on the one Scripture or we will be led astray. The above Scriptures also say, only those who know Him will enter the Kingdom of Heaven, only those who do His will, and only those who repent. We only know Him based on time spent with Him. Remember, it is not about just believing in Jesus. satan believes in Jesus, but that is not what He means. If you really believe in something, you will die following that which you believe in your heart. The main thing is that you know Him intimately. To know Him only happens as you gain knowledge through studying His Word. If you don't know Him, He doesn't know you either. You can continue reading in Matthew 7 to be able to see this is true. To know Him, we must seek until we really find Him. *(Matthew 7:7-8)*

The unbelievers flock into these churches and never gain any wisdom or knowledge of Scripture, and they are discouraged to read and study themselves, as they are trained to follow that man. These unbelievers by the multitudes believe that they are saved and going to heaven.

Warren, as well as many of these leaders, teach that these churches are not for those who are saved. They teach that once they say their little prayer for salvation, that the church is no longer about them. One of his tag lines is, *"It's not about you!"* This slogan mainly means that these churches that are in mega-proportions, are established to bring in the multitudes by whatever means is necessary. In order to bring in the multitudes that are goats, you pretty much have to make these churches look like the world, and they have done this!

Many of the churches today spend thousands of dollars in order to bring the same entertainment of the world inside of their sanctuaries. They put on an elaborate performance with secular music. Much of the elements used are composed of the pop culture of today which is part of man's methods of marketing strategies, business techniques, and demographics rather than Biblical instructions. There are pastors who use a humanistic psychology and self-esteem theology which appeal to the masses. They develop brochures, videos, etc., in order to entice this generation. All of these methods are geared towards enticing the unchurched and providing a place for those who would otherwise not attend the kind of church that Jesus built. This is the church for the unbeliever, but is there such a thing as a church for those who do not believe? According to the new growth movement, the church is not for believers because these visionaries are quick to let believers know that God is interested in the unchurched. However, when Jesus prayed to His Father for those who followed Him, He was very explicit in saying that He did not pray for those in this world, only for those that the Father had sent to Him. If that be the case, Jesus was NOT praying for the unchurched; He was praying for those who were His disciples. He was praying for those who followed His lead in doing the same things that He did. This is the difference between believers and unbelievers. Jesus did NOT pray for those who did NOT believe. He only prayed for those who His Father sent to Him not to just anyone and everyone in this world.

John 17:9-10 (ESV) I am praying for them. I am not praying for the world but for those whom you have given me, for they are yours. ¹⁰All mine are yours, and yours are mine, and I am glorified in them.

John 14:12a (ESV) "<u>Truly, truly</u>, I say to you, whoever believes in me will also do the works that I do.

Jesus did NOT pray for the world and the true church is NOT for the world. These churches should not even be called churches according to Scripture because the church is NOT for the unbeliever. The New Testament church is for the equipping of the saints and unbelievers are not considered the saints.

We see in Scripture that the church is sent out into the world but does not bring the world into the church. *(Matthew 28:18-20)* Our calling was never to build the church, much less to fill it with unbelievers. In Matthew 16, we see this by Jesus' response from the question He asked Peter. Jesus knew Peter's heart and that his answer was genuine because he had come to that intimate knowledge to know and truly believe in Jesus Christ.

Matthew 16:18 (NKJV) And I also say to you that you are Peter, and on this rock I will build My church, and the gates of Hades shall not prevail against it.

We all have choices, we can either seek to find Him intimately as Peter did, or we can play church each week believing in that man or woman at the pulpit. Whichever you choose, that will be who you serve, man or God?

These mega-churches today are congregations filled with people by men who have used worldly measures to fill their pocket books and bring them fame. These are nothing more than cults that will be destroyed in God's timing. The church grows as those who follow Biblical principles, go out into the world to share the Truth as written in the Word of God. The majority will reject truth but the true church will stand through all persecution because Jesus Christ intercedes on behalf of those who are truly His. *(John 17:1-26)*

Warren, like many other megachurch leaders, seldom teach anything on Jesus and when they do use His name, their statements are many times unbiblical. Jesus said to beware, that these false teachers would rise up and that the wolves were already among us. *(Matthew 7:15-20)*

We are told in many Scriptures that if they deny Christ, they are false teachers. We think just because someone may say the name of Jesus that this shows they have not denied Him, but we must look at what that word means. Deny is the state where one refuses to admit truth or existence from. When these *"so-called"* preachers or leaders stand before the multitudes and teach heresies, they have denied Christ. Robert Schuller, who passed away in 2015, stated in the article referenced at the back of this book, that there was certain language in the Bible that he would not use because it would make the people angry, and they would leave.[5] Schuller was interviewed and the responses of his answers are noted. At one point, he shut down and quit answering the questions. The point is, Schuller in his own words did not take the Bible or what Jesus said as literal. He made his own religion to bring people to church by making them believe that it's all about God wanting them to be happy. Schuller did not believe in telling people that they were sinners because those words should not be used. My favorite quote that Schuller used in the interview was, *"Just because it is in the Bible doesn't mean you should preach it."* I will also have to say, Schuller quoted that he was very proud of who he was and that he had not broken any of the ten commandments or teachings of Jesus Christ.[5] This is quite amusing as it reminds me of the rich young ruler who declared the same thing to Jesus. Jesus told the rich young ruler to sell all he had and follow Him, but the rich young ruler was unable because he had much wealth. In Matthew 9, Jesus also tells us that he did NOT come for those who were well but for those who needed a physician. Those who claim they are without sin believe themselves to be well and so, Jesus did not come for them. He came for those who are lowly and humble, those who believe they need a savior.

In Warren's book, *The Purpose Driven Church*, his method of going door-to-door to see what the unchurched wanted in a church, was influenced by Schuller's book, *Your Church Has Real Possibilities.* Schuller had gone door-to-door in 1955 asking hundreds the question, "Why don't you go to church?" and *"What do you want in a church?"* Warren capitalized on Schuller's method but came up with 5 questions to ask which have been utilized among thousands of churches today using this same method.[6]

Their methods of teaching are based on giving the people a sense of a god that they would serve not by giving them the true God. If the name of Jesus were used and shared in true Biblical content, the people would not stay just like they did not remain when Jesus shared truth! By teaching false doctrine, these leaders of the modern megachurches deny Jesus Christ every single time they stand before the people. Their churches are NOT churches but they are congregations of demonology.

Matthew 10:33 (NKJV) But whoever denies Me before men, him I will also deny before My Father who is in heaven.

Titus 1:16 (NKJV) They profess to know God, but in works they deny Him, being abominable, disobedient, and disqualified for every good work.

2 Peter 2:1 (ESV) But false prophets also arose among the people, just as there will be false teachers among you, who will secretly bring in destructive heresies, even denying the Master who bought them, bringing upon themselves swift destruction.

1 John 2:22-23 (ESV) Who is the liar but he who denies that Jesus is the Christ? This is the antichrist, he who denies the Father and the Son. ²³No one who denies the Son has the Father also.

Christ is the title given to Jesus which merely means that He is the Son of God, the anointed One who came in order to save and redeem those who would choose to follow Him. When these false teachers stand up and teach heresies, it not only denies the teachings that Jesus gave but also it diminishes the power behind the true gospels that bring salvation to those who seek Him, not man!

Philippians 2:9-11 (ESV) Therefore God has highly exalted him and bestowed on him the name that is above every name, ¹⁰so that at the name of Jesus every knee should bow, in heaven and on earth and under the earth, ¹¹and every tongue confess that Jesus Christ is Lord, to the glory of God the Father.

In my references I have given recognition to an article written by Alan Roebuck[1], which was noted towards the beginning of this chapter. I do encourage you to read Alan's article in full, which is very well written. In his article, there is also a link to watch a video which is quite extensive but well worth the time. The video by Elliott Nesch can be accessed through Roebuck's article or by visiting the second reference at the end of this book.[2] Nesch has many video clips by many of the pastors I have written about in this chapter stating the facts in their own words which I have shared to an extent.

CHAPTER FIVE
VISIONARY LEADERS

There is much being said today about visions. Is this Biblical?

Joel 2:28 (KJV) And it shall come to pass afterward, that I will pour out my spirit upon all flesh; and your sons and your daughters shall prophecy, your old men shall dream dreams, your young men shall see visions.

Yes, having or seeing visions is Biblical. However, just because something is Biblical does not mean that we just accept any and everything we are hearing or being told. Remember, we are warned strongly by Our Lord and Savior that in those days, what days? In these days we are seeing right now—there will be many led astray. Why are they led astray? I know that I cover these things over and over again but the point is that these things need to be said over and over again because we know in the end, the majority will be in hell.

Matthew 24:24 (KJV) For there shall arise false Christs, and false prophets, and shall shew great signs and wonders; insomuch that, if it were possible, they shall deceive the very elect.

I would say it is very possible that the majority will be led astray because they trust in man and his philosophies on Scripture instead of seeking themselves. We are told to seek and we shall find. If we are merely seeking a man's philosophy and a man's religion, and a man's visions, then we are NOT seeking Jesus Christ. We are told to seek and we shall find. That Scripture does not say to seek man and you will find; however, you will find but it won't be Jesus Christ. We only find what we seek after. If your religion is based off of someone else doing the work of reading and studying the Bible for you, then yes, you will find a man—let's say a mere man because that is all that he is. You will not find Jesus.

You will not stand before Him one day for Him to say, *"Well done,"* on the contrary, He will say, *"Depart from me for I never knew you."*

Today, in this age, spiritualism has become the popular thing where everyone wants to seem mystic as they are attending the right church and following these great men who have a direct connection to God. These men lay out their visions and people seem to go full force in helping that man grow his church to become great among men. Let me tell you, there is nothing great about a man! Man did not create man, he didn't create the heavens nor the earth, he did not create anything we can see. Man made things from what God created. God is perfect and man is fallible. Yet, people are hungry to be fed something, and they say they want truth but they look to man that is fallible to receive that which they perceive to be truth. The only problem with this is that God is truth and outside of Him there is no truth.

I could touch on many articles out there today where there are businesses developed to help man grow his empire. I will say empire because man is full of greed, and they may only want a small slice of the pie but once that is achieved, they decide they want more. This is our sinful nature and that is what controls our life until we submit our will over to God's will. These organizations out there to help businesses thrive are not a bad thing, as long as they are helping those who own a business. Yes, learning to be a visionary leader in your place of business, company, organization, is not a bad thing. If there are businesses that are going under, hiring a company to come in to show you how to be a visionary leader, is a good thing. However, it has gone a step too far when we are now using man's method to grow a business in the church segment. Jesus never said to turn to man to learn how grow your church. For one thing, if in fact the leaders in your church are really hearing from God, they do not need a man to tell them how to grow their church because it is NOT their church. In fact, as we know, we are the church, for it is not a building. We are the church if we are really hearing from God. If we are not reading and studying and seeking Jesus, we are not hearing from God. Sometimes, I feel as though I say the same things over and over again but maybe by repetition, some who are reading this may actually get it. Perhaps, that light bulb will go off and you will understand that this is life and death and not a joke about how big *"my church is."*

These companies that are for hire, they use a man's model of success that has worked in the industry to help businesses thrive and not go under. It was never our job to grow the church anyway. Jesus' church and He needs no help in growing His church. In Matthew 16, Jesus told Peter that on this rock, He would build His church. It is His church not a man's church but His. He will build it and does not need our help. The problem with this is that most churches out there today want to be grand! They want to grow and thrive and be luxurious where their church stands out in the community and they are lifted up and increased with praise for the glorious things they are doing in the community. Those that desire to be increased and glorified on earth, will be cast down and not enter heaven. In John 3, John tells us that he is not the Christ and that Jesus must be increased and he must be decreased. In these visionary churches, they desire to be increased and increased and increased. They lead the multitudes astray by their false teachings and they show no glory unto God. Whose church is it anyway? Mans or Jesus'?

Walking with our Lord and Savior, we listen for His voice, that small quiet voice. He still speaks today, yet the majority seldom hear His voice. You will not hear His voice when your motives are for increase. That means when you are striving to be a Christian but your motives are for yourself, you will NOT hear His voice. Jesus came humbly to live among those who followed Him. He is the same today. When our motives for going to church, giving tithes or money are merely to belong to this church or that church, be a part of this ministry or that ministry, be blessed beyond measures, we will NOT hear His voice. Yes, you will hear man's voice because they are out there by the dozens striving to find all the puppets they can to control and take their money. They make promises that they cannot keep, but then they are not telling you that they will fulfill your wishes and you will be blessed beyond measures. It is God, they say that will bless you and increase your money when you help grow that ministry. I say all these things because I have been there, but I questioned everything. I am glad I had the experience from the inside which was necessary for me to know much about what goes on inside these churches. I will tell you that the majority of what is taught does NOT line up with Scripture.

These visionary leaders are very talented. Yes, they are smart people but not smart enough because in the end, they will not win. They have a certain personality. You know the type, those that seem to be able to talk anyone into doing anything. At some point in all of our lives, we meet these kinds of people. In the workforce, I was the kind of person that could run with something and get the job done. These traits are not bad traits, but they have no place in Christianity. Like I said, it is Jesus' church not man's.

In the work place, it takes those who are driven to get the job done. However, why would we be driven to grow a church? Remember, the church is NOT a building, but the church consists of all those who follow in the same pathway as Jesus Christ, hopefully. God already knows what is going to become of the church, it is in the Word of God. It is and never will be a man's or a visionary's job to be driven to usher in a new way to do church or a new way to grow the building that we call *"church"* to be an empire of thousands of *"unbelievers."* Sorry, but that job was not given to us. We are merely told to go and make disciples. Yet, the church building has become an easy place to drop our money in the offering plate and walk out the door believing that we have done what we are called to do. I am going to tell you, being a real Christian is NOT easy. It is hard because it takes your sacrifice. No one else can help you get to heaven. On the contrary, we already know that the majority will stand before Jesus one day as He tells them to, *"depart from me."* Jesus does not know the majority who claim to be Christians. Why? Because they only knew of Him by what someone else said. It takes YOU making the decision that YOU want to know Him.

Big Picture Leaders

Being a leader in a *"big church"* takes those who have a *"big picture."* To grow any business, it takes those who can see a bigger vision. However, we do not have to see the *"big picture"* in serving Jesus Christ because God already has that under control. We only have to believe, by walking in faith, that there is a bigger picture that we CANNOT see because Jesus is the author, creator, and finisher of what is to come. *(Hebrews 12:2 KJV)* We only follow as we are led by the Holy Spirit, not by man.

I share from time to time about the puzzle and have done so in Chapter two. The picture is all the same thing. It belongs to God, the picture, the puzzle—whatever you want to call it. We are all in that same picture and the large portion belongs to God. It is only our little bitty piece that fits in. When we try to create the big piece, we are trying to be God. We are only called to do our own part not take on the world and try to convince every lost soul out there that they are saved. If they are not seeking Him themselves, they are as lost as a goose. No ministry is going to save them, but woe to the ministries out there that try to convince the lost they are saved. Woe to those who are not leading the people to Him! You see, we can't save people, only God can. We can only lead them to Him, but we cannot make them drink of the water that is going to save them. Beware—it is not man's job to save them, but it is our job to lead them to seek and find Him! If any man or woman standing at those pulpits are not leading them to find Him but instead, they are leading them to believe they are saved without finding Him—beware because your days are numbered!

People want to attend the churches that look like they are thriving, but they gauge this by outward appearance. Man's methods to gain the multitudes have become to build these vibrant churches to attract the majority by their appearance on the outside and all the latest technology to appear as the world. You see, those churches are telling people, you don't have to give up much and you don't have to change much. We have brought the world into the mega-churches for you. It has only worked because the majority will never be saved anyway. It's Biblical, read it!

We look at success based on what the world tells us. What do we consider success as Christians? It has nothing to do with numbers, as I have shared but everything to do with man's heart as he seeks Jesus Christ intimately. A mere man cannot usher in new ways to do church and think he is pleasing God when we are told that Jesus is the only one that will build His church. We are NOT God as I have discussed; we are to be followers of Jesus Christ not of man! *(John 13:12-17)*

These big picture people make awesome CEO's of companies in order that the business thrives, and they are paid very well in doing so. The church was never meant to be a business but that is what these mega-churches have become. When we turn church into something that man has built, then we have cut *"Jesus"* out of the equation because He builds His church His way, and the actual church is the people who come together as one body in communion with our Lord. Never was the church about creating buildings and building them to be gigantic-monumental-architectural landmarks of any city. Not to mention, these churches spend thousands each year making every single thing within the building attractive in order to draw in the *"unsaved."* I have already briefly noted that the church, the body of Christ is NOT for unbelievers, and I will further emphasize this in the next chapter. *(1 Corinthians 12:27; Romans 12:4-5; Colossians 1:18)*

These visionary leaders are to change the course of that business by transformation, reorganization, restructuring, developing new methods and ideas. They must be able to sell their product. What is their product? Their product is the church, as there are evidently churches that come to a plateau and growth ultimately stops, and then there are also those small churches that will never grow. Let me emphasize that the churches which choose to share the same bold messages in which Jesus shared will NOT grow to mega-proportion. They will NEVER grow to be large because the majority do NOT really want to serve the real God! However, it is not that they cannot be megachurches, the norm is that they will never grow to that capacity unless Jesus is the author and finisher of their faith. I do have to say, that John MacArthur, pastor of Grace Community Church is California, is a megachurch. However, MacArthur teaches Calvinist theology, not lined up with a denomination, and he also speaks out against the prosperity gospel and emerging church movements. The difference is that Jesus can build His church where many come, but it will still only be the few that make heaven. We do not know what few means Biblically, but when the Word of God says that the many who believe themselves to be Christians stand before God one day, they will be sent away and only the few will be welcomed into heaven. We may not know what that number looks like, but we do know by the words *"many"* and *"few,"* that there will be more who believe themselves to be Christians not allowed to enter the narrow gate than those who will be allowed. This means that even though MacArthur may teach Truth from his pulpit, he knows there are many that come week after week that leave and do not really know Jesus. It will never be a mere man that can save someone, only Jesus and only when man truly desires to know Him intimately. So, in reality, the church not being a building but man, there are still few within MacArthur's congregation that will actually make heaven and that are actually the true church.

Charismatic Leaders

Those who are visionary leaders are normally very charismatic where they are gifted in a business setting to be able to take that establishment to a new level. As we have already learned, many of these leaders have gone door to door to see what the *"unchurched"* want a church to look like. Once these leaders know what the unchurched want, they go back and get their leaders on board to follow them as they begin their transformation of building church according to the vision by man. Their plan begins as they put into motion building a church that looks like the world. Oh, and it works as the people that are *"not saved"* begin to buy into their product which is a really cool atmosphere that feels like what they are used to in the world. These movements may call themselves church but according to Scripture they are nothing more than false prophets who have made a really awesome place for others to gather together to socialize. Their worship is not lifted up to the heavens but rather they worship man and his man-made ministry that went by motives also created by man! Nowhere in Scripture will you find anything of the sort. If you follow the ministry of Jesus Christ, you will see that His messages and methods of ministering to people turned the majority away because they really wanted a god that would allow them to continue in their sin, they really wanted a god that looked like the things they loved in the world, which they never would have given up that way of life anyway. This my friend is the world in which satan is their god! As we are told in Scripture, that the *"falling away"* will come prior to the return of Christ, which is what we are seeing today! *(2 Thessalonians 2:1-12; Matthew 4:10; John 6:25-27; John 6:66-67; Matthew 27:24-26; Matthew 7:13-14)*

These mega-churches always have projects going with their visions that continue to increase growth and funds where they can continue with more development, as they strive to bring in the masses where they are recognized by man to be one of the greatest churches of all times. Please never think that these men do not have every intention of being the greatest. It is in the nature of man to be on top and to be praised but as Christians, we are to be lowly and humble ourselves because we are NOTHING without truly walking with Jesus Christ and being of His humble nature.

They are charismatic leaders that know how to manipulate and sell their vision where others come on board having the sense that they are part of ushering in this huge mega-church, with all of the components that are attractive to the majority. Wait a minute, did I just say attractive to the majority? Yes, I did and we already know that Jesus tells us that only the few will find heaven. I guess the majority have already found their heaven, as they walk in the doors of their magnificent mega-churches with all the entertainment, glamour, seduction, etc. They all feel like one big family and that they are so lucky to have found this awesome church building, so that they can have fun singing their worldly music as they tell everyone, *"If you are happy, then God is happy too!" "If you are smiling, then God is smiling too!"* I think there are so many people out there that are truly looking for something real, but the sad truth is that if you really want what is real, it will take effort on your part to find it! Like seeking Jesus Christ for one!! *(Matthew 7:13-14; Matthew 5:3; Isaiah 66:1-2; Matthew 7:7; 1 John 2:15-17; Mark 8:34-37; John 3:27-30; Galatians 2:20)*

There's always a larger picture and these visionaries already know what that looks like and that is how they sell their product. However, the larger picture which is about life after this world, only God has that answer. Yes, you can study Scripture and learn a lot about heaven, but there is also a hell mentioned in the Bible, as well. This one life that we have here on this earth, it can either be your heaven or hell, but if your choice is to choose heaven for your time here on earth, be sure to know that you will face hell once you leave your earthly body. What do I mean by that? This earth in all its beauty and everything that God created for man to enjoy while here, the majority are very busy enjoying the things in which man created out of the things that God made from nothing. So, you can live this life as if it is one big party every single day on this earth, and this will be the only pleasures you will ever enjoy because your after-life has nothing to do with God's big picture in heaven. God's big picture for life after death are for all those who have chosen to give up their life for Christ's sake while here on this earth. In other words, this life on earth can be your hell but that is okay because your heaven awaits you after death. The larger picture to follow will be the one that is Biblical, not what a man has envisioned for those who chose to follow his ministry. It is NOT a man's ministry, the church and those who are true followers know that they have ONE God and they hear ONE voice and that is NOT the voice of a mere man! *(Matthew 7:13; 1 John 2:15-17)*

Let me emphasize something here that I use from time to time. My oldest daughter was killed at age 25. For most of her life, I had raised her according to the Word of God and 10 days prior to her death, she told me that she had been praying and knew that there was something that God had chosen her for but was unsure what that was. I gave birth to my daughter at age 17 and while I was pregnant my mother had died. It was a very hard time in my life, as I was not raised in a Christian home. There was much sadness in my life and I made miserable choices, as I did not have Jesus in my younger years. Many of my choices resulted in my oldest daughter having to live through things which none should have to live through. The good thing is that Jesus found me and saved me through His grace and while my daughter was still very young, she was able to experience Jesus Christ for much healing and pain that she had lived through for many years. Her life had been much torment and her years cut off much too soon. When she was killed, I never blamed God, I only wanted to know why. The *"whys"* are not important to what I want to share, as the importance of this story is to impart how God literally transformed my life because of her death to a place it could have never been. I have said many times, as a public speaker sharing my experiences and walk with Jesus, that if given the chance to go back, would I change things where she would not have died? My answer to that question was *"absolutely not"* because my daughter's life on this earth had been much hell and her life after was with Jesus. Do you understand that our life here can never be as heaven because earth is NOT heaven! My daughter is not in pain anymore and is living her heaven right now. Why would I want to bring her back to live in pain on this earth? You may say that Jesus doesn't want our life to be pain on this earth and in a way, I agree. He loves those who are His, but Jesus' life while on this earth was pain. He lived persecuted and hated and He tells us that we will too, if we belong to Him. So, if you consider yourself one of His, you should also accept that you are going to be hated and persecuted because this is NOT your heaven.

Building Their Team

These visionary leaders must build a team, and in doing so, their team must be bought into the visionary's ideas and concepts. These men who are very gifted at manipulating people, know how to choose and pick those who will devote their time for that same vision. Visionaries are gifted people, but their gifts are not being used to purpose God but rather to glorify satan. However, they are excellent sales people and are the kind of people that large corporations hire because they know how to sell, and they know how to select the right people that will follow their lead and buy into their vision. They cannot be successful without putting the right team together and transforming that team to believe in them, where they would give up everything for that visionary's cause. I remember spending 7 days a week at the church when I was a leader; even though, I worked a full-time job and was raising my first granddaughter. I was at the church every single evening and every single weekend. I gave everything for that vision because I had come to believe in the man that was over that vision, and we were all one big family. However, those who hear His voice, the Lord's, and know His voice, will eventually walk away because there are thousands of Scriptures that discount what is being taught on those pulpits weekly. *(Luke 14:27-30; John 14:6; Matthew 22:37; Philippians 2:1-11; Matthew 7:15; Ezekiel 13:8-11; Jeremiah 23:16-22; 2 Timothy 4:3-4)*

Notice, a visionary will do all in their power to accomplish the goals or visions in which they have described to those who follow. Of course, in these mega-churches, the people are taught that God has given them the vision, but we have already discussed this in chapter 4. Just to emphasize, we are to follow but ONE God and we do so through Jesus Christ. We are warned and warned about being taught by man because there are so many false prophets. Yes, we can learn about Jesus Christ through others that are on that narrow pathway, but if all we are doing is listening to a mere man and not asking, seeking and knocking ourselves, we will fall astray. Your life is too precious to live by chance based on any man's philosophies without hearing from God Himself. Yes, He does speak in that still small voice, but if we do NOT know His Word, we will be led astray. The multitudes are led astray! Oh, and by the way, man has no power unless it comes down from heaven. He can operate with that which is false when he is following the wrong voice himself, but the only way to know what voice any of us are following is to go back to the Word of God and see it for yourself. Do not take one Scripture and assume you know the meaning. It takes deep study to really know the meaning based on all the Word of God. *(2 Timothy 4:3-4; Acts 20:28-30; 2 Peter 3:14-18; 1 John 2:18-19; 1 John 4:1-6; Matthew 7:7; Luke 24:49; Acts 1:8; 1 Corinthians 3:18-21; John 10:2-5)*

These leaders focus on motivating others to be invested. A better word to use should be more like manipulating others to be invested growing that church building. Visionaries are very good at manipulating but in doing so, they must of course sell their vision first to those who will be their leaders and fight for their cause. This has nothing to do with living for Jesus Christ because for one, Jesus did not build a church for the unbelievers. A charismatic person has that gift to be able to inspire others. Those who choose to follow also have certain characteristics, as well. Many of those who follow a visionary were lost souls looking for purpose in their lives and then the big, bad wolf came along and devoured them just like he did in the original version of *Little Red Riding Hood*.[1] A good allegory to use, as the original Brothers Grimm version was written in the 1st century where the girl and her grandmother were both miraculously saved by the lumberjack who cut open the wolf, and they were still alive in the beast's stomach. Jesus is our Savior and will still miraculously save those who choose to walk away from following wolves in sheep clothing, instead of following the teachings in the Word of God.

However, many of those who follow these false teachers are so devoted to that particular visionary, they would lay down their own lives for the sake of their leader. We are only asked to lay our lives down for Jesus Christ, the difference? To lay your life down for a man, you won't have to give up much. Your life can pretty much continue where life is pretty good in this world, not many complaints. However, to lay your life down for Jesus Christ, it will cost you everything. Salvation being a free gift is not so! It is a free gift but Jesus had to pay for it with His blood, meaning it has already been paid for so you cannot buy it! However, salvation demands that you give up your life as you know it today and you walk according to the ways of Jesus Christ. Just as it cost Jesus His life, it will also cost you your life. If the way you are living is not the way He lived, forget salvation because Jesus came and died for us. He suffered for us. He was persecuted for us. He bore our sins that we might have life and the life in abundance that the Word speaks of has nothing to do with money, my friend. Like I said, you cannot look at one Scripture and think you know Jesus intimately. Look at all those in the Bible who truly followed Him. They also all died for Him. To follow Him, you may be known but not famous, as in others want to be like you. Jesus was known but He was hated by the majority, and I will never be loved by the majority who read these words because they are offensive. My friend, the Bible is the most offensive book ever written. It would pay you to really study it word for word, day in and day out to see for yourself what real Christianity is all about. It is not about God being happy when you are happy; God smiling when you are smiling! It is not about this life here on earth and what we can gain, but it is about the life after and that we will spend eternity in heaven. Living an abundant life here on earth is not about riches but about living our lives through Him as we become more like Him. Our abundant life will be one of eternity living in paradise created by God. This earth is far from paradise, and you better be sure to know that eternity in hell will definitely not be paradise. *(Ephesians 2:1-3; Matthew 16:24-26; 1 John 3:16-18, 23-24; John 14:15; Luke 6:46-49; Matthew 7:21-23; 2 Timothy 3:12; James 1:12-15; John 16:33; Luke 14:27, 33; Romans 5:1-5; Romans 8:35-39; 1 Peter 1:1-7; 1 Peter 2:24-25)*

The Abundant Life Biblically

I wanted to add to this Scripture where Jesus came to bring us life, an abundant life.

John 10:10 (NKJV) The thief does not come except to steal, and to kill, and to destroy. I have come that they may have life, and that they may have it more abundantly.

Jesus first taught about the thief which is satan. satan came to steal, kill and destroy. Jesus' life was never about material wealth; it was about people. A thief, he breaks in for material possessions, but those things mean nothing when you are on your death bed. We even see this when Jesus answered the young, rich ruler. He told him to sell everything and give it to the poor, then follow Him. *(Matthew 19:16-22)* Jesus knew he would walk away because his possessions meant far too much to him. Jesus tells us that the thief will destroy, but He *(Jesus)* will give life and that life is abundantly. He is not telling us that if we follow Him, we will be blessed with the riches of this world, why would He say that? Jesus tells us that we are not of this world, so why would we want this world more so than the world to come, if we are really desiring to follow in His footsteps. Jesus never acquired riches of this world. His promise is a *"life of abundance."* Abundance in the Greek is *perisson*, which means exceedingly, very highly, beyond measure, a quantity so abundant as to be more than expected. In other words, Jesus promised that our *"life"* would be greater than we could ever imagine. Are we not able to see on front pages of tabloids how those who are rich and famous do not have a life of abundance? The majority of what we see are lives full of deceit, divorce, cheating, and I could go on and on. They do not possess the peace of God in their lives. In that Scripture, Jesus is not referring to wealth since the Bible clearly shows us the attributes that God looks for in those who are called to do great things, and He is not looking at those who have accomplished greatness through their own means, such as gaining wealth and power of this world.

1 Corinthians 1:26-31 (ESV) For consider your calling, brothers: not many of you were wise according to worldly standards, not many were powerful, not many were of noble birth. ²⁷But God chose what is foolish in the world to shame the wise; God chose what is weak in the world to shame the strong; ²⁸God chose what is low and despised in the world, even things that are not, to bring to nothing things that are, ²⁹so that no human being might boast in the presence of God. ³⁰And because of him you are in Christ Jesus, who became to us wisdom from God, righteousness and sanctification and redemption, ³¹so that, as it is written, "Let the one who boasts, boast in the Lord."

Our abundant life will far exceed all expectations when we walk through that narrow gate to spend eternity with Him.

If a visionary leader can ever get your attention, they will do everything in their power to keep those following focused on their vision. If we stay busy enough, especially doing something we believe is God, we will be too busy to actually hear His voice because of the distractions of this world. Let me say and have probably already said this, visionary leaders build worldly empires and name it a church when in fact, it is nothing of the sort. When your focus becomes on building a man's vision, you will never hear the Lord's voice because in this world there are many distractions, and the worst distraction and most dangerous of all are the false teachings of the *"so-called"* prophets. Their god is satan and because they have chosen to bow down to him, their kingdoms have advanced. However, this advancement is only for a season. Woe to those who have ears and do not hear, eyes and do not see, for your day will come when all the demons in hell will not be able to come against Jesus, as He rides in on His white horse to destroy all the works of the enemy. *(Mark 4:18-19; Romans 12:1-2; 1 John 2:15-17; Colossians 3:1-3; 2 Timothy 3:1-9; Revelation 19:11-16)*

Jesus never needed a good visionary. In fact, Jesus picked those who were lowly because He is God. God does not need man nor his wisdom to build His church. These leaders that are being followed are really good for a worldly business, but God despises the works of man as it relates to loving this world. We are to walk away from man's pleasures in this world and focus on God's vision for man according to the Word of God in its entirety.

1 Corinthians 3:18-21 (ESV) Let no one deceive himself. If anyone among you thinks that he is wise in this age, let him become a fool that he may become wise. [19]For the wisdom of this world is folly with God. For it is written, "He catches the wise in their craftiness," [20]and again, "The Lord knows the thoughts of the wise, that they are futile." [21]So let no one boast in men. For all things are yours.

The Bible tells us that we have no strength outside of God. He is our strength not man. The wisdom of this world is foolish and those who adhere to it, shall perish.

Psalm 46:1 (NKJV) God is our refuge and strength, A very present help in trouble.

Proverbs 18:10-12 (ESV) The name of the LORD is a strong tower; the righteous man runs into it and is safe. ¹¹A rich man's wealth is his strong city, and like a high wall in his imagination. ¹²Before destruction a man's heart is haughty, but humility comes before honor.

1 Corinthians 1:19 (ESV) For it is written, "I will destroy the wisdom of the wise, and the discernment of the discerning I will thwart."

Proverbs 16:25 (NKJV) There is a way that seems right to a man, But its end is the way to death.

Defining Weaknesses

As I have said, when I was in a large church, we hired a man to come and spend about a week with all the leaders. Like I said, there are companies out there that have a business model to help companies that are going under or merely to help companies that desire growth. There is nothing wrong with that, but the church is not a man-made business. One of the things they teach is the weaknesses to look for. Let's think of this in a business sense. If your business has areas of weakness, yes, you would want to eliminate those areas immediately. However, those areas of weakness are not Biblical for the Christian. Doesn't the Bible say when we are weak, He is strong? *(2 Corinthians 12:10)* Or, perhaps the Scripture that says that the Lord is my strength. *(Psalm 28:7)* And then there is the Scripture that says with man this is impossible, but with God all things are possible. *(Matthew 9:26)* My point is that we must recognize that we only have strength through Him. It is okay to be weak because if we trust in Him, He brings us through everything.

For the business model, having a one-track mind is a weakness. However, if we have eyes to see and ears too hear, our mind should be a one-track mind. When we walk with Jesus and are one of His, our spirit will connect with His Spirit and our mind will be one with His mind. There is no such thing as being all over the place when all we have to do is submit to Jesus Christ, for then the Holy Spirit will lead our lives daily for His pleasure not for ours.

Matthew 13:14-17 (ESV) Indeed, in their case the prophecy of Isaiah is fulfilled that says: "You will indeed hear but never understand, and you will indeed see but never perceive." 15For this people's heart has grown dull, and with their ears they can barely hear, and their eyes they have closed, lest they should see with their eyes and hear with their ears and understand with their heart and turn, and I would heal them. 16But blessed are your eyes, for they see, and your ears, for they hear. 17For truly, I say to you, many prophets and righteous people longed to see what you see, and did not see it, and to hear what you hear, and did not hear it.

Romans 8:16 (NKJV) The Spirit Himself bears witness with our spirit that we are children of God.

1 Corinthians 2:16 (ESV) "For who has understood the mind of the Lord so as to instruct him?" But we have the mind of Christ.

We are told in Scripture that we are to only think on today. Our focus should be on the NOW! We are not to dwell on the past nor worry about tomorrow.

Isaiah 43:18 (NKJV) "Do no remember the former things, Nor consider the things of old."

Matthew 6:34 (ESV) "Therefore do not be anxious about tomorrow, for tomorrow will be anxious for itself. Sufficient for the day is its own trouble.

Let me add something here that is very prevalent among these mega-type churches. Most build their vision statement. What vision statement? Where is that in the Word of God? I would love for someone to show me where Jesus said, *"When you build your church, be sure to develop a vision statement."* To be clear, the Bible doesn't even tell us to go out and build our own church. We are told that Jesus would build the church. I know I keep saying this but evidently, it needs to be repeated often to wake some people up.

Concerning the vision statement, we can have a statement, but the only statements that we can use must be listed word for word in the Bible where it is NOT taken out of context. One vision statement I shared in chapter 4, pretty much stated that their church was built on the vision that God gave to their pastor, and they would aggressively defend their unity and that vision. Where is this in the Word of God? I'm going to tell you that it is NOT there because this is NOT the way to do church! Jesus is the church and no man will ever be able to bring Him down, but woe to those who are false because they will be brought down!

1 Timothy 4:1 (ESV) Now the Spirit expressly says that in later times some will depart from the faith by devoting themselves to deceitful spirits and teachings of demons.

2 Corinthians 11:13-15 (ESV) For such men are false apostles, deceitful workmen, disguising themselves as apostles of Christ. ¹⁴And no wonder, for even satan disguises himself as an angel of light. ¹⁵So it is no surprise if his servants, also, disguise themselves as servants of righteousness. Their end will correspond to their deeds.

Proverbs 24:16 (NKJV) For a righteous man may fall seven times And rise again, But the wicked shall fall by calamity.

Jeremiah 23:1 (NKJV) "Woe to the shepherds who destroy and scatter the sheep of My pasture!" says the LORD."

Jeremiah 50:6 (ESV) "My people have been lost sheep. Their shepherds have led them astray, turning them away on the mountains. From mountain to hill they have gone, they have forgotten their fold."

Ezekiel 34:11 (NKJV) "For thus says the Lord GOD: "Indeed I Myself will search for My sheep and seek them out."

I encourage any who are reading this book to also take advantage of the Scriptures I have noted in the above paragraphs. I pray that you research them yourselves as sheep that desire to know Him greater and not be seduced by that which is false.

CHAPTER SIX
THE CON-ARTIST

In the Word of God, Jesus used the analogy of a wolf in sheep clothing for us to be able to see that these were people that believed themselves to be Christians, or they were people who claimed to be Christians in order to gain the fame and fortune from the masses. *Matthew 7:15* clearly warns us to beware because these false prophets inwardly are wolves. Notice, it's not what it seems on the outside because on the outside, these wolves look just like sheep. If they look like sheep on the outside, you will not be able to tell that they really are not Christians—unless, you have enough of the Word of God inside of you to know what comes out of their mouth is false and will deceive the many. They are *smooth talkers*, but we know that their heart is evil which means truth will not be spoken.

Matthew 7:15 (ESV) Beware of false prophets, who come to you in sheep's clothing but inwardly are ravenous wolves.

These *"feel good"* messages which are sugar-coated are far too often being infiltrated inside of the buildings that we call church today. These messages are all about portraying God as someone who is happy when He knows we are happy. In fact, God is all about making our world a happy place where His children have all the riches of this world, and He has sent all these false teachers to impart man's wisdom on the vision that God has evidently given to them in order to carry out God's plan—for one big happy world.

There are many problems with this concept, beginning with the teachings that this world is about us instead of about God. We are NOT all His children, and He definitely is not smiling down on the multitudes that are creating a *"god"* that they desire to follow because that god has made it all about them!

Wait—that god has made it all about them—until they say that simple little *"tag line"* for salvation and then the church is no longer about them! I'm really laughing here because this is so foolish and what makes it even worse is that the multitudes are following the most aggressive *con-artists* that this world has known. Of course, these con-artists are following the master con-artist which is satan. Even so, this is reality because the Bible teaches us that the majority will be blinded by truth and if they are blinded, then this is very, very real!

Most have probably never thought about these false teachers as being merely con-artist. Let's examine what a con-artist looks like. You can google, there are many definitions and signs that describe a con-artist out there today—one who operates to gain the confidence of others where they will choose to follow them. Everyone at some time in their life will more than likely come face to face with a con-artist, and I believe it is imperative as Christians that we are wise to their dealings. I will touch on some of the most obvious signs of a con-artist in this chapter.

Attracting the Masses

One sign is that they are smooth talkers, as I said above. A con-artist cannot con people if they are not good at talking. They will be very charismatic. A charismatic personality is one that overflows with charm. It is the power that brings about delight and admiration in others. I am not saying that a charismatic personality is a bad thing, but in someone who is a con-artist, it gives them an advantage to attract others and gain a certain amount of control. They are smooth talkers, meaning that they know what to say and how to say it where others will follow their lead. They are very pleasant, easy-going, and friendly while they infiltrate among others while striving to gain trust.

How do they con the masses? Simple, they are able to hold the attention and control over the masses by inventing the method of all being as one together. They form teams. You will hear their expressions referring to their followings as *"we"* or *"us."* Think about that, the megachurches grow to astronomical size because they form this mighty team that reaches out with the pastor's insight *(vision)* in order to bring in the many. They use it to get closer to their victims by creating the illusion that they're all in the same boat. They also know that most people will not go against a majority, this way they keep the masses in line. Within the church buildings, a church which is being led by a con-artist, the messages will not line up with the Bible. It is very simple; however, the majority today have little concept of what the Bible says since only the few really study the Word of God. This is another topic which was discussed in Chapter three on how few really read or study the Bible. What we need to understand is that the con-artist's messages are going to be geared at growing that ministry—the importance of growing that ministry. Yet, a true Biblical teacher will stand up and portray the gospels, in order that the people know truth that will change their lives in that they will know the importance of developing that intimate relationship with Jesus Christ. Here is the difference—one church will teach to grow his ministry while the other church will teach to grow the people to desire to read the Bible and draw closer to Jesus Christ. One is a true sheep while the other is a wolf in sheep clothing. One keeps their flock intact and grows in numbers due to manipulation methods, while the other need not strive to keep the flock intact because it is not his job. Pastors or preachers are only to bring truth—Jesus Christ will build His church and needs not a man to do that for Him. Jesus Christ will keep His flock together, again, it is not man's job to do so. *(Matthew 16:18)*

I have said this many times and will probably say it more, that the church is NOT a building. We, as believers, are the church. Jesus builds His church, but we have many false teachers out there that believe the church building is for those who do not believe. It is for the lost souls to come in and manipulate until they buy into man's vision on what a church is to look like. Many of these churches are geared to attract the unbeliever in order to gain more bodies which translates into more money and fame for their ministry. However, biblically speaking, the church is for believers not for those who do not believe. In the Bible, the word church is never referring to a building as I have said. It will never be about where God's people meet but about them coming together to meet. If you have a group of believers get together, then they are the church. According to Scripture, the *"church"* are believers.

1 Corinthians 12:27 (NKJV) Now you are the body of Christ, and members individually.

Romans 12:4-5 (ESV) For as one body we have many members, and the members do not all have the same function, ⁵so we, though many, are one body in Christ, and individually members one of another.

Colossians 1:18 (ESV) And he is the head of the body, the church. He is the beginning, the firstborn from the dead, that in everything he might be preeminent.

In order to grow a huge ministry as the megachurches have, the messages must be geared to bring in those who are NOT believers in order to grow to great numbers. The true Biblical teachings will never preach messages that assure those listening that they are right with Jesus Christ. In fact, a true minister of the Gospels will always assume that those sitting in the congregation may not be in the right place with God. With that assumption, a true minister will preach a true Biblical message which will be bold just like those that Jesus taught. If those listening are really His *(Jesus')* sheep, as true followers, they will also be sharing true Biblical teachings as they walk forth as a true Christian. The churches that teach truth will not conjure up methods to entice the many and to satisfy the flesh in order to keep them, as you see in the vast entertainment aspect of these megachurches today. As they broaden their views which bring the world inside the building, then they capture the minds of the unbelievers in order to bring them into the fold. It is only through the characteristics of the church looking like the world that entices the unbelievers where they desire to attend in masses. The true church will look like that which we see in the New Testament which began with the teachings of Jesus. Jesus taught wherever He was whether it was in a building or outside, but His teachings attracted many but few followed. The majority will always go away because the majority are goats and not sheep—not my words—His Words. *(Matthew 7:13-14)*

Controlling the Flock

There is always the control that a con-artist uses. When they sense that a particular person is questioning their methods, if that person is of value to the ministry, they then use manipulation to strive to gain that control back where they keep their flock following their lead. I can only give an example based on my own walk when I was a leader of a big church that was striving to grow in great numbers. As a leader, when I began to question what was being taught, I was immediately brought to the pastor's office for a consultation. When he saw that he was losing ground on what I believed based on true Biblical teachings, his demeanor completely changed whereas he noted that my teachings on Revelation brought fear to those who were sitting in my class that I held once a week, and we should never put fear in people. In fact, he never taught on Revelation just as many of the large churches will not because Revelation brings fear upon those listening—Revelation is NOT a *"feel good"* message! However, Revelation should bring fear upon those listening in order that people get it right where they make it to heaven. This pastor went on to say, that I could remain and could continue with my class but only if another leader read through my lesson each week. In another leader doing so, they would make changes to what I could and could not teach. His method began with an insult which was that I was not teaching according to how I should BUT—here was an ultimatum in order to remain part of that family of believers in the true teachings of that pastor, I could remain on conditions. Those conditions were to follow that pastor and only teach what I was told I could teach. This was followed by a compliment, which was nothing more than manipulation. It was a method to con me where I could stay and go along with their teachings. The compliment he noted was that out of his 48 major leaders, there were only 3 that really heard the voice of the Holy Spirit with me being one of those, and he hated to lose me. This was meant to make me feel that I was a valuable part of his ministry, but it was nothing more than a con to get me back in line with his teachings and to control me by manipulation. If a con-artist is ever losing ground, they will look at ways to pay compliments to make those they are addressing feel good about themselves. Once that is achieved, they can then instill conditions to continue controlling a member. Remember, they do not desire to lose any of their following and will use any method of manipulation to keep those under control. It is funny to see how people immediately change their demeanor when someone begins to pay them compliments. Beware—we are told to beware! I really thought about what he said when I walked out of that meeting, but I also wondered why he would have so many leaders that were overseers of his huge congregation when he knew they did not hear the voice of the Holy Spirit. This is the blind leading the blind, and the con was to bring about the insult whereas he could then throw out a huge compliment in order to keep me, as long as he could control what I taught. Since those days, I have watched friends leave over the years and others be conned by the same method that was used with me, where they remained. Of course, I walked away and my journey with God since that day has been amazing.

As I have noted, charm is one of the greatest assets of a con-artist. Everyone loves being around those who are delightful and charming. I dare say, few would have enjoyed walking with Jesus during Biblical days, for He did not use charm to acquire those who followed Him. Jesus' methods were very bold, hard-core, and in fact, offensive. If we are to teach the Bible, it is the most offensive book that has ever been written which is perhaps, the reason why the majority do not really want to follow those teachings. Most messages from the pulpits of the megachurches are spoken with charm and niceness because they give the people the image of a god that is just loving and forgiving. In the church where truth is proclaimed from the pulpit, there is not always a lot of people saying, *"amen"* nor laughter, as the hard-core message is sharper than any two-edged sword cutting through bone and marrow, as is Biblical.

Hebrews 4:12 (ESV) For the word of God is living and active, sharper than any two-edged sword, piercing to the division of soul and of spirit, of joints and of marrow, and discerning the thoughts and intentions of the heart.

The Word of God in truth does not bring about a message that doesn't slice through the heart of man but rather one that does, where those who have ears to hear receive that truth in order that they make the choice to turn from the wickedness in this world and to Jesus Christ who brings salvation to their soul.

Selling Their Product

The con-artist is huge at selling his product each week as he stands on the pulpit. His messages are geared for that particular ministry in order to capture the attention of those listening to his ideas, his beliefs, his doctrine, his visions where they will seldom search Scripture themselves to clarify what is being taught. This is huge because the con-artist is giving many false teachings that if the hearer were actually to study their Bible, they would be able to see the lies coming forth from these pulpits. Have you ever been around a true salesman that was trying to convince you that their product was worth purchasing? There are massive amount of phone calls these days by businesses using mass telemarketing in order to try and make sales of their products. I receive these kind of phone calls almost daily where I seldom will even answer the phone if I do not recognize the caller. Telemarketing is a huge business these days through internet, phone calls, and perhaps there may still be some who go door to door. They are trained to go on and on about their product to make sales. I've often wondered if people really buy into this, but it is evident that it must work because they spend millions every year investing in this type of marketing to sell products. Those who have been trained know that the longer they can keep you on the phone or the more they can entice you to read when you receive advertisements through emails or mail, they can make a sell. The same is true on that pulpit each week. If that man or woman can entice you with their message that goes on and on with foolishness, they will sell themselves where you will follow them. When I say foolishness, those are not my words but God's Word.

Proverbs 12:15-17 (ESV) The way of a fool is right in his own eyes, but a wise man listens to advice. ¹⁶The vexation of a fool is known at once, but the prudent ignores an insult. ¹⁷Whoeveer speaks the truth gives honest evidence, but a false witness utters deceit.

These megachurches stand up week after week sharing their visions that give the listener promises of who God is, how to be saved, and how to live out their life which a huge part is going to be all about the support of their vision which is NOT Biblical. They lead people to salvation through a watered-down message that is not Biblical where those who recite this line leave with a promise of going to heaven one day, but the truth is that no one will see heaven that merely stated some small *"tag line"* that is NOT Biblical. True salvation comes from hearing and hearing the Word of God. It does not come from hearing that man or woman on the pulpit. It comes from many, many readings and studying of the Holy Scriptures that bring truth to the soul where you feel His presence inside of you, as He speaks to you. It is a heartfelt experience that only can come through the Holy Spirit and never through a mere man or woman.

These con-artists stand up on their pulpits week after week convincing the multitudes that their church has created a place of refuge where they can come to feel good about themselves. These men and women are charming, and they also know how to get close to those they are deceiving. In getting close, they come to know them personally and know their needs. In doing so, they give them a message that speaks to their heart. Meaning, they give the people a message that they want to hear instead of a message of truth—what they need to hear. These are the days that we live in. People are searching for answers and con-artist are giving them what they want to hear.

2 Timothy 4:3 (AMP) For the time will come when people will not tolerate sound doctrine and accurate instruction (that challenges them with God's truth); but wanting to have their ears tickled (with something pleasing), they will accumulate for themselves (many) teachers (one after another, chosen) to satisfy their own desires and to support the errors they hold.

The con-artist provides what the people want, what they desire to hear, and also an avenue to socialize with others and be part of their massive entertainment and growth, but it all comes with a price. Once you get sucked in, the church needs your money to continue bringing in the masses, in order that you are part of the growing movement where you are a family and it really feels good to your flesh!

It is not in the vocabulary of a con-artist to be told *"no."* When they have a vision and there are those who want to continue to say *"no"* to their vision, they will soon find themselves on the outside very quickly unless their *"no"* becomes a *"yes,"* and they choose to go with the flow. The con-artist's vision will be what ultimately leads and controls their flock, and it will be his vision not God's that leads that congregation.

These megachurches have come up with a new way to present Christ's message to the world. What was wrong with the old way? Jesus taught us the way; the Bible clearly tells us that He is the way, the truth, and the life.

John 14:6 (NKJV) Jesus said to him, "I am the way, the truth, and the life. No one comes to the Father except through Me.

So, your choice, you can either choose to follow Jesus according to His teachings or you can choose to follow those who have altered the pathway which leads to salvation. Of course, if you never study the Bible, you will never know if you are truly right with God anyway.

Rick Warren, after walking door to door to find out why people do not come to church, decided to give the world what they wanted. They didn't want a traditional church with pews and organ music. His messages had to be geared towards entertaining the unsaved in order that they would return.[1] Instead of hard-core, bold messages like Jesus gave, many pastors today have changed that method and replaced it with the *"feel good"* messages which make people laugh and feel good about themselves. I'm not saying that church should make people feel bad about themselves, but if you study Scripture, Jesus' messages did NOT bring smiles and laughter to those who were beginning to know Him. Why is this? The reason is because Heaven and Hell are very real, and Jesus wanted to make sure that those He ministered to understood that if they did not get their life right, they would never see heaven. To clarify, I am not saying that true Christians will never smile nor laugh—on the contrary, be around my family for very long and there will be much laughter. Your personality does not change when you find Jesus Christ. He needs all personalities out there to bring about His purpose. In fact, in creating you—your personality was also given to you. Mine—over the years, well, I am not even sure what to say—my personality has always had much humor and much happiness. My friends over the years will tell you, I make them laugh—it is just something in me, created by Him. I am generally a very happy individual, but my joy came to a much greater degree walking with Jesus instead of walking alone. Notice the word *"joy,"* my joy came from Him. This is Biblical. In Him we find that joy, true joy. Jesus tells us in John 15, that His joy may be in us and that our joy may be full. It is only through Him that we truly find that kind of joy.

The Evolving Church

The state of what we call the church today, keeps changing according to the ways of man—not according to the Bible. Many churches today do not even want crosses reflected in their church. They do not teach hard core messages on subjects such as the crucifixion or repentance. These pastors have devised a plan to build churches where the world would come. Robert Schuller wrote the book, *Self Esteem*, where he teaches that the church will never succeed until it fulfills every person's hunger for self-value. So, now the church is to be built to give people self-value? The Bible says we must die to self, how can we serve a ministry that teaches contrary to the Word of God?

Luke 9:23-24 (ESV) And he said to all, "If anyone would come after me, let him deny himself and take up his cross daily and follow me. 24For whoever would save his life will lose it, but whoever loses his life for my sake will save it.

Warren, in *The Purpose Driven Church*, states that anyone can be won to Christ if you can discover the key to their heart, and that most people are not looking for truth but for relief.[2] This concept is nothing more than using marketing techniques to satisfy the consumers. If these churches can convince people that Jesus died to meet their needs, they will buy into their products. However, Jesus did not come to increase people but to decrease them by bringing them to the Cross.

1 Corinthians 1:18-19 (ESV) For the word of the cross is folly to those who are perishing, but to us who are being saved it is the power of God. ¹⁹For it is written, "I will destroy the wisdom of the wise, and the discernment of the discerning I will thwart."

John 6:26-27 (ESV) Jesus answered them, "Truly, truly, I say to you, you are seeking me, not because you saw signs, but because you ate your fill of the loaves. ²⁷Do not work for the food that perishes, but for the food that endures to eternal life, which the Son of Man will give to you. For on him God the Father has set his seal."

John 3:30 (NKJV) "He must increase, but I must decrease."

These pastors are of this world! God is not their father!

John 15:19 (ESV) If you were of the world, the world would love you as its own; but because you are not of the world, but I chose you out of the world, therefore the world hates you.

There will be more discussed later in this book about those who have gained love and popularity from the world. My point is that these pastors have gained enormous followings, they are gaining the world which in turn is also gaining the riches of this world by satisfying the people's felt needs. These pastors are seeking to please men not please God.

1 Thessalonians 2:4 (ESV) but just as we have been approved by God to be entrusted with the gospel, so we speak, not to please man, but to please God who tests our hearts.

Galatians 1:10 (ESV) For am I now seeking the approval of man, or of God? Or am I trying to please man? If I were still trying to please man, I would not be a servant of Christ.

Warren also wrote a column in the March, 2005 issue of the *Ladies' Home Journal* where he states that we are to accept ourselves, love ourselves, be true to ourselves, forgive ourselves, and believe in ourselves.[3] However, Warren begins *The Purpose Driven Life,* with the words, *"It's not about you!"*[4] Warren has a humanistic approach which puts his teachings where it is about you. Of course, his methods are to reach the unchurched, as I have said, and they do not put God first. All of the emphasis in the *Ladies' Home Journal* article teach us that everything is about putting *"us"* first. These are not the teachings of the Word of God.

2 Tim 3:1-2, 8 (ESV) But understand this, that in the last days there will come times of difficulty. ²For people will be lovers of self, lovers of money, proud, arrogant, abusive, disobedient to their parents, ungrateful, unholy. ⁸Just as Jannes and Jambres opposed Moses, so these men also oppose the truth, men corrupted in mind and disqualified regarding the faith.

Today, churches can hire someone to come in to show them what they are doing wrong, in order that they too can increase to great numbers. No wonder the church has a bad name and is referred to as nothing more than a massive business that capitalizes on manipulating people to support and increase it by astronomical measures. Hiring companies to come into the churches to assist with growth has become a huge business where many pastors desire to be recognized as a great empire among their community. As a leader within one of these churches, the Scripture, *"You will know them by their fruit,"* was taught to mean that this meant numbers within the church. If you were doing what God called you to do, the multitudes would follow you and that was your fruit. However, the only fruit I know of in the Bible referred to the change within each of us. We gain the fruit of the Holy Spirit which meant we become more like Jesus.

Galatians 5:22-23 (ESV) But the fruit of the Spirit is love, joy, peace, patience, kindness, goodness, faithfulness, 23gentleness, self-control, against such things there is no law.

In many of the larger churches, people are considered your fruit, it's all about numbers. A successful church was considered a church of huge numbers. I can remember where the pastor would teach the leaders that there were certain elements to the Word of God that could not be taught to the whole congregation because the people would leave, and the people were needed to pay the bills. I remember questioning so much of what was being taught. I can remember time and time again, hearing the voice of the Holy Spirit as He would give me Scripture that conflicted with what I was being taught. You see, you can gain quite a following when your messages are the *"feel good"* messages giving the people what they want to hear instead of what they need to hear. Jesus taught bold and harsh messages because He was all about people getting their act together, in order that they would be saved from eternal death and able to enter into the gates of heaven. His messages were never about gaining the wealth of this world and living on earth as if it were heaven, on the contrary, Jesus' messages were about life after this world, and He imparted these same teachings to those who followed Him. Paul said it this way—

2 Corinthians 10:1-6 (ESV) I, Paul, myself entreat you, by the meekness and gentleness of Christ – I who am humble when face to face with you, but bold toward you when I am away! – 2I beg of you that when I am present I may not have to show boldness with such confidence as I count on showing against some who suspect us of walking according to the flesh. 3For though we walk in the flesh, we are not waging war according to the flesh. 4For the weapons of our warfare are not of the flesh but have divine power to destroy strongholds. 5We destroy the knowledge of God, and take every thought captive to obey Christ, 6being ready to punish every disobedience, when your obedience is complete.

John 28:36 (ESV) Jesus answered, "My kingdom is not of this world. If my kingdom were of this world, my servants would have been fighting, that I might not be delivered over to the Jews. But my kingdom is not from the world."

1 John 2:15 (ESV) Do not love the world or the things in the world. If anyone loves the world, the love of the Father is not in him.

Colossians 3:2 (NKJV) Set your minds on things above, not on things on the earth.

No Need That Anyone Should Teach You

When pastors teach out of context, there are many Scriptures that are scanned over and never mentioned. In fact, there are three such Scriptures which warn us about being taught the Bible by man that are never mentioned from the pulpit, or at least, I have never heard them in all my years as I sat under man's teachings. I teach on these myself many times and within my books. Two of the Scriptures are located in the New Testament, but one is in the Old Testament as well.

1 John 2:26-27 (ESV) ²⁶ I write these things to you about those who are trying to deceive you. ²⁷ But the anointing that you received from him abides in you, <u>and you have no need that anyone should teach you. But as his anointing teaches you about everything, and is true, and is no lie—just as it has taught you, abide in him.</u>

Hebrews 8:10-11 (ESV) ¹⁰ For this is the covenant that I will make with the house of Israel after those days, declares the Lord: I will put my laws into their minds, and write them on their hearts, and I will be their God, and they shall be my people. ¹¹ And <u>they shall not teach, each one his neighbor and each one his brother, saying, 'Know the Lord,' for they shall all know me, from the least of them to the greatest.</u>

You can read Jeremiah 31:33-34 in order to read these same words in the Old Testament. However, if you will read 1 John 2 in depth, you will see that John was first teaching about the dangers of loving this world. When our desires are for this world, we will live for this world and Jesus takes back stage in our lives. He continues from that point to teach about all of those who will come and teach you falsely, and he continues to tell you that there is NO need that any man should teach you. Like I said, John was not the first person to teach this because it began in the Old Testament. Jesus knew that men would arise to teach out of context, and the multitudes would follow those teachings because the multitudes look to man to learn of God and not to the Holy Spirit who is to be our ultimate teacher. If you have the Holy Spirit living within you, God's presence, you should be hearing His voice and not having to sit up under a ministry to learn what God wants to teach you. Yes, be joined together with other believers but that should be for encouragement, prayer and above all discipline. Yes, it is also alright that we teach and listen to teachers, but we must also learn that our ultimate teacher is the Holy Spirit. We should always go back to the Bible on anything that we learn from man. The church building does have its place among the Christian community, as long as it is geared to increase Jesus Christ not a man standing at the pulpit. Also note that coming together as the church can be any place where two or more are gathered together, it does not have to be a building that we call church. When I go into the streets to minister Jesus Christ, I am the church coming together with other believers who are also the church.

Therefore, we are warned that we have no need to be taught by man because we are to be taught by the Holy Spirit, so that we are not deceived by false teachings. Yes, I do attend various church services but am very selective on where I will go. However, I study the Word of God diligently so that I am able to judge the words being said from the pulpit to know if they are right or wrong. I can tell you that if I sit at a particular church and week after week the words being taught are out of context, I don't go back. Why on earth would I want to waste my time sitting among a group of people who are in agreement with what is being taught, and I could give several Scriptures to prove it is false? I desire to be around God's people but also to be among those men standing at the pulpit who are striving to teach according to the Word of God and not to teach it out of context, in order that their gain is for wealth in this world.

Think about this, you spend your life going to church putting your trust in another person instead of looking to Jesus for Truth. The problem with this is that the man or woman you have chosen to listen to could be wrong, and many will follow them right to hell. If the pressure is put on you to know Truth, suddenly you will strive to know God deeper and you will question every voice you hear. Why on earth would we trust another human being with our life, especially someone we do not know intimately? Most Christians who have been raised in church have been taught by their own family what denomination is accurate based on the traditions of that family. Most of the time, these Christians continue to go to the same denomination as they were taught and their children, as well. However, there comes a point when we must step out from the traditions of man and seek God ourselves. I used to resent the fact that I was not raised in church until I came to know Jesus Christ intimately. I soon realized that most people in church who were raised in certain denominations were programmed from the time they came into this world to know Jesus Christ based on what they were taught by that family—the traditions of that family. The sad truth about this is most Christians today will tell you they have never heard the voice of God, which is really the Holy Spirit. The Holy Spirit was sent to us after Jesus died on the Cross and ascended into heaven. The Holy Spirit is God's presence within us. Or at least, it should be His presence living inside of us.

Romans 8:9 (ESV) You, however, are not in the flesh but in the Spirit, if in fact the Spirit of God dwells in you. Anyone who does not have the Spirit of Christ does not belong to him.

Would it not be better to break the cycle and begin raising our children to know God intimately? Would it not be better that we seek after God to a degree where we hear His voice ourselves instead of putting our whole life in the hands of someone that may be wrong? I tell those I minister to all the time that they do not have to believe anything I say, but they should not believe what others say either. I tell them that I am not their God and if all they listen to is me week after week, when they stand before the true God one day, they will hear Him say, *"Depart from me, I do not know you!"* You cannot get to heaven based on my relationship with God, it must be your relationship with God.

Matthew 7:21-23 (NKJV) 21 "Not everyone who says to Me, 'Lord, Lord,' shall enter the kingdom of heaven, but he who does the will of My Father in heaven. 22 Many will say to Me in that day, 'Lord, Lord, have we not prophesied in Your name, and done many wonders in Your name?' 23 And then I will declare to them, 'I never knew you; depart from Me, you who practice lawlessness!'

Goats Vs. Sheep

Not every ministry is correct, yet every flock of people are the same as they choose to follow that one person that is over their church and that person is not Jesus Christ. Man can never be over the church of Jesus Christ and when a mere man is over the church, the church will not stand forever. There may be enough money to keep that church going for a time, but all those churches that are not leading the people to an intimate relationship with Jesus Christ will NOT stand.

As I left one such church many years ago, I continually hear of others who were leaders leaving as well. Those who are really sheep will hear His voice and eventually their eyes will see what is false. I know myself that even though I was questioning many things, I remained because I felt that the pastor evidently knew more than I did, and I must be wrong. However, the voice I was hearing time and time again kept showing me Scripture after Scripture until I no longer could deny that what I was being taught was not accurate. Until the day that Jesus comes back for those who are His, the true sheep will continue to seek out for a church teaching truth. They will continue to find fellowship with those who also see Truth as they see Truth!

The majority of our churches in America are made up of a few sheep and many goats. Jesus tells us that His sheep will hear His voice. Sheep follow one voice whereas goats desire to be in control and lead. *(John 10:27)*

If you study sheep in the natural sense, they follow one master but goats in the natural desire to be the leaders. I did a study on sheep and goats which makes a lot of sense when you look at the condition of the church in America. We see among the many congregations where goats are trained to act as sheep but putting on that costume to play the part of a sheep will never make you a true sheep. As good trained sheep, they will steer clear of anyone that tries to steer them away from whatever denomination or ministry they are following. If your eyes are always feeding on what you have been trained to believe or things of this world, then those things are what your heart is full of. The company we have chosen to keep will also keep us blinded from being able to see Truth. What we choose to watch, read, and listen to is what our heart is made of. We may not be living as we once did in sinful ways according to the world, but remember to God, if you are not listening to the voice of the Holy Spirit but rather a mere man, you are just as much a part of that false doctrine as they are. What you have been programmed to believe is what is in your heart and those things will come out of you to also fill others with that which is false.

There will always be those areas of weakness that the enemy will use to entice us to believe in something that is NOT God. He will cause us to stumble over and over again when we choose to allow a man to lead us instead of our one and only Shepherd, Jesus Christ.

Distinguishing the goats from the sheep, you will always notice that goats want to be the one in charge. The majority of the churches we see today are being heavily run by goats not sheep. In the natural, goats are never satisfied and are always looking for greener grass on the other side. We see this in several aspects, it would be those who continually become angry at the church and look for another church expecting it to be more vibrant. It would also be those who feel that their leadership is not being allowed to grow under that pastor, and they seek for a church that will allow them to lead. Finally, it would also be those who are leaders within a particular church but are never satisfied with where the church is currently and are always coming up with man's methods to enhance the church in order to become wealthier, more vibrant and to also use man's methods to snare those who are looking for a church family. These are the most dangerous because they are always looking to snare the lost, those from other congregations, as well as manipulating the true sheep. Those goats who are given positions in the church to be in charge of an area, they will remain as long as their authority is not brought down.

Years ago, my husband and I owned a female goat and two males. We lived in the country and had different farm animals from time to time. The goats were the unruliest of all the animals we owned. They were constantly breaking out of their fence and destroying our garden. They were always fighting among each other on who would be the dominant one. It did not take long until we sold them to make our life easier.

Goats are always looking for more and never satisfied with less. This is probably why the larger churches are full of goats. Most goats would not be satisfied in a small church that did not seem vibrant on the outside, unless they were given something great to be in charge of. A goat is really good at keeping the flock intact which is why they make great leaders within the churches so that the people remain. The goats will use manipulative measures to remain in charge and to remain over the flock of those they are given charge of in order to maintain the control needed so that the people remain. I have been there and seen this type of manipulation many times. I have seen the manipulation and control when someone in a group would begin to look elsewhere and have been in the midst of this myself. At one point, I was even threatened that if I chose to listen to messages outside of the church where I was a leader, I would never again be a leader in that church. I have seen really ugly things take place among leaders quarrelling over whose fruit a particular person was when that person would choose to sit under another's leadership in the small groups outside of church. First of all, people are not fruit. People do not belong to a particular person but to Jesus Christ if in fact, they are truly sheep. The goats that are put in high places within many of the churches today, are always the ones right and those not in charge are wrong. Whereas, the Bible should be the ultimate source on determining what is right and what is wrong. Yet in the large churches, those not in high places are to follow the voice of those who are. The problem with this is that sheep only will follow one voice and that voice is not a man or pastor nor any leader within the *"so-called"* church. The church was never meant to be where a man was increased and lifted up to be head over that body of believers.

The voice we choose to follow will ultimately either keep us on the wide road or lead us to the narrow road. Our lives are determined by voices, who are you following today? Are you following your own voice, which will be all about what's in it for you? Are you listening to parents, friends, teachers, associates, pastors, etc.? Is the voice you are following leading you down a good path or evil path? Is that voice a wolf in sheep clothing or is it a true sheep? Is the voice you are listening to leading you only to Jesus Christ to be your ultimate leader? Your ears will determine where you will go in this life, and your eyes will take you down the pathway of whatever voice you choose to listen.

Matthew 7:24-27 (ESV) Build Your House on the Rock
[24] "<u>Everyone then who hears these words</u> of mine and does them will be like a wise man who built his house on the rock. [25] And the rain fell, and the floods came, and the winds blew and beat on that house, but it did not fall, because it had been founded on the rock. [26] <u>And everyone who hears these words of mine and does not do them</u> will be like a foolish man who built his house on the sand. [27] And the rain fell, and the floods came, and the winds blew and beat against that house, and it fell, and great was the fall of it."

We all make choices in this life every single day. Our choices are based on the voices we have chosen to listen to. Those beliefs and philosophies are what our heart is full of. What you listen to will affect what you choose to read, watch on television and social media. Your associates will ultimately affect the lifestyle you choose which basically will be the road you also choose to remain traveling—wide path or narrow path. Just because it looks like you live a good life does not mean it is a GOD life! Making the right choices which will lead to eternal life will only happen if you are truly listening to the One true voice! A watered-down message that feels good to our flesh will never lead you closer to God like a bold fire and brimstone message as Jesus Christ taught. Either the messages will be geared to storing your treasures here on this earth or storing them in heaven. When we listen to any other voice than the true voice of the Holy Spirit, our desires will be filled with the pleasures and desires of this world and those treasures are stored on earth! Our ears will never follow the voice of our Master when our soul is filled with the things of this world. Our soul will be filled with the things of this world when our ears are continually listening to everything but the Holy Spirit.

This world cannot save you; mere men cannot save you; pastors or priests cannot save you, and this book or anything I am sharing with you cannot save you! However, it is important that you listen to men and women that are going to tell you truth not what you want to hear but what you need to hear. It is also important that you seek the Scriptures yourself to build that relationship with the ONE true God in order that you come to know Him intimately which is the only way you can become saved.

During the last days which are the days we are currently living—Jesus warns us that many would be led astray. It is not enough to claim that you love Jesus if all you are doing is placing yourself among the goats and following the wrong voice. If you are not building that intimate relationship, you will never even find that narrow path.

Matthew 24:11 (NKJV) Then many false prophets will arise up and deceive many.

Matthew 7:13-14 (ESV) "Enter by the narrow gate. For the gate is wide and the way is easy that leads to destruction, and those who enter by it are many. ¹⁴For the gate is narrow and the way is hard that leads to life, and those who find it are few."

There has always been and always will be only one pathway that will lead to heaven. Yet, so many people claim they are going to heaven and do not even know the Scriptures. Those that do stumble on someone out there preaching the bold messages, the majority do not really want to walk the narrow pathway because it requires giving up and letting go of the life they have.

When I began questioning and began seeing things from the narrow road standpoint, I can remember the battle within my own soul of letting go of the things in this world that the Holy Spirit began to show me. It was a battle, but it was also a choice. Do we really want to be saved? Do we really want that intimate relationship with God? I have had people come to me when they desperately needed prayer for something they were going through and felt that I had a direct connection to God. In other words, they felt that God would listen to my prayers before their prayers. I tell you that I am one to be straightforward because I will not pray for God to fix anyone's problems. I will tell them to stop fighting their storm and learn to endure the storm. Thank God if you find yourself in a storm because that means He hasn't given up on you yet, and those storms are His way of getting you to wake up and seek Him that you find Him. He desires that intimate relationship with you!

Conformed to this World

We can either seek Him to find Him or we can choose to serve a god like the majority of people in this world who really have no relationship with the true God whatsoever. Every single person in this world is following something. They are either following their own desires which are worldly; following their friends as in dressing like others, hair trends, music types; following their family in like manner; following a persona as in trying to be someone they are not by the way they act, talk, etc.; following a particular kind of denomination, religion, or group of people; and those who truly choose to follow Jesus Christ. If we are following anything other than Jesus Christ, we are trying to be conformed to this world and are warned not to be conformed to this world.

Romans 12:2 (ESV) Do not be conformed to this world, but be transformed by the renewal of your mind, that by testing you may discern what is the will of God, what is good and acceptable and perfect.

The world categorizes people as either the rich and high-class, the educated, the middle class and the poor. Once again, the majority desire to be classified as either the rich or the educated. There are many who are content with being classified as middle class but probably few would choose to be in the class of the poor. However, God does not categorize like the world.

Matthew 9:9-13 (ESV) Jesus Calls Matthew ⁹ *As Jesus passed on from there, he saw a man called Matthew sitting at the tax booth, and he said to him, "Follow me." And he rose and followed him.* ¹⁰ *And as Jesus reclined at table in the house, behold, many tax collectors and sinners came and were reclining with Jesus and his disciples.* ¹¹ *And when the Pharisees saw this, they said to his disciples, "Why does your teacher eat with tax collectors and sinners?"* ¹² *But when he heard it, he said, "Those who are well have no need of a physician, but those who are sick.* ¹³ *Go and learn what this means, 'I desire mercy, and not sacrifice.' For I came not to call the righteous, but sinners."*

If God did categorize, it would look more like this:

- You think you are rich, but you are really poor *(Revelation 3:17)*
- You think you are educated, but your wisdom is foolishness *(1 Corinthians 3:19)*
- You think you are straddling the fence, but that makes you lukewarm *(Revelation 3:15)*
- You think you are poor, but you are really rich *(Revelation 2:9)*

I know this steps on toes because it stepped on mine years ago as well, but we need to stop trying to fit into this world if we claim to be Christians. We are told that we do not belong to this world.

John 17:16 (NKJV) They are not of the world, just as I am not of the world.

We also need to stop categorizing people and stop looking at ourselves as more than we are. Was this not what the disciples desired in Matthew 10 when they wanted to know who would sit on his right hand and who on his left in heaven? What was Jesus' final reply to them?

Matthew 10:43-45 (NKJV) Yet it shall not be so among you; but whoever desires to become great among you shall be your servant. 44And whoever of you desires to be first shall be slave of all. 45For even the Son of Man did not come to be served, but to serve, and to give His life a ransom for many."

I encourage you to read the complete story in Matthew, but I wanted to emphasize Jesus' reply to man's desire to be great. If we go over to Matthew 18, Jesus gives us a glimpse of who is the greatest among us.

Matthew 18:1-6 (ESV) Who Is the Greatest? At that time the disciples came to Jesus, saying, "Who is the greatest in the kingdom of heaven?" 2And calling to him a child, he put him in the midst of them 3and said, "Truly, I say to you, unless you turn and become like children, you will never enter the kingdom of heaven. 4Whoever humbles himself like this child is the greatest in the kingdom of heaven. 5Whoever receives one such child in my name receives me, 6but whoever causes one of these little ones who believe in me to sin, it would be better for him to have a great millstone fastened around his neck and to be drowned in the depth of the sea."

If you think about this, children are nothing like adults. They grow up to be like us but while they are children, they have an innocence about them that we do not have. They trust and have faith in those who care for them. They do not judge people but rather love all man-kind rather rich or poor. It is as they grow that they begin to form an opinion based on their surroundings and what they have been taught. Jesus wanted us to understand that a small child comes into this world very humble because they have nothing. They are born without knowing anything until they are taught and are easily persuaded as they grow to believe like those they are around. We are to draw closer and closer to Christ that our influence and our lives look like His life because that is what a small child looks like. I will give you one example but I do write extensively on this subject in another book. You can put a small child up high on a counter-top and back up a bit and say, *"Jump to me."* What do they do? They reach their little arms and hands out and without even thinking about danger, they jump right out into thin air trusting that you are going to catch them. On the other hand, most who call themselves Christians try to make deals with God. *"Who will be the greatest in heaven, Lord?"* What they really wanted to say was, *"If I were to know that Jesus would pick me to be the greatest, then I could go all out and give up everything because I know my reward awaits me in heaven."* However, as true Christians, it should never ever be about what we receive here on earth and it should never be about caring who or what we will be in heaven. I bet if you could talk to someone in hell, they would tell you that they would have given anything to be in heaven, even if it meant that they spent eternity serving others and were the lowest rank in heaven. Think about that!

Of course, we are all children in the eyes of God if we are truly His and according to the Scripture above, *"Woe to those who cause any of God's children to stumble."* False teachers, preachers, prophets, they are all leading people astray and some of those are actually God's children. If we already desire to be greater here, are we not in that same mindset as the disciples were? What would Jesus speak to us or what is He really saying to us, and we are choosing not to listen?

The Biblical Church

Let's look at the church according to revelation. Jesus had good things to say about the small churches that saw themselves as poor with little strength. On the other hand, what He spoke to the churches that saw themselves as rich and alive was a different story.

Churches that are considered poor:

- Church in Smyrna – I know your works, tribulation, and poverty—but you are rich. *(Revelation 2:9 NKJV)*
- Church in Philadelphia – I know your works. See, I have set before you an open door, and no one can shut it; for you have a little strength, have kept My word, and have not denied My name. *(Revelation 3:8 NKJV)*

Churches that are considered rich:

- Church in Sardis – I know your works, that you have a name that you are alive, but you are dead. *(Revelation 3:1b NKJV)*
- Church in Laodicea – Because you say, 'I am rich, have become wealthy, and have need of nothing' – and do not know that you are wretched, miserable, poor, blind, and naked. *(Revelation 3:17 NKJV)*

We should be thankful if our fellowship is among those churches that are small but the teachings are bold. Likewise, we should feel blessed if we do not fall up under the class of the rich in this world, as long as our relationship with our Creator is strong. God is so much more than material wealth in this world. A few things to ponder:

- Be proud if you are poor because God is so much more!
- If you are middle class, be satisfied with less so that you will be blessed!
- If you are rich, give it away where maybe you can find heaven someday!

Please do not take my notes to ponder literal because there are those who have more and use it to glorify God. There are times that God will bless some with more because He knows their heart is in serving and giving. However, riches in this world somehow change the heart in such a way that causes us to never see heaven. We have to really think about this. I know I have over the years and have prayed that God never allow me to have the riches of this world, if it would change my heart. God knows that we cannot serve Him and mammon. He knows that wealth changes people. In fact, there are ministers in this world today that at one time preached the bold messages but as growth took a hold of them, their messages changed. At that point, they became blinded because they believed that God blessed them with the riches for being faithful. There are times that God will allow us the desires of our heart; however, many times those desires turn to striving to gain more and more of this world, and we are no longer following the voice of the Holy Spirit. Also, satan is totally okay with us gaining the desires of our heart, especially if the deception causes us to remain on the wrong pathway.

We will never be able to have the best of both worlds. When you find yourself surrounded by the wrong voices, stop listening! When you make the choice that it does matter what you choose to listen to and you step out to walk away from those wrong voices, your eyes will stop looking at the riches of this world desiring to have more and being content with less. When you begin to listen to the right voice, your desires will not be for the things in this world. You will find that your ears will hear the Master's voice and as sheep, your desire will be to follow that One voice!

Matthew 6:19-24 (ESV) Lay Up Treasures in Heaven [19] *"Do not lay up for yourselves treasures on earth, where moth and rust destroy and where thieves break in and steal,* [20] *but lay up for yourselves treasures in heaven, where neither moth nor rust destroys and where thieves do not break in and steal.* [21] *For where your treasure is, there your heart will be also.* [22] *"The eye is the lamp of the body. So, if your eye is healthy,* *your whole body will be full of light, ²³ but if your eye is bad, your whole body will be full of darkness. If then the light in you is darkness, how great is the darkness! ²⁴ "No one can serve two masters, for either he will hate the one and love the other, or he will be devoted to the one and despise the other. You cannot serve God and money.*

I know this is not an easy road because I have been there, but when you begin to pour so much of the Word of God into your soul, you will find that your desires will change. Of course, satan will try to entice your eyes to cause you to stumble, but that is okay because as you continue to pour into God's Word, it will be harder for satan to cause you to stumble. Your focus eventually will be on following that One voice. Please know that salvation is a journey and with any journey, the trials never cease until you have reached that destination. Our ultimate journey will be the day we stand before our Creator. If you have done all you know to do as you strive to follow that One voice, your journey will end in good hands. Your Creator will welcome you into heaven, and all those hardships and trials you endured were well worth the effort of being able to stand before your Creator with open arms.

Remember, God does not desire that we should fall. *(Psalms 37:24)* Of course, this is for those who are striving to know Jesus Christ. We are told that we may stumble, but He will not let us fall. It's not about missing it and feeling worthless or that you will never be able to make it, it is about getting back up. A true soldier that is fighting for something he believes in, nothing will ever be able to bring him to the place where he quits. In this journey, we continue to keep our eyes focused on the One true master, no man or woman standing on the pulpit. On this journey, if you are truly following that One voice and not being persuaded by man, you will remain through the trials and tests, storms and persecution on the pathway chosen for you.

The majority today choose every single day to follow the voice that the multitudes follow, but that voice leads them many times to follow a particular denomination. If we are following anything other than the voice of the Holy Spirit, we will be led down the wide pathway where the multitudes travel. The voice less traveled will never be the choice made by the multitudes, as their focus remains on the con-artists who have captured their loyalty. However, for the few that dare seek out to know Jesus Christ intimately, will hear His voice and their journey will lead to salvation.

CHAPTER SEVEN
GATEKEEPERS

In biblical days, there were gatekeepers. Gatekeepers were watchmen who were to protect the Lord's house in several areas. One of those areas was defending the truth of the gospels. Gatekeepers were bold to speak out against the sins of the church. Those who are gatekeepers or watchmen of the church, they know the Scriptures well as they spend much time in the Word of God.

In Old Testament times, they guarded various gates of a city as to keep any danger from entering. These men had to be trustworthy and dedicated to the Lord.

1 Chronicles 9:23 (NKJV) So they and their children were in charge of the gates of the house of the LORD, the house of the tabernacle, by assignment.

Gatekeepers were also to stand guard over the storehouses.

Nehemiah 12:25 (NKJV) Mattaniah, Bakbukiah, Obadiah, Meshullam, Talmon, and Akkub were gatekeepers keeping the watch at the storerooms of the gates.

The storerooms or storehouses as in other translations in Biblical days were where the tithe was brought by the people; however, the storehouses were not referring to a church building as we perceive it today. In fact, the tithe had nothing whatsoever to do with money but rather with crops and livestock. The Hebrew word for storehouse has several meanings in the Old Testament dependent upon the Scripture location. The most prevalent that is used in the modern-day churches that pastors recite in order for people to give money would be the Scripture in the Old Testament in Malachi 3:10. The Hebrew word in Malachi for storehouse is *o-tsawr* which means a depository, armory, cellar, garner, or store. In fact, for the church, there is only one mention of the word storehouse in the New Testament which is in Luke 12:24. Once again, the mention in Luke is referring to food as the Lord declares that the ravens have no storehouse or barn, yet God still feeds them. The New Testament being written in Greek, the word in Luke is *tameion, tamiasor,* or *temo* which means chamber on the ground floor used for storage or privacy, a spot for retirement, secret chamber, closet, or storehouse. There is never a mention in Hebrews or Greek that bringing tithes into a storehouse refers to giving money to a building called the church. In fact, in Malachi, that Scripture is also used as it relates to robbing God because there were many who did not tithe their crops and livestock. The purpose of the tithe was that there was food in God's storehouses in order that His people had food. I will not get into this as it pertains to so much more in our world today, especially America where we have thousands on the streets that go hungry because our way of government has abandoned the Word of God and succumbed to a society that has taxed people in order to create Welfare which has crippled the poor to be dependent upon a democracy that could care less about its people, as they rob the poor and middle class to become the wealthy.

To get back to my purpose of disclosing the storehouse was because in Biblical times, the gatekeepers who watched over the storehouses where the tithe was brought, did so in order that the food supply was protected. However, to be clear, the tithe in the Old Testament was to bring forth crops and livestock, which proves that the only meaning of the storehouse was some type of structure that livestock and crops could be stored; it was not referring to the church. With that said, gatekeepers or watchmen are those who guarded those gates or doors which were of great importance in the Old Testament times.

Move forward into the New Testament times, and you will more often see the wording as watchmen which are basically the same thing depending on what translation you are reading. Jesus coming on the scene, became the watchmen over those souls who belonged to Him. After Jesus died on the Cross and ascended to heaven, the Holy Spirit came down to those who belong to Jesus, in order that they be filled with His presence and become those watchmen guarding the truth of the gospels. Therefore, those who have truly found Truth through the Word of God will be unafraid to stand up for that which is not Biblical. Meaning, those who are on the narrow pathway that leads to heaven, will be the few that are radical when it comes to standing up for Truth in our society. Standing up for truth will be those who are unafraid of the consequences because today, we need watchmen that will stand up to our government and the corruption behind the scenes. We need watchmen who will stand up for the corruption within what people refer to as the church where most are as corrupt as our government. We need those who are rebels that stand up and shake the very grounds we stand on in the name of Jesus Christ. True followers will be watchmen over the souls of those who are being led astray as sheep to the slaughter. Jesus commanded us to go and share truth. In doing so, we have become the watchmen to guard the lost sheep and bring them back into the fold. This of course will only be those who truly have eyes to see and ears to hear, but we go forward none the less proclaiming that which is true and that which is false.

Before I go further, let me clarify that we are to obey our government which is Biblical unless our government goes against the Bible. I see many who claim to be Christians fighting against our government on many issues which have nothing to do with the Bible. We may not always agree with our government's methods, but we better believe what the Bible says and it is very clear about obeying our government.

Romans 13:1-2 (NKJV) Let every soul be subject to the governing authorities. For there is no authority except from God, and the authorities that exist are appointed by God. [2]Therefore whoever resists the authority resists the ordinance of God, and those who resist will bring judgment on themselves.

God's laws prevail over man's laws, but if we are not being told to break the commandments that we live by, we submit to man's laws. Yes, the government has broken many of God's laws such has killing the unborn, changing laws which allow same sex marriages, taking God out of the schools and public offices, etc. We stand on God's laws pertaining to those things and as citizens, we have the right to be able to vote. Our votes should never be to put those men and women in office that carry out the evils of this world. Yet, as far as anything else that our government does or does not do, it is in God's hand. He appointed them in those positions which ultimately, we all know the ending to this story—if in fact, we are true believers. If so, according to Revelation, our world as we know it one day will end and this is part of God's plan to redeem those who truly belong to Him. Yes, our world will go through much tribulation and our fighting through social media on trying to stop the birth pains will not happen. Jesus warns us in Matthew 24 that the birth pains will come. This is all part of God's plan and as Christians, we are to live by the Word of God knowing that one day, the end is going to come.

Going back to my topic, in Biblical days, watchmen were mocked and hated by those within the church, and we will also be hated. It is no different today, as in the days of the first disciples. When there is one that is willing to stand up and go against the majority that claim they are Christians, they are persecuted and kicked out of those congregations. The sad part is that the majority will dare to stand up against those false prophets over these mega-churches. I can tell you that any time I have suffered persecution and hate, it has been from those who call themselves Christians. Jesus said that we would be hated and persecuted. This persecution comes from those who claim to be followers of Jesus Christ far more than from those who do not believe at all.

Matthew 10:16, 22 (ESV) "Behold, I am sending you out as sheep in the midst of wolves, so be wise as serpents and innocent as doves. ²²and you will be hated by all for my name's sake. But the one who endures to the end will be saved."

Let me say here, we are already told in Scripture that there will be many who look like sheep on the outside but inwardly, they are wolves in Matthew 7:15. These are wolves portrayed as Christians. In the Scripture above, we are warned to be wise as serpents and innocent as doves. Why? The reason is that our battle today is not with this world. Our battle is within those buildings that we call church. Our battle is with the deadliest of enemies—it is the enemy that portrays themselves to be Christians and in doing so, they have captured the majority. It is no wonder that our Lord tells us to be wise and innocent. If we are not wise, we will be led astray. If we are not innocent, we will fall to their prey. It is of utmost importance that we stay strong through the Word of God where we will not fall captive. Yes, there is a battle in the world, as well. Yet, that battle is only with our will. When we stay strong with the Lord, we are able to overcome sin of this world and our desires to be close to Jesus by walking away from temptation.

1 Chronicles 9:26 (ESV) for the four chief gatekeepers, who were Levites, were entrusted to be over the chambers and the treasures of the house of God. ²⁷And they lodged around the house of God, for on them lay the duty of watching, and they had charge of opening it every morning.

In Old Testament times, the gatekeepers were in charge over that which was sacred, which was the chambers and the treasures of the house of God. They were bold and unafraid to tell the Truth of God's Word in hopes that people would remain on the right pathway and not drift away from the Lord. Even the messages that Jesus gave were bold and harsh not watered-down messages as we see today. They were not messages that the people wanted to hear but rather bold messages that they needed to hear in order to be saved from the eternal fires of hell. They were not messages that the majority prefer to hear today. Pastors do not want to give the people what they need but what they want. The church has merely become another means of shopping for what makes us feel good and pastors capitalizing on our needs in order to grow in numbers to be great and fill their pocket books. Bold messages never were what was popular in Jesus' day, and they are still not popular today. Bold messages will not keep the goats intact because goats are blind and deaf. They have not eyes to see nor ears to hear. It is the goats that are needed to build the empires that bring in the masses, and the true gospel message will fall on deaf ears to those who do NOT belong to Jesus. However, Jesus called us to a ministry which requires that we die to self. This requirement many times will step on our flesh because it is about letting go of this world. *(Romans 12:2; Luke 9:23-24)*

Like with anything, we have a choice. We either can follow a man or follow Jesus Christ. It is only because of Christ dying on the Cross for mankind, we can come to Him and lay our sins at the Cross and make that choice to follow Him. It is not about following a man but following the One True God! When we make that choice by laying down our own life and choosing a life with Him, we have chosen to die to self. Only through knowing Him do we come to know the Father. As one with Him, we become one Spirit united and the very presence of God no longer resides in the sacred sanctuaries as it did in Old Testament times, His Spirit resides within us.

Romans 8:9 (ESV) You, however, are not in the flesh but in the Spirit, if in fact the Spirit of God dwells in you. Anyone who does not have the Spirit of Christ does not belong to him.

It is only through His presence within us that our mortal bodies are able to do away with the old nature of sin and rise with Him in a new nature.

Romans 6:6-7 (ESV) We know that our old self was crucified with him in order that the body of sin might be brought to nothing, so that we would no longer be enslaved to sin. ⁷For one who has died has been set free from sin.

It is only through this new life of His presence within that we truly come to know Him and are able to walk as He walked. The temptations that once enslaved us no longer have dominion over our bodies as we are alive through His presence, the Holy Spirit. It is at this place that the Holy Spirit becomes the gatekeeper to our hearts, and we have confidence that He watches over us and guides us through this new life.

Psalm 32:8 (NKJV) I will instruct you and teach you in the way you should go; I will guide you with My eye.

Psalm 121:8 (NKJV) The LORD shall preserve your going out and your coming in From this time forth, and even forevermore.

Jeremiah 29:11 (ESV) For I know the plans I have for you, declares the LORD, plans for welfare and not for evil, to give you a future and a hope.

John 16:13 (ESV) When the Spirit of truth comes, he will guide you into all the truth, for he will not speak on his own authority, but whatever he hears he will speak, and he will declare to you the things that are to come.

As we grow in His love and grace, we become the gatekeepers or watchmen over His Word which is the only Truth in this world.

Making Choices

John Bunyan, an English writer and Puritan in the 17th century, the author of *The Pilgrim's Progress,* was also the author of *The Holy War,* where he describes the various gates in which our soul interacts, our 5 senses noted as the *Ear-gate, Eye-gate, Mouth-gate, Nose-gate*, and *Feel-gate*. I have written many times about the openings to our body, as being the very avenues that make the choice to either allow that which is good to enter or that which is evil. I liked Bunyan's metaphor as it is used to show that as the Holy Spirit is the gatekeeper over those who truly belong to Christ, we must play a part to this because we are given choices daily. As true Christians, we only draw our strength through the Holy Spirit and time spent in the Word of God which fills us with that which is good and not evil. Another choice in this life is to walk away from true spiritual growth and choose the things in this world which will ultimately bring death to our senses that we are no longer alive with Christ but dead. If we are not gatekeepers joined with the Holy Spirit over our senses, we are no longer alive through Christ.

In Biblical days, there were always gatekeepers who guarded the most holy of places, the treasures of God. As a true disciple of Jesus Christ, you are a treasure to Him and He has given you the presence of God to dwell within your mortal bodies that you are dead to sin. Our choice, we either live for Christ in these natural bodies or we are dead to Christ and alive to sin.

1 Peter 2:9 (NKJV) But you are a chosen generation, a royal priesthood, a holy nation, His own special people, that you may proclaim the praises of Him who called you out of darkness into His marvelous light.

Psalm 141:3 (NKJV) Set a guard, O LORD, over my mouth; Keep watch over the door of my lips.

Gatekeepers also were charged to keep watch for the Master's return. They were mindful to watch for the signs of the times. They studied diligently in order to gain the wisdom needed in the Word of God so that they would hear the voice of the Holy Spirit to be able to understand what the signs meant. The messages today should be bold and should be equivalent to that of John the Baptist. John gave up all to follow the voice that was guiding him to be a gatekeeper to prepare the people for the coming of Jesus Christ. We are to be preparing the way for the second coming of Jesus Christ. We are to be gatekeepers. When you know truth and you hear the voice of the One calling you, that calling will be to gain the tools needed in order that you have ears to hear and eyes to see Truth. When you can truly see the Truth, you go forth as John the Baptist went forth in order to bring that same Truth to all people that God sends across your path. Those pastors that want to try and teach their followers how to live a good Christian life here on this earth are nothing more than false teachers. As followers of Jesus Christ, we are to boldly go where most will never go in order that we proclaim the gospels in all boldness and truth. If this means that we suffer, then we suffer for Jesus Christ.

2 Timothy 2:12 (NKJV) If we endure, We shall also reign with Him. If we deny Him, He also will deny us.

1 Peter 2:21-22 (NKJV) For to this you were called, because Christ also suffered for us, leaving us an example, that you should follow His steps: 22"Who committed no sin, Nor was deceit found in His mouth."

If our messages are bold and harsh as Jesus' messages were, the majority are not going to follow you just as they did not follow Jesus.

John 6:66-67 (NKJV) From that time many of His disciples went back and walked with Him no more. 67Then Jesus said to the twelve, "Do you also want to go away?"

The multitudes came but the multitudes also left. Why would we think that we can build a ministry of thousands when Jesus could not? I'm using that number hypothetically to merely indicate that the Bible tells us that few will find the pathway leading to heaven whereas the many will not. However, man continues to come up with methods trying to entice the many. Oh, and they will come but they will not all remain if the teachings are equivalent to the Words of our Savior. You see, man learned a method to give the multitudes what they want in order that they would remain. I suppose if Jesus had of tried man's methods, they would have remained. Jesus did not come to be lifted up as a king, but he came humbly. You can see this as he chose to ride in on a donkey which in Biblical days portrayed a lowly animal, a symbol of peace. In those days, donkeys related more to the common people whereas horses were in relation to kings.

John 12:14-15 (NKJV) Then Jesus, when He had found a young donkey, sat on it; as it is written: 15"Fear not, daughter of Zion; Behold, your King is coming, Sitting on a donkey's colt."

Jesus had no desire to be lifted up by man, and we should have no desire to be acknowledged and increased either. If our heart is right with God, our motives will be also. The Bible tells us that Jesus is Truth. He was in the beginning; He was Truth and Truth came to live among us.

John 1:14 (NKJV) And the Word became flesh and dwelt among us, and we beheld His glory, the glory of the only begotten of the Father, full of grace and truth.

The people came, and the people rejected the Truth because the Truth required that they die to self. That message has not changed today, even though most churches do not teach it as such. To live with Christ is to die to self, to our own desires of this world.

Every single day when we awake, our day begins and ends with making choices. We seldom even think about lining those choices up with the Word of God. We have been programmed in this world to live according to the standards which we have become accustomed to and not those standards set down by Jesus Christ. Our choices daily are based on what voice you choose to follow. As I have said, most claim they have never heard the voice of God which is really the voice of the Holy Spirit. Yes, Jesus tells us that His sheep will follow His voice, but He also told us that it was better for Him to leave because One greater would come. That would be the Holy Spirit. The Holy Spirit is God's presence within us. When we hear that voice deep inside of us which lines up with the Word of God, it is the voice of the Holy Spirit. However, Jesus also tells us that they are ONE!

John 17:20-23 (NKJV) "I do not pray for these alone, but also for those who will believe in Me through their word; 21that they all may be one, as You, Father, are in Me, and I in You; that they also may be one in Us, that the world may believe that You sent Me. 22And the glory which You gave Me I have given them, that they may be just as We are one: 23I in them, and You in Me; that they may be made perfect in one, and that the world may know that You have sent Me, and have loved them as You have loved Me."

We are to be ONE with them! If you are truly a sheep, you are to be ONE with them. I explain it like this – the Bible tells us that when a man and woman get married, they no longer are two but one. *(Mark 10:6-8)* We see two, but they are one when joined together. The trinity is one as well and Jesus desires that we be one with them. The trinity is in union together which means agreement. Unity is the state of being united as a whole, meaning as one. We may see things differently as someone we are in unity with, but the way we see it must still be in agreement. To look at the marriage between a man and a woman, they are in unity and should be as one. This does not mean they will see everything through the same eyes because men and women tend to see things differently which concludes the meaning of *"opposites attract."* In bringing together a union between two people, there will be strengths in the man where the woman may be weak and weak areas in the man where the woman has strengths. The two brought together is to complement each other where they are joined together for a holy completion. The importance of a marriage truly withstanding the temptations of our day is that they are joined with our Lord and Savior, where they are brought together as one with the trinity. Our weaknesses are strengthened as we grow in truth as one with God the Father, God the Son, and God the Holy Spirit.

Being in unity with the trinity takes place when man sees themselves as nothing outside of the relationship with Jesus Christ. To become one with them takes man decreasing as he increases Jesus Christ. To be in unity will be man looking to the Bible as the ultimate authority of truth where there is no disagreement with God. God is God and His Word stands as the ultimate truth; whereas, man has no truth within him unless he is joined through the Holy Spirit to Jesus Christ. A man and a woman married should be in unity together and will be, if they know their roles as husband and wife according to the Word of God. There would be no divorces if those married truly found Jesus Christ and developed that relationship, where they were following the right voice.

As I said, there is God the Father, God the Son and God the Holy Spirit. I know this is taught so many different ways, but this was an analysis that God gave me years ago to teach in order that His people would understand. I have heard other teachings that were close to mine but not exact, but really, what we should gain out of this instead of arguing about who is right and who is wrong, is that Jesus was trying to teach us that the Holy Spirit was sent for us, in order that we hear that voice and adhere to that voice so that we do not fall up under all the false teachings that will ultimately lead you to hell. There can be disagreements with the interpretation of the Word of God, but as long as those different analysis do not keep you from traveling the narrow road, there is no need to argue. My point here is that our walk with Jesus Christ should be based on relationship and that relationship should be sought after by you. Your walk should be one where you strive to know Him and strive to hear the voice of the Holy Spirit. If we go through this life and we only follow the voice of a pastor or man/woman we choose to listen to, we will surely die because there is no relationship. Being one with someone is being one in agreement. Why are they one? They are one because of unity. A man and a woman should be in unity together when they get married. They should agree. They should complement each other whereas when you see one of them you see them both, separate they are not complete but together they are strong and stand as a pillar alongside their Savior. This is only true when a married couple is not just two but three. It should be Jesus Christ as the head of the man and the woman up under her husband. Our marriages today are all a mess because the head is not where it should be, and each spouse is not operating under the leadership they should.

All Are Called

As we develop that relationship with our Savior, we should adhere to the calling that He places on our lives. I know many will be saying that they are not called to be a gatekeeper. I will disagree with you on that. We are all called to be gatekeepers or watchmen but in what capacity will depend on your individual calling. Not everyone is called to be a pastor, priest, etc., but Jesus tells us that we are all called to go. Jesus tells us that if we are His, we will feed the sheep, lambs, etc.

John 21:17 (NKJV) He said to him the third time, "Simon, son of Jonah, do you love Me?" Peter was grieved because He said to him the third time, "Do you love Me?" And he said to Him, "Lord, You know all things; You know that I love You." Jesus said to him, "Feed My sheep."

This was not just for Peter; this was for all who would call themselves believers in Jesus Christ. If we truly love Him, we will go out into the world and feed His sheep. We will share the truth in the Word of God.

I know many times people have said that they are the hands because they are called to use those hands to feed others, take care of the sick, etc. However, if you have hands, you are called to use them. Otherwise, there is no need that you have hands. It's time that those who claim to be Christians understand that we were not placed in this world for our own pleasures but for His. When you stop using something, it can be taken away. *"Thank you, Lord, I have hands to go out into the street and use those hands to feed others, to bring comfort with a hand on their shoulder or to hug those who need to feel the touch of another person that cares about their circumstances."* Of course, we share Jesus because ultimately, He is the only One that can bring completeness to all people going through any and all circumstances. In other words, in the midst of any storms in this life, Jesus is the answer but it takes those willing to go and be the feet to take them there, the hands to show compassion, the mouth to share the answer, etc. We are all called to be gatekeepers because a gatekeeper is merely one that says, *"Lord, send me I will go into the world and share your love and goodness with all those you send across my path, and I will defend the truth of the Word of God!"*

You see, Jesus went from place to place where His feet would take Him. The people came to Him. The people came when they heard He was there. The people came because they knew He had the answers to their storms. This does not mean the people became saved. We are all human and our main objective is to fix our problems. If we hear there is someone coming to our city that is a minister of Jesus Christ and they can lay hands on us and heal us, we go. If we hear that someone is coming to our city that is well-known because of their teachings, we go in hopes that they have answers to our storms. However, the majority that go also leave. The majority that go never come to know Jesus Christ intimately. Those who come to minister to the people also come with a price-tag, meaning that those conferences cost money to attend. You must pay to hear what that speaker has to say. In this day and time, we are so programmed to believe that a mere person can have the answers to fix our circumstances when the answers are in the Word of God. We run to this person and that person who claim to be called by God to heal or called by God to have the answers to fix our problems. However, Jesus did not charge to share with the multitudes what His Father's Words were. Jesus did not claim to anyone that everyone could be healed just by asking or running to someone to have them lay their hands on them. Jesus claimed many times that your faith has made you whole but He also said, *"Go and sin no more!"* I believe there is a lot to be said about healing and if God is going to heal anyone, it will take that intimate relationship between them and Him.

My point is that we do not have to run to a mere man for the answers because God is waiting to give us the answers if we will just seek Him.

My point is that only those who truly seek God will find Him. It is not about spending one week pouring into the Word of God in order that you may get your answers to get you out of your current storm and when God doesn't move in your life in that week, you claim, *"Well, I tried that 'God stuff' and it didn't work for me!"* God is not something you try. It is a way of life for those who hear that calling. His sheep will hear His voice. His sheep may be sitting under false teachings, but they are going to continue to hear that voice where they keep questioning everything until they answer that calling. His sheep will seek deeper to know more. His sheep will follow because they are called not because there is something in it for them. His sheep will have compassion for man-kind which will lead them as gatekeepers to share the gospel of Jesus Christ to all who are sent across their path.

Truth Will Set You Free

Jesus did not go seeking people, they came to seek Him. Not all remained but those truly called either remained or went out to share with others. When you have something so great as the Word of God burning inside of you where you actually understand what you have come to know, you cannot keep it inside of you. When there is something great that happens in our lives, we cannot wait to share it with others. The same with knowing—really knowing Truth! The Truth will set you free, but the only way we are set free is by abiding in His Word. Abiding means that we remain in His Word, it is lifelong, continual, standing firm on truth, steadfast.

John 8:31-32 (NKJV) Then Jesus said to those Jews who believed Him, "If you abide in My word, you are My disciples indeed. 32And you shall know the truth, and the truth shall make you free."

I could go deep into that one Scripture, but the point is that we can be set free from many things, but the most important thing we are set free from is being able to see with our eyes and hear with our ears. You see, the majority of those who claim to be Christians are living in a world of deception. I have lived in this world myself from following a man instead of my own knowledge gained by the Holy Spirit. As you step out to really begin to study to know Him, there will be days and days that something you once thought is revealed in another light. Your eyes begin to see clearly and your ears begin to cipher everything that you are being taught to know truth from that which is false. Knowledge comes from knowing something which happens when there is time spent studying the Word of God, and wisdom comes from walking in that which you have come to know. The last part is understanding. As you spend time in Scripture to really know God and you spend much time walking in the knowledge you have gained—living each day by the Truth of the Word of God as taught to you by the Holy Spirit, there will be times that you begin to understand why

God allows certain things and why you must go through certain circumstances. At this point, it all becomes worth it. At this point, the persecution is worth it. At this point, letting go of certain areas of your life and dying to self becomes worth it. At this point, you grow stronger and are ready to be the mouth, hands, feet, etc.

Have you ever heard the saying, *"Birds of a feather flock together?"* This means that our associations, those we hang out with, are normally those who are like us. We are not comfortable hanging out with those who are different. God's people are different, they are set apart from this world.

Romans 8:30-39 (NKJV) Moreover whom He predestined, these He also called; whom He called, these He also justified; and whom He justified, these He also glorified. [31]What then shall we say to these things? If God is for us, who can be against us? [32]He who did not spare His own Son, but delivered Him up for us all, how shall He not with Him also freely give us all things? [33]Who shall bring a charge against God's elect? It is God who justifies. [34]Who is he who condemns? It is Christ who died, and furthermore is also risen, who is even at the right hand of God, who also makes intercession for us. [35]Who shall separate us from the love of Christ? Shall tribulation, or distress, or persecution, or famine, or nakedness, or peril, or sword? [36]As it is written: "For Your sake we are killed all day long; We are accounted as sheep for the slaughter." [37]Yet in all these things we are more than conquerors through Him who loved us. [38]For I am persuaded that neither death nor life, nor angels nor principalities nor powers nor things present nor things to come, [39]nor height nor depth, nor any other created thing, shall be able to separate us from the love of God which is in Christ Jesus our Lord.

Openings to Our Heart

There are 5 senses as noted, but there are 3 openings into our body—our eyes, ears and mouth. The Word of God tells us that what goes in the mouth is not what defiles the body but what is in our heart defiles us.

Matthew 15:11 (NKJV) "Not what goes into the mouth defiles a man; but what comes out of the mouth, this defiles a man."

We are defiled by what in in our heart. What is in our heart is determined by what we are feeding it and this is determined by our eyes and ears. What we choose to read, watch and listen to will be what is on the inside of us. Then what proceeds from our mouth when we speak, will come forth from what has been stored in our heart by what we have read, watched and listened to. This is not just about social media, computers, televisions, etc., this is also about our associations—those we choose to hang out with to include what we listen to within the buildings we call church. satan is very good at making sure the *"so-called"* Christians are not fed truth, in that there are so many false teachings spreading throughout our country. satan does not have to keep us out of the church building, all he has to do is corrupt the *church building ministries* through the men and women who call themselves ministers but do not hear the true voice. All satan has to do is defile the church. satan was able to defile the church in Biblical days, and he is still able to do so today. When I say church, I am merely referring to those ministries that claim to be the church; however, true Christians are the church! My point is that if satan can keep our eyes focused on this world, a particular ministry, a particular denomination, desires of this world, etc., we will never find the narrow road. If our eyes are blinded by truth, our ears will only choose to listen to what we have come to believe is truth! When we are following that which is false, we are conformed to this world and our desires are no different than this world. When our desires are filled with the pleasures of this world, our treasures are stored on earth not in heaven.

Matthew 15:13-19 (ESV) ¹³ He answered, "Every plant that my heavenly Father has not planted will be rooted up. ¹⁴ Let them alone; they are blind guides. And if the blind lead the blind, both will fall into a pit." ¹⁵ But Peter said to him, "Explain the parable to us." ¹⁶ And he said, "Are you also still without understanding? ¹⁷ Do you not see that whatever goes into the mouth passes into the stomach and is expelled? ¹⁸ But what comes out of the mouth proceeds from the heart, and this defiles a person. ¹⁹ For out of the heart come evil thoughts, murder, adultery, sexual immorality, theft, <u>false witness</u>, slander.

What is in your heart that defiles you? Remember, Jesus tells us that if we have had thoughts in our mind of sexual immorality, we have committed adultery; He also tells us that if we hate our brother, we have committed murder. Let's be honest, how pure are your thoughts today? Are you being fed truth which fills your heart with good instead of evil, or are you no different than this world? Are you disciplined to make choices in reading and watching those things which bring life instead of death to your soul, or are you no different than this world? We must look at ourselves truthfully and decide if we are blind and being led by the blind or if we are securing our salvation by following that which will produce pure thoughts within our heart. Who and what are you following today? Are you listening to those gatekeepers that were called to bring real truth even though it is hard on your flesh, or are you just following the crowds?

John 12:40 (NKJV) "He has blinded the eyes and hardened their hearts, Lest they should see with their eyes, Lest they should understand with their hearts and turn, So that I should heal them."

John 14:26 (NKJV) But the Helper, the Holy Spirit, whom the Father will send in My name, He will teach you all things, and bring to your remembrance all things that I said to you.

Yes, the Holy Spirit was sent to be our teacher and to remind us of all truth. If we are not hearing His voice, we are more than likely deceived. satan wants the world to be deceived. When we never study to know God, we more than likely will be sitting up under a man who is teaching out of context than one who is teaching the truth. I believe it would be safe to say, if you are not listening to the voice of the Holy Spirit, you are more than likely listening to the voice of satan. There are 3 voices that will lead us in this life. One is your own voice which will be selfish and about you. The other voice is satan's which will be contrary to the Word of God but if you do not study Scripture, you will never know that. The other voice is that of the Holy Spirit. Of course, we will hear the voice of other people every single day, but the voices of those will either have been influenced by their own selfish voice, satan, or the Holy Spirit.

Old Testament Gatekeepers

In Old Testament times, we can read about those who were called to be gatekeepers/watchmen over the soul of people. We know that the voice Abraham followed was not his own voice or that of satan. Abraham gave up his life to live a life full of God. He listened to God's voice time and time again and chose to follow that voice. Abraham had hardship but that did not stop him from going forth as a gatekeeper. Abraham followed the pathway chosen for him no matter how hard it was at that time. God provided everything needed for Abraham and his family. God made promises to Abraham that are still being carried through to this day. God promised that He would make him a great nation. He promised him that He would bless him and make his name great, and that he would be a blessing. God promised He would bless those who blessed Abraham and curse those who did not. There are many more blessings, but these are carried through generations as they are for those who follow in the footsteps of our Lord and Savior. If our lives do not lift up Jesus Christ, we are promised that we will be cursed.

Noah would have been another gatekeeper or watchman, as he stepped out and gave up his own life to do what God called him to do. Building the arch took many years, some believe that number to be 120 years based on the Scripture in Genesis 6:3; however, Bodie Hodge in the website, *Answers In Genesis,* has an analysis which is Biblical where his estimation is somewhere between 55 to 75 years.[1] Even at 75 years, that is a lifetime for today. During this timeframe, Noah was ridiculed and persecuted over and over again. The persecution never stopped him from going forth daily to do the calling placed upon his life. These men along with many others including women gave up their own selfish desires to follow an inner-voice that required letting go of this world. It required living a life knowing that you would be hated and ridiculed. Every single one of Jesus' disciples made the choice just as Moses did which was to follow that inner calling placed upon their lives. This calling will always be about other people. Jesus Christ came to suffer and die for people. We are called to use the talents we have in order to share Jesus Christ with people. We are called to be the *"John the Baptists"* sharing Jesus with the world, in order that we prepare them for the second coming of our Savior. We are all called to let go of this world and give what it takes to be seen as the light among darkness. Being a gatekeeper will be one that seeks and finds, asks and receives, knocks and the doors open. *(Matthew 7:7-8)*

In Old Testament times, those men of God were called to be the watchmen over the house of Israel. They were called to speak truth, to speak words that would turn men away from their sin and towards the only God that could save their soul. If the watchmen failed to speak up and defend the Word of God, the blood was on their own hands of those who died because of the weakness of man not speaking up.

Ezekiel 33:7-9 (ESV) "So you, son of man, I have made a watchman for the house of Israel. Whenever you hear a word from my mouth, you shall give them warning from me. [8]If I say to the wicked, O wicked one, you shall surely die, and you do not speak to warn the wicked to turn from his way, that wicked person shall die in his iniquity, but his blood I will require at your hand. ⁹But if you warn the wicked to turn from his way, and he does not turn from his way, that person shall die in his iniquity, but you will have delivered your soul."

Today, we are also called by Jesus Christ to follow in His footsteps. We are to awaken a generation to truth, to proclaim the truth, to stand up to false doctrine. In the Old Testament, there were watchmen who were blind just as they are today.

Isaiah 56:10-11 (ESV) His watchmen are blind; they are all without knowledge; they are all silent dogs; they cannot bark, dreaming, lying down, loving to slumber. ¹¹The dogs have a mighty appetite; they never have enough. But they are shepherds who have no understanding; they have all turned to their own way each to his own gain, one and all.

Shepherds with no understanding, each to his own gain. The era has changed but the ways of man has not. Many, many of those who claim to be watchmen over the souls of man, have construed their own doctrine to tickle the ears of those under their ministry. What profit a man if he gains the world but loses his soul?

2 Timothy 4:3-4 (NKJV) For the time will come when they will not endure sound doctrine, but according to their own desires, because they have itching ears, they will heap up for themselves teachers; ⁴and they will turn their ears away from truth, and be turned aside to fables.

Mark 8:36 (NKJV) For what will it profit a man if he gains the whole world, and loses his own soul?

True watchmen over the souls of man today, we should know them by their way of life and by their way of faith. One thing that will always hold true is that true watchmen will never attempt to change the ways of Jesus Christ, but they will submit to every commandment and way of life as our Lord and Savior when He walked this earth.

Hebrews 13:7-8, 17 (ESV) Remember your leaders, those who spoke to you the word of God. Consider the outcome of their way of life, and imitate their faith. [8]Jesus Christ is the same yesterday and today and forever. [17]Obey your leaders and submit to them, for they are keeping watch over your souls, as those who will have to give an account. Let them do this with joy and not with groaning, for that would be of no advantage to you.

Our lives will never be about this world but about the world to come. Our lives will never portray selfishness but selflessness. As those who claim to be Christians, we should all examine our lives and seek a holy God that desires we come to Him to give everything for the sake of those we love and the strangers that will cross our path. In America, our lives have become so cluttered with stuff, that our focus is far from living a life as a gatekeeper. I pray that each and every person reading this book comes to a place where they seek out for that intimate relationship with our Creator until they find Him.

CHAPTER EIGHT
TWO PATHWAYS ~ TWO CHOICES

There are two pathways and two choices in this world. You will either be on one or the other. One pathway will lead you to heaven and the other one will not!

As people who call themselves Christians, we all want to believe that we are on the right pathway. In my walk with God, there have been times that I believed I was on the right pathway. It is much easier to believe you are on that right path when you are sitting up under a man's teachings that try to convince the people that when they die, they will surely see heaven. Of course, there came a time when I began to question what I was being taught and stepped out for my own sake to make sure that I was traveling the pathway to heaven. When we begin to question and begin to seek God minus man, this can be a great place to be but also very terrifying. Seeking God deeply, you will always find more than you bargained for. However, I would much rather find truth instead of going through the motions only later to realize that I missed heaven, as I am sure most would agree to this. Yet, most people will never do what it takes to ensure their salvation. Why spend your life going through the motions of some false Christianity when seeking Him deeply can lead you to the Truth that will ultimately set you free and save your soul.

Jesus tells us that His sheep will follow His voice as discussed in chapter 3. However, if we are not really following in His footsteps, are we not His sheep? That depends—if we have the deep desire to really know Him and really find Him, then we will hear His voice many times as we are sitting up under false teachings. When we hear that voice, He is trying to tell us to question the words. When I was sitting under false teachings, I can remember over and over again Scriptures coming to my mind that proved what was being taught was not true. Of course, I was studying Scripture and like I have said, if you never study and never seek, you will never find Truth. If you never find Truth, you will never be set free from the bondage of man or the bondage of that which is false. Without Truth, you are on that wide pathway instead of the narrow pathway that leads to heaven.

I know it took me years to walk away from my *"so-called"* church family because I had roots there, and I felt that I was being used by God. However, I was being used by man to further his own motives of building an empire that had some man's name all over it. Helping to build a man's empire only makes that man great—not Jesus Christ!

In seeking God to a deeper level, there were many things He taught me about the choices of the two roads. I think we get so caught up in doing what the majority does that we seldom acknowledge what the pathway even looks like that we are traveling on. When you go on a road trip, you must pay careful attention to all of your surroundings. Why is this? A road trip is going someplace that you are not familiar with. That means you will be on many different types of roads such as interstates, highways, country roads, etc. You will drive through places that are very congested with people and traffic, and you will drive through areas that are deserted and abandoned. We pay a lot of attention to those things when we travel into places unknown to us but our everyday walk where we assume that we are walking with Christ, we seldom pay any attention to our surroundings.

Many times, since God has given me great revelation in this area, I have asked others what they think the narrow road to heaven looks like. I do this simply because I know that the majority have never even thought about that or asked that question. Remember, I was there once and never even thought about what the road to heaven looked like. I believe as Christians that are striving to seek Jesus Christ, we must always be asking the questions. If salvation is so important—and it is, our minds should be full of questions to ask to God.

If we are not asking, we are not seeking either. He tells us to ask, seek, and knock. Why are we not doing this?

Matthew 7:7-8 (ESV) [7]"Ask, and it will be given you; seek, and you will find; knock, and it will be opened to you. [8]For everyone who asks receives, and the one who seeks finds, and to the one who knocks it will be opened.

Of course, this Scripture has been used out of context so much by false teachers where people have begun to believe that we use this verse for our own pleasures. Most people who sit in church services regularly are familiar with this verse because it is used often in the mega-churches. This Scripture is often used to stand in agreement with, where they believe for what they need and want. However, when the majority desires to know what a Scripture really means, they tend to ask their pastor or some other man or woman the questions that they desire to know about the Bible, instead of seeking God themselves. Scriptures do not teach us to ask, seek and knock to our pastor or anyone else. Scriptures teach us to ask Jesus Christ, to seek Jesus Christ, and to knock on the door for Jesus Christ to open it. Men or women should not be our God. Yes, we can go to men and women for prayer or for counseling but if we are NOT seeking the Scriptures, we will be blinded to Truth. I'm going to tell you that there are very few men and women out there that I would ask for directions on anything to do with the Bible. I'm not saying that there are not people out there that will lead you in the right direction, but as people who desire to really know God, we cannot find Him through a mere man or woman. He desires that YOU seek Him and not man! However, there are those and it is few, that I will listen to their teachings that I have found because what they teach does line up with the Word of God. Of these that I do listen to, it is satisfying to my soul to know there are those out there that are really walking this same narrow road and have chosen to let go of this world. If you seek for those who are teaching truth, God will help you find them. Remember, the few are the true church not a building.

As I have asked others what they believe the narrow road looks like, I've never heard anyone say anything that made it sound like they had a clue about what that road looked like. There came a time in my walk as I was seeking God to a deeper level that I decided I wanted to know what the wide road looked like and what the narrow road looked like. Yes, we should also know what the road to hell looks like because it may surprise us that we are on the same pathway as the world, and the world is blinded from being able to see that their pathway is leading them to hell.

I came to a place after sitting under so many false teachings that I desired to know Truth and to hear it from God – no one else! I had to seek Him for days and even months. I cried out to Him time and time again through this period as I was hungry for knowledge in His Word. He led me out to the desert area where I lost all my *"so-called"* Christian friends, family, etc. I was alone! I became the enemy to the Christian population that I had been connected to for years and was perceived as hearing the wrong voice. At this place, normally the Christian community thinks you have totally lost it, and they choose not to associate with you. It was just me and God, but it was a great place to be. If you are someone that feels like you cannot live without man's approval daily, you will never find God. God will not send you out to a desolate place indefinitely, but He will send you for a while. Just like John the Baptist, he was alone for some time before others began to come to him. Jesus Christ, He went into the desert for 40 days, but it was only for a season. Today, I have friends but I choose to not have many close friends. It's not because I don't want many friends but because I don't need many friends. I have those few that I am close to but in reality, if you are doing what you are called to do for Jesus Christ then you will not have time to be popular. Truthfully, none of us were ever called to strive to be popular. Jesus Christ should be the One that we lift up and increase, not ourselves and as Scripture tells us, those who are a friend to the world are an enemy to God!

James 4:4 (NKJV) Adulterers and adulteresses! Do you not know that friendship with the world is enmity with God? Whoever therefore wants to be a friend of the world makes himself an enemy of God.

The Wide Road

After some time went by as I was seeking to know what the narrow and wide roads looked like, God gave me an analogy on both roads which made sense. To begin with the analogy on the wide road, it would be compared to an interstate highway. When we travel on any interstate, what do we see? There are always many distractions as many people are traveling to get to various cities and states. You have cars, trucks, eighteen wheelers, motorcycles, RV's, etc. We must be very careful and pay attention at all times because we know that the interstate highways are one of the most dangerous of all road systems in the United States when it pertains to casualties. You are more likely to be killed in an accident on interstate due to the fast speed limits than on road systems that do not travel at those high speeds. As you are traveling along, there are many other distractions besides the traffic such as bill boards, road signs, etc. There are entrances and exits which all lead to various other locations. As you approach cities, you must pay close attention to the various signs to know what lane you must be in based on the direction you are heading or the exit you may need to be taking to get you from point A to point B, etc. Traveling on interstate highways, your mind must be alert and focused at all times. However, your focus will be on those things of this world, and your life will be full of busy-ness. This is the pathway that the majority of this world travels. Included on this road are those who do not believe in any god or the true God whereas they believe in a false god.

The interstate highway road system is filled with those who do not believe in Jesus Christ, those who do not believe in life after death, and also those who say they believe in Jesus, but they have never really studied to know Him. They may even read their Bible from time to time and attend church, but they only know Him based on what they have heard from others. There is much enticement and much temptation on this road. Those who travel this road, their mind is entangled with all the distractions that keep them focused on their day to day choices. This pathway which the majority of this world are traveling, keep them conformed to this world. This pathway keeps those who claim to be Christians focused on storing their treasures on earth and not in heaven. Let me clarify, the interstate system includes those in this world that do not believe in Jesus Christ, as well as those who claim to be Christians yet their walk in this life is one and the same, as both are conformed to this world.

The interstate system, offering so many distractions and choices in this life, is the road where people are focused on gaining all they can gain as they store up treasures on earth. Their storehouses that they are watchmen over are filled with earthly treasures. How do we store our treasures on earth? When we are distracted just as this world is distracted, our focus is on all those bill boards or road signs. Let me clarify once again, on the interstate system, the signs and bill boards you are following are leading in the same direction as this world. You are not following the narrow path which leads to heaven, as our Lord teaches but rather the same pathway as this world. The interstate system will lead you to hell with the rest of the world. An example on bill boards or road signs could be an advertisement for a new movie being played at the theater or perhaps, advertising a concert coming to your area. Maybe, the advertisement is giving you the day and time that your favorite sports team will be playing. You may be thinking, what is wrong with that? There is nothing wrong with that if your focus in this world is to live like this world. However, we were called to not be like this world. As a Christian, we are to be set apart and stand for something far greater than this world, but the majority in this world have sold out to be connected to this world. The majority in this world who label themselves as Christians do not know the voice of God, and they follow the wrong voice. Please go back to chapter 3 if you do not understand that there are different voices out there and only one voice that will lead you to heaven. The majority of Christians choose to follow false teachings which have blinded them from truth and in their defense, they want to throw out there that Jesus also associated with the world. No, you are wrong. Jesus was in the world but not of the world.

John 17:14-18 (ESV) 14 I have given them your word, and the world has hated them because they are not of the world, just as I am not of the world. 15 I do not ask that you take them out of the world, but that you keep them from the evil one. 16 They are not of the world, just as I am not of the world. 17 Sanctify them in the truth; your word is truth. 18 As you sent me into the world, so I have sent them into the world.

In John, Jesus is praying to His Father and He is praying for those who belong to Him. He says that we are not of this world. If He has chosen you, His Word will abide in you and this world will hate you because you are not of this world!

Jesus ministered to all who listened, but He did not choose them nor associate with them. The definition for associate is someone who connects with someone else. In other words, they link with them, couple with them, relate to them, identify with them, etc. Jesus did not associate with those who chose the world and not the way which leads to heaven. He did not link with them because they were of this world and He was not; He did not couple with them, relate to them or identify with them. To relate and to identify is connecting to something. How could Jesus connect to those of this world when they stood for everything against God? Yes, He associated with sinners, but we are all sinners. Those He associated with saw something greater, and they wanted what He had to offer. In order for them to gain what He had to offer, they chose to walk away from the world and from their sin. Jesus tells us that He is not of this world which means He will not connect with this world. There is a huge difference in ministering truth to the world and agreeing with the world. To connect, you would be in agreement, and Jesus was never in agreement with the ways of sin. To add to that or to clarify, Jesus was also not in agreement with being conformed to this world in any way.

Pay attention to those who He chose. Jesus chose those who were willing to leave all behind to follow Him. You cannot follow Jesus when you want to hold on to this world. You cannot follow Jesus when you make the choice to have two sets of friends—the friends who are Christians and the friends who blatantly choose to follow satan. We are not to associate with those who openly sin and have no desire to change because if we do, we will be in agreement with them. If we choose to connect to this world and walk with this world, then we choose to link to this world. This means that we choose to be part of this world, and if we are part of this world, the truth does not abide in us. Yes, we can minister to this world but there is a huge difference to inviting them into your home and hanging out with them on a daily basis. Friends of the world are not friends of Jesus. Beware who you invite into your home—many times, those you allow in have no desire to know Jesus Christ; however, satan does have the desire to bring destruction to you and your family when you allow that which is not of God into your surroundings. Do you know the reason that those who followed Jesus had to leave all behind and go? Jesus required this because He had to separate them from the world in order to pour into them. In other words, if we desire to KNOW that we are really on the road to heaven, there must come a time where we are willing to be set apart from this world, in order that we can be filled with His Word—the true Word of God. As long as we are trying to hold onto certain things or certain people in this world, we are limiting the time we spend with God and the time it takes for us to be filled with His presence. As long as we continue to pour more and more of this world into our lives, there is only limited space that we can take in His Word. It is the Word of God inside of us that will change our lives, but it first takes those things in our heart being removed for us to begin to understand and allow the Holy Spirit access. We limit God when we are not willing to *"go."* We limit God when we are not willing to let go of those things inside of us which will only keep us from finding that road, which leads to heaven and ultimately ensures our salvation.

Am I going to tell you that you will not go to heaven if you do the same things as the world does or you choose to be friends with the world? Like I said, there is only one voice to follow and if you are hearing the voice of the Holy Spirit as Scriptures tell us, your choices will be like those in Biblical days who stood out from the crowds and were persecuted.

2 Timothy 3:12-13 (ESV) [12]Indeed, all who desire to live a godly life in Christ Jesus will be persecuted, [13]while <u>evil people</u> and <u>imposters</u> will go from bad to worse, deceiving and being deceived.

Who are those people who do evil? We are all evil if we are not transformed by the Word of God where our choices in this life become for His good. His Word says that no one does good, not even one.

Romans 3:12 (NKJV) They have all turned aside; They have together become unprofitable; There is none who does good, no not one."

Who are the imposters? The imposters are those who are spreading false messages. The imposters are those who claim to be followers of Jesus Christ, but their messages do not line up with the Word of God. The imposters are those who have sold out to fulfill their own agenda in this life whether it be for fame, fortune or some other agenda, but their walk in this life is not the same walk that Jesus walked while here on this earth. The imposters are merely false prophets, false teachers, etc. This world is full of them, and they capture the minds of the majority because the majority who claim to be

Christians are so busy trying to fit into this world that they seldom spend time seeking the true God and never hear His voice.

If you go back and read 2 Timothy 3 in full, you will see that he sums up those who are of this world to name a few— people who are lovers of self, lovers of money, unholy, lovers of pleasure rather than lovers of God, etc.

Name Above All Names

Who exactly do we think is being increased among the Christian community that the majority are following? Pastors, evangelists, and Christian artists to name a few—are they not lovers of self? You may say no because you see their good works, but we must examine what those works are and who is being increased? Are their works really considered good according to Biblical standards? When those who fit in this category are in control such as a pastor, it is NOT Jesus being increased. When their name is being lifted up all over the world and they have gained fame in their name, who is being increased? Whose name is supposed to be increased? Who is supposed to be humble? We see in Philippians 2 Christ's example of humility.

Philippians 2:1-10 (ESV) So if there is any encouragement in Christ, any comfort from love, any participation in the Spirit, any affection and sympathy, [2]complete my joy by being of the same mind, having the same love, being in full accord and of one mind. [3]Do nothing from selfish ambition or conceit, but in humility count others more significant than yourselves. [4]Let each of you look not only to his own interests, but also to the interests of others. [5]Have the mind among yourselves, which is yours in Christ Jesus, [6]who, though he was in the form of God, did not count equality with God a thing to be grasped, [7]but emptied himself, by taking the form of a servant, being born in the likeness of men. [8]And being found in human form, he humbled himself by becoming obedient to the point of death, even death on a cross. ⁹Therefore God has highly exalted him and bestowed on him the name that is above every name, ¹⁰so that at the name of Jesus every knee should bow, in heaven and on earth and under the earth.

It seems that the majority of Christians today are following names that are above the name of Christ, names that are in the highlight, names that are blasted all over the radio, social media, etc. Whose name is supposed to be above all names and who is supposed to be humbled as a servant counting others more significant than themselves?

Let's also look at lovers of pleasure. This is huge among the world to include the majority who claim to be Christians. Lovers of pleasure are going to be all those who choose to live in sin because of the desires in their heart which are evil. Those desires for pleasure are normally fulfilling the lusts in their heart for things that are unholy to God, such as satisfying their sexual appetite whether it be adultery, sex outside of marriage, homosexuality, etc. On the other hand, lovers of pleasure are any who live out their lives daily seeking anything which brings them pleasure to fulfill the lusts of the flesh. To take it down a notch, that could mean those who live to eat instead of eating to live. Perhaps it is those who find pleasure in spending foolish amounts of money on the latest fashions, jewelry, etc. Does this not also satisfy our fleshly desires? I think you get my point; it is not just about those who have sexual pleasures but also about anyone whose lifestyle is based around fulfilling those things which bring them satisfaction and have nothing to do with increasing the name of Jesus Christ.

The final category in 2 Timothy are those who strive to gain the riches in this world, lovers of money. I always like to bring up the fact that when Jesus shared to the multitudes His Father's Word, He didn't ask for money, and He didn't charge people to come and be entertained. Yes, we should be giving to those who are true disciples, even though the tithe has nothing to do with giving money to a church. However, any who step out to *"go"* as Jesus taught, they were to go from place to place taking nothing with them for those who truly desired to know Jesus, would feed them and give them a place to rest. You can read the story in Luke 9, but my point is that if we are gaining knowledge and wisdom from a true man of God, by all means we should give to that man who has sacrificed his life for the good of others. Today, this would be in the form of money because there are pastors out there that do not work to make money, as they have sacrificed their life unto the ministry daily. As for 10% of our earnings, this is not Biblical, but we should give as the Holy Spirit speaks to our spirit and that may be more than 10%.

My point I wanted to make, was that as Jesus did not charge people to hear His messages, men and women today should not be charging us to hear their messages either. We have famous pastors that travel where multitudes come to hear them and there is a fee to be able to attend. This is absurd! Where are the lowly and poor sitting in these events? Do any of these pastors or Christian artist give free tickets to the homeless, so that they can sit perhaps on the front row? I'm just saying, when the Holy Spirit began pouring into me to write books, I will never forget the words I heard, *"How dare you put a price on the words I gave you!"* Yes, you can buy my books, but I tell you right now, I give more of the books I have written away than I sell because I am not in this to make money but to do the calling placed on my heart. How dare that I would tell someone who has very little in this world that they cannot have one of the books I have written unless they have money to purchase it. You see, my books are NOT my books, if He gave me the wisdom and knowledge that is written in these pages. The glory should go to Him. However, do we not see the multitudes of Christians flocking into *"so-called"* Christian concerts having to pay high dollars for their ticket to see their favorite *"idol"*—Christian artist. We also see mega-preachers and evangelists who travel to be guest speakers at various venues, and they charge an admission. What about that person who is seeking Jesus Christ deeply because God has been dealing with their heart, and they have no money? You will never see them sitting in these concerts or attending these services that charge an admission because they cannot afford it. This is probably a good thing as most of these entertain false doctrine. Those who have become wealthy, many times publicize their charitable organization that they send money to where people can see their good works. In fact, you can probably google to find what charity any of your favorite idols give to because it is more than likely out there for all the world to observe their good works. However, what does the Bible say about doing works or helping those less fortunate in this world? Let's read in Matthew.

Matthew 6:1-4 (NKJV) "Take heed that you do not do your charitable deeds before men, to be seen by them. Otherwise you have no reward from your Father in heaven. ²Therefore, when you do a charitable deed, do not sound a trumpet before you (OR ADVERTISE IT ON YOUR WEBSITE) *as the hypocrites do in the synagogues and in the streets, that they may have glory from men. Assuredly, I say to you, they have their reward. ³But when you do a charitable deed, do not let your left hand know what your right hand is doing, ⁴that your charitable deed may be in secret; and your Father who sees in secret will Himself reward you openly.*

Every time those who are in the spotlight give and it is seen by all in this world as good works, they are seen by God as hypocrites and their reward has already been received on this earth, there will be nothing further for them. First, I want to say that there are many who have used the name of Jesus to become rich and famous. Such, are those *"so-called"* Christian preachers or ministers of the Bible that travel in their jets and live in their million-dollar homes to include the famous Christian artist/musicians. We dare look at these men and women as being sent by God? They are not sent by God. They are wolves in sheep clothing and making millions off of deception all the while keeping the multitudes listening to every word they speak—buying tickets to hear them, buying every book they print, and sending money to continue to help grow their empires. Jesus is NOT being increased but that man or woman is being exalted in this earth—false prophets and teachers!

How can these *"so-called"* ministers sleep at night knowing that they are only giving their time for the person that can afford to listen to their teachings or their concerts? I can tell you how they sleep, their god is NOT Jesus Christ but satan. satan has no trouble sleeping at night for deceiving those who believe they are following Jesus. I could name many out there that are wolves in sheep clothing and you could as well if you studied the Scriptures because all of a sudden you would be able to see what category they fit in. Do we really want to fit in with this world? Do we really want to be a friend to the world? Do we want our idols in this world to be those men and women who have cashed in on using the name of Jesus or God for their own agenda where they have millions in the bank, mansions, and huge followers? I tell you now, I would rather be among the broke than for my life to be as such. The good news is that those whose life in this world is considered poor, we are told in the Bible that they are rich! There are many Scriptures that teach on being rich such as:

- *Keep your life free from the love of money, Hebrews 13:5*
- *Those who desire to be rich fall into temptation and a snare, 1 Timothy 6:9*
- *He who loves money will not be satisfied with money, this is vanity, Ecclesiastes 5:10*
- *Better is a little with the fear of the Lord than great treasures and trouble with it, Proverbs 15:16*
- *Take heed, and be on guard against all covetousness, for one's life does not consist in the abundance of the things he has acquired, Luke 12:15*

- *For where your treasure is, there your heart will be also, Matthew 6:21*
- *How much better to get wisdom than gold and to get understanding is to be chosen rather than silver, Proverbs 16:16*
- *What is desired in a man is steadfast love, and a poor man is better than a liar, Proverbs 19:22*
- *The little that a righteous man has is better than the abundance of many wicked. For the arms of the wicked shall be broken, but the Lord upholds the righteous, Psalm 37:16-17*
- *Do not overwork to acquire wealth; be discerning enough to desist, Proverbs 23:4-5*
- *Riches do not profit in the day of wrath, But righteousness delivers from death, Proverbs 11:4*
- *For the love of money is a root of all kinds of evils, 1 Timothy 6:10*
- *No one can serve two masters, for either he will hate the one and love the other, or else he will be devoted to the one and despise the other. You cannot serve God and mammon, Matthew 6:24*
- *Let the lowly brother boast in his exaltation, and the rich in his humiliation, because like a flower of the grass he will pass away, James 1:9-10*
- *I know your works, tribulation and your poverty (but you are rich), Revelation 2:9*
- *I know your works, that you are neither cold nor hot. I could wish you were cold or hot. So, because you are lukewarm, and neither cold nor hot, I will vomit you out of My mouth. Because you say, 'I am rich, have become wealthy, and have need of nothing' – and do*

> *not know that you are wretched, miserable, poor, blind, and naked, Revelation 3:15-17*

The sad part is that the *"so-called"* Christian community has poured millions of dollars into the hands of these *"so-called"* ministers/teachers and Christian artists where they travel the country to have revivals and/or concerts in the name of who? In their own name that's who! Let's not forget that they also sell their merchandise with their own names all over it such as on the cover of their CDs, posters, t-shirts, etc., and we also have those *"so-called"* pastors selling their books with their picture plastered all over the front cover to be known and recognized as great among men. They are only increasing themselves and they have no problem letting it be known that they use part of their riches to give to those certain non-profits of whatever they are compassionate about. Therefore, the Christian community tends to look at their works, as doing great things for those who are less fortunate. However, the Christian community fails to read and study Scripture. We see those famous artists or those famous ministers preying upon the people to give them more of their money on a daily basis and all the while we believe that their works are good. They are not good! When we truly give from our heart, there is no one that needs to know this but God unless you are trying to gain a reputation with this world as being good. This is striving to gain popularity with the world. Yes, we are to give to the poor and there are many Scriptures that confirm this fact, but if we are truly walking with Jesus, we have no desire to gain the recognition of this world.

Let's go a bit farther, those in this world who strive to gain a place in this world and to be seen by man as something great, they are not of God! There is NO truth in them. The Scriptures are black and white when it comes to this, there is no middle ground. We are told if you are of this world, your father is satan.

John 15:19 (NKJV) If you were of the world, the world would love its own. Yet because you are not of the world, but I chose you out of the world, therefore the world hates you.

John 8:42-44 (ESV) Jesus said to them, "If God were your Father, you would love me, for I came from God and I am here. I came not of my own accord, but he sent me. 43Why do you not understand what I say? It is because you cannot bear to hear my word. 44You are of your father the devil, and your will is to do your father's desires. He was a murderer from the beginning, and does not stand in the TRUTH, because there is no TRUTH in him. When he lies, he speaks out of his own character, for he is a liar and the father of lies.

John 14:24 (NKJV) He who does not love Me does not keep My words; and the word which you hear is not Mine but the Father's who sent Me.

To touch on a few things briefly, those who desire fortune and fame in this world have no love for Jesus because that is NOT His purpose for the true church! Those who have sold out to the world, have done so for their own gain! They are blinded by truth because God has allowed this. Their desires line up with the desires of this world and their father is the god of this world!

John 12:40 (NKJV) "He has blinded their eyes and hardened their hearts, Lest they should see with their eyes, Lest they should understand with their hearts and turn, So that I should heal them."

The last thing I want to expound on to a greater degree is what the Scriptures have to say about those who claim to be Christians yet their lifestyles are no different than this world. I touched briefly on John 17 where Jesus was praying to His Father for those whom He was given. I want to go a little deeper into this Scripture as I have the whole passage in full, for I believe this Scripture is very important to study.

John 17:1-26 (ESV) When Jesus had spoken these words, he lifted up his eyes to heaven, and said, "Father, the hour has come; glorify your Son that the Son may glorify you, ² since you have given him authority over all flesh, <u>to give eternal life to all whom you have given him.</u> ³ And this is eternal life, that they know you, the only true God, and Jesus Christ whom you have sent. ⁴ I glorified you on earth, having accomplished the work that you gave me to do. ⁵ And now, Father, glorify me in your own presence with the glory that I had with you before the world existed. ⁶ "I have manifested your name to the people whom you gave me out of the world. Yours they were, and you gave them to me, <u>and they have kept your word.</u> ⁷ Now they know that everything that you have given me is from you. ⁸ For I have given them the words that you gave me, and that I came from you; and <u>they have received them and have come to know in truth</u> believed that you sent me. ⁹ I am praying for them. <u>I am not praying for the world but for those whom you have given me, for they are yours.</u> ¹⁰ All mine are yours, and yours are mine, and <u>I am glorified in them.</u> ¹¹ And I am no longer in the world, but they are in the world, and I am coming to you. Holy Father, keep them in your name, which you have given me, that they may be one, even as we are one. ¹² While I was with them, I kept them in your name, which you have given me. I have guarded them, and not one of them has been lost except the son of destruction, that the Scripture might be fulfilled. ¹³ But now I am coming to you, and these things I speak in the world, that they may have my joy fulfilled in themselves. ¹⁴ <u>I have given them your word, and the world has hated them because they are not of the world, just as I am not of the world.</u> ¹⁵ I do not ask that you take them out of the world, but that you keep them from the evil one. ¹⁶ <u>They are not of the world, just as I am not of the world.</u> ¹⁷ Sanctify them in the truth; your word is truth. ¹⁸ As you sent me into the world, so I have sent them into the world. ¹⁹ And for their sake I consecrate myself, that they also may be sanctified in truth. ²⁰ "<u>I do not ask for these only, but also for those who will believe in me through their word,</u> ²¹ <u>that they may all be one, just as you, Father, are in me, and I in you</u>, that they also may be in us, so that the *world may believe that you have sent me. ²² The glory that you have given me I have given to them, that they may be one even as we are one, ²³ I in them and you in me, that they may become perfectly one, so that the world may know that you sent me and loved them even as you loved me. ²⁴ Father, I desire that they also, whom you have given me, may be with me where I am, to see my glory that you have given me because you loved me before the foundation of the world. ²⁵ O righteous Father, even though the world does not know you, I know you, and these know that you have sent me. ²⁶ <u>I made known to them your name, and I will continue to make it known, that the love with which you have loved me may be in them, and I in them</u>."*

There is a lot to say about Jesus' words to His Father. I have underlined many of the words above to emphasize a few points. Those who receive eternal life will be only those whom the Father has given to His Son. Those who belong to Him will keep His Words—not some of His Words but they will live in a manner to please Him and not please this world. They will daily strive to know Him deeper and seek Him to the degree that they are able to overcome the strongholds in their lives. They gladly receive His Word and that lightbulb goes off in their mind where their eyes are open and ears are open to see and hear truth and know the truth in their heart. This is a supernatural experience that can only happen through the Holy Spirit, as those turn from this world and cry out to Jesus Christ for redemption upon their lives. When our lives cross over, Jesus Christ is glorified through us because He is lifted up and increased—His name above all names and our name is NOT up there in lights!!

Philippians 2:9 (NKJV) Therefore God also has highly exalted Him and given Him the name which is above every name.

Whose name is above every name? I don't think the Bible tells us that a *"so-called"* preacher/teacher or Christian artist's name is above every name, but Jesus Christ's name is above every name! We live out this walk (according to the Word of God) which is evident in our lives! The evidence that your Christianity is real and is from the God above, not the god of this world, is that the world will hate you! Look around at all those in the spotlight whom claim to be Christians and see their name lifted up and see their great followings as this world loves them!! This world only loves them because their father is the god of this world, satan! This world accepts them and does not persecute them because they are of this world.

In John 17 above, Jesus continues to pray not only for those disciples that He walked with but also for every disciple to come that would leave all behind and choose a lifestyle according to His Word and have no desire to gain the riches, popularity, fame and fortune of this world that is perishing! This is love! This is the only true love that there is in this world. God is love and without a true sincere relationship with Jesus Christ, there is NO God in you and there is no real love! Who are we following these days? What idols have we placed in our lives? We want to believe that we can love God and love this world but we cannot!

1 John 2:15 (NKJV) Do not love the world or the things in the world. If anyone loves the world, the love of the Father is not in him.

People want to say that we are to pray for those who are out there lost. Yes, I believe that we are to pray for those who are truly lost and seeking, but I am not going to pray for those who are leading the multitudes astray with false messages because their father is satan. It is written in the above Scripture that Jesus said Himself that He did NOT come to pray for the world but for those His Father had given Him! If I am to be Christ-like, I will pray for those that Jesus Christ places on my heart to pray for but not for the world in general. If you are walking close with Jesus Christ, you will hear that voice, and He will let you know who you are to be praying for.

God Hates Sin and The Sinner

Among all the false teachings today, we are led to believe that God loves everyone, but that is contrary to His Word. Scriptures teach us that God not only hates sin, but He also hates the sinner! We want to believe that because God is love, that He is looking down from heaven on all these false prophets with compassion, but that is not the God of the Bible at all!

Proverbs 6:16-19 (ESV) 16 There are six things that the LORD hates, seven that are an abomination to him: 17 haughty eyes, a lying tongue, and hands that shed innocent blood, 18 a heart that devises wicked plans, feet that make haste to run to evil, 19 a false witness who breathes out lies, and one who sows discord among brothers.

In reading this Scripture, we have all sinned and come short of the glory of God, but it is what we do once we sin. Do we run to God or continue on our path of destruction? The Scripture says He hates the eyes, tongue, hands, etc., does that mean He actually hates the person or the sin? That may be that He actually hates the sin, but as we read the last part of that Scripture, we see that He hates that person who is a false witness. Beware, if we are not studying and spending time in the Word of God to really know Him, what is coming out of our mouth may be false and if it is, remember that He hates the false witness. Does that mean He will not forgive that person? Perhaps He will forgive, but it is by far better that we run from those who are false witness' so that we do not fall into a trap. I believe that God knows each man's heart. After all, He is God and He knows everything. With that said, He already knows if those who teach false messages will turn from their wickedness. Like Judas who had the desire for riches, there are also those out there where their gain in this world has become so great which has resulted in their heart becoming tainted. I believe once you go so far into your sin, that He gives you over to that sin because His Word says that He has blinded their eyes and hardened their hearts. Just like the rich young ruler standing before Jesus Christ could NOT walk away from his earthly empire which he had built, there will also be many that cannot walk away from their own empires. We must beware of our choices in this world because gaining the riches can lead to our destruction and following false teachers will keep us conformed to this world. As we spend time allowing that which is false access to our eyes and ears, we will be filled with that which is false. When we are filled with false messages, that is what our heart is full of because we have allowed access through the openings of our body. At this place is where we will also share with others that which is false!

I will not tell you what you should or should not do, but the interstate system is full of those who label themselves as Christians yet they do not seek Jesus Christ and do not hear that small quiet voice. I know that there are many who would stop reading this book at some point, especially when it hits home and they find themselves having to make a choice between being a real Christian vs. a counterfeit Christian. The disciples of yesterday, they did not travel on an interstate highway that distracted their calling to doing all kinds of things for entertainment, instead of following Jesus Christ down the road that was not popular at all. You see when we compromise, that means we choose to follow Jesus Christ when it fits into our own schedule but when it conflicts with our personal plans with friends, family, etc., we tend to look away. In fact, we tend to ignore the fact that just maybe we are not really on that narrow road at all.

Conformed to This World

To emphasize on being conformed to this world, let's examine that further. Jesus tells us if we belong to Him, we will follow in His footsteps. We are told that if we are His, we will be hated by this world. We will not be accepted by this world because we will be different, yet all those idols that we listen to that claim to be sending Jesus to the world are accepted by the world and loved by the world—false prophets, teachers, and artists! Unless the Word of God is not really true, how can we read that THOSE who are following in Jesus' footsteps will be HATED by this world and not be able to see when they are loved by the world that something isn't quite right with the picture? Again, how can we believe that those who have used the name of Jesus to gain fame and riches in this world are not false prophets? Either the Word of God is true or it is a lie. If it is a lie, why are you even trying to follow anything that claims to be spreading the Word of God, yet the evidence is that it is NOT God? However, if you consider the Word of God to be truth, why are you making idols of people who are merely false prophets, teachers, and artists?

On the interstate system, we can recognize many live conformed to this world—yet, far too often they have never heard the voice of the Holy Spirit. They call themselves Christians based on what they have been taught by man. The majority of those will tell you they have never heard the voice of the Holy Spirit and some do not even believe that you can hear His voice. Some believe they are good in their walk with Jesus and will go to heaven because their belief system is based off of a message they have heard within the modern-day churches. *"All who desire to be saved, come to the altar and ask Jesus into your heart!"* Sorry, but that in NOT in the Bible. The only difference in their walk on the interstate system and those who do not believe in Jesus Christ is that maybe from time to time, they do attend church or maybe they even regularly attend church. Perhaps, they even give tithes to the church to help build up that ministry and perhaps they even give money to help with missions and feeding the poor; however, giving money to help increase a ministry that is teaching false, is not good works. Even if it was good works, we cannot be saved by works alone. Works will never assure your salvation because there are even those on the interstate system that do not believe in Jesus that give money for good causes.

Ephesians 2:8-9 (ESV) For by grace you have been saved through faith. And this is not your own doing; it is the gift of God, ⁹not a result of works, so that no one may boast.

There are also those who believe that if you are a good person, God will not send you to hell. Yet, according to the Word of God, none are good.

Romans 3:10-12 (ESV) as it is written: "None is righteous, no, not one; ¹¹no one understands; no one seeks for God. ¹²All have turned aside; together they have become worthless; no one does good, not even one."

As shown in Scripture, our good, will never be good enough and that is why we need a Savior. Having a Savior is not a *"get out of jail"* card. It is not claiming that you know Him; it is really knowing Him. To ensure your salvation, you need to study to know Jesus Christ intimately and understand that on the day Christ returns, there will be many that He tells to depart because He never knew them.

Matthew 7:21-23 (ESV) "Not everyone who says to me, 'Lord, Lord,' will enter the kingdom of heaven, but the one who does the will of my Father who is in heaven. ²²On that day many will say to me, 'Lord, Lord, did we not prophesy in your name, and cast out demons in your name, and do many mighty works in your name?' ²³And then will I declare to them, 'I never knew you; depart from me, you workers of lawlessness.'

Jesus was speaking to those who gave themselves a title of being a Christian but being a Christian has to do with your relationship with Jesus Christ. Many are called but few are chosen.

Matthew 22:14 (NKJV) "For many are called, but few are chosen."

If we are traveling the interstate system and have never heard His voice, beware because that pathway is the wide road which leads to hell. Your walk on the wide road will be all about living in this world trying to gain as much of this world as you can gain as you dress like this world, desire the same things as this world, like the same movies that the world likes, desire the same fashions, cars, motorcycles, boats, etc. as this world. This my friend is called being conformed to this world and we are warned that this is NOT the narrow road which leads to heaven.

Romans 12:1-2 (ESV) I appeal to you therefore, brothers, by the mercies of God, to present your bodies as a living sacrifice, holy and acceptable to God, which is your spiritual worship. Do NOT be conformed to this world, but be transformed by the renewal of your mind, that by testing you may discern what is the will of God, what is good and acceptable and perfect.

I will continue to elaborate on the definition of the word *"conform"* because this is crucial to walking according to the Word of God. When we choose to conform to this world, we are accepted in the society of this world. Step out and be different than this world, and you will see how few friends you actually have. People do not want to run with the few that are causing friction in their society. People want to blend in with the crowds many times and not attract attention to themselves, unless they are those who strive to step out to gain the wealth and fame. However, it is those that have gained the wealth and fame that society desires to follow. The majority of Christians choose to also follow the pathway that is acceptable by society. They follow the traditions and customs. They strive to adapt and follow the crowds. The majority fit in with what is the norm for our society. Very few will go against the customs set out by the standards of a society.

Two Choices Two Losses

Our whole life is about choices. There are two choices and two losses. Yes, both choices result in losing something, and we must make that choice of what we are willing to lose and what we are not willing to lose. One of your choices will be to continue on the wide road that is not the narrow road and you will lose your chance for heaven, but you will gain your place in this world. The other choice is to lose your influence, recognition, popularity, and your will – the things you desire in this world, but you will gain heaven. Yes, it is a hard choice and one that the majority will not choose to really follow Jesus Christ because the majority do not really want to give up their own life—it's called selfishness. We are a selfish people and even during the days that Jesus walked the earth, the majority came and listened but after He was finished sharing with the crowds how to have everlasting life through Him, the majority walked away. They wanted a savior, but they wanted one that would allow them to continue living their own selfish life and not require them to give up those things and desires they enjoyed in this world. Today is no different, we see many carry the title of a Christian camped out in the mega-type churches because they want to believe it must be God due to the crowds that follow those teachings. Yet, Jesus was not able to capture the crowds if you will study the Scriptures. If we are to follow Jesus, why did the crowds walk away? You will see why in John.

John 6:60 (NKJV) Therefore many of His disciples, when they heard this, said, "This is a hard saying; who can understand it?"

On hearing what? On hearing Jesus share what we must do to inherit the Kingdom of Heaven. At this point, there were many of His disciples that chose to walk away. I am not talking about the 12 but about other disciples.

John 6:66-67(ESV) From this time many of his disciples turned back and no longer followed him. ⁶⁷"You do not want to leave too, do you?" Jesus asked the Twelve.

In another Scripture, Jesus speaks out to the crowds that had come looking for him once again on the second day, same crowd, that their reason for trying to find Him was not because they desired to follow Him but it was for their own selfish reasons.

John 6:26-27(ESV) Jesus answered, "Very truly I tell you, you are looking for me, not because you saw the signs I performed but because you ate the loaves and had your fill. ²⁷Do not work for food that spoils, but for food that endures to eternal life, which the Son of Man will give you. For on him God the Father has placed his seal of approval."

These are the Scriptures where multitudes came, but they left and here is a particular scene where the same crowd went seeking for Him on the following day and Jesus responded to them. He knew that they were not interested in hearing what He had to say but interested in getting their fill. This was the majority, the masses that people will try to tell you followed Jesus. They did come and they did go away. They did not want the spiritual food but the natural food. This is the same thing we see today. It is always about, *"What's in it for me?"* You see, the message Jesus gave the crowds that day is still the same message today. What is that message?

John 6:54-58 (ESV) Whoever eats my flesh and drinks my blood has eternal life, and I will raise them up at the last day. ⁵⁵For my flesh is real food and my blood is real drink. ⁵⁶Whoever eats my flesh and drinks my blood remains in me, and I in them. ⁵⁷Just as the living Father sent me and I live because of the Father, so the one who feeds on me will live because of me. ⁵⁸This is the bread that came down from heaven. Your ancestors ate manna and died, but whoever feeds on this bread will live forever."

How do we feed on the bread? It is the Word of God which produces life not death. This should never be interpreted to the communion of literally eating and drinking of the bread which will not produce life. The communion was not instituted at that time. The bread is life; Jesus is the bread of life. Our minds are to feed upon the flesh and blood of Jesus Christ. In order to do this, we feed upon the Word of God because it will bring life not death. When we spend little time or even no time pouring into His Word, there will be no life in you but only death. It does matter what we are feeding upon these days just as it did in Biblical days. Jesus could not capture the minds of the majority in those days because they did not really want to listen to His Words, as He spoke. Why do we think a man or woman of God can capture the minds of the people and it be real Christianity when Jesus Christ could not? It is because those mega-type churches are bringing them a savoir that walks the wide road where they do not have to really give up their life! People want to believe that they can serve Jesus Christ one day a week or maybe even two days, but they really do not have to give up their own lifestyles to make it to heaven. So, the pastors teach what the people want to hear instead of what they need to hear. The pastors are no different, they too desire to only give Jesus Christ a certain amount of their time because they also desire to continue living their own life being conformed to this world as the majority.

The Country Road

Now to take a look at the narrow road which is the wilderness road as discussed in chapter 2. I prefer to look at the narrow road as a country road. A wilderness road could be a pathway where cars are unable to go, such as a remote area which is an awesome analogy of the narrow road that leads to heaven. However, there may be many people who have never walked such a road whereas they have probably at some time experienced a country road in their car. Therefore, to be able to get a visual, we will call the narrow road a country road which can be very lonely at times in our travels because few today travel these roads. On this road, there is not much excitement going on but there is a lot to look at as I discussed on my road trip with my granddaughter. The things you will see on a road trip have God all over them. They are not man-made things but God created things such as the beautiful sceneries, trees, forests, mountains, lakes, rivers, animals, etc. The analogy that God gave me to this pathway was a small lonely dirt road where there were no distractions other than that of nature. Only the simple pleasures of life were all around you. Occasionally, you may see other people traveling this same road but not often, for there are few. Most of the time, it is just you and God alone for long periods. This road can seem very lonely at times, but it allows you to really seek God to know Him deeply.

I remember, the road trip that I had taken with my granddaughter I chose many times to take back highways that had been heavily traveled at one time prior to the interstate system. I was very surprised that we seldom saw any traffic because the majority are more interested in getting from one destination to another, as fast as they can without enjoying the scenery in between. On these roads, we would see old abandoned buildings that at one time had been opened due to the amount of people who traveled prior to interstates. It was quite a site as I could remember when I was just a child stopping at some of those locations that were no longer open. Yes, it took us longer to get to our destination, as we also stopped at times to take pictures of all of God's glorious natural creations. It was well worth the extra time when your focus is not on a particular activity but rather on exploring that which is natural.

When we make the choice to step out from the majority and seek that quiet pathway, we will actually question if we are really hearing the voice of God, whereas on the heavily traveled type of roads, we seldom question anything—we just go with the flow. In fact, on the narrow road, you will actually spend a lot of time seeking God because there may be no one else that you even know traveling this same road for some time. As I said, normally God will send you into the desert area alone because He desires to spend quiet time with you, so that you can come to really know Him. After some time, others will cross your path that are actually on this same road. However, we should always be questioning if we are hearing the voice of God instead of listening to other people. God desires that we find Him, and He loves the opportunity when we make the decision to step out of what is comfortable to man and go into a wilderness setting to seek Him deeper. The danger with remaining on the wide road is that everything looks so good and is comfortable to our flesh, that we will seldom seek God to a greater degree and never question what we have been taught. After all, if those brothers and sisters in Christ are all beside us, what is there to question? If the road looks good and we have been trained that this is what sheep look like, then why should we question?

When I was on that wide pathway, I never questioned anything for some time. However, on the narrow pathway, you will continually question because you may have no one walking side by side with you to assume that you are on the right road. It is much easier to believe you are right when you have close friends or family walking beside you and harder when you are alone.

The Poseidon Adventure

Let me share something that God showed me during this time in my life. Most of you will probably not be familiar with an old movie called *"The Poseidon Adventure."* It was during my time of deeply seeking God and questioning everything when He brought back this movie to my remembrance. God works that way. Things you have lived through or perhaps incidents you have done in your past, God is really good at using those things to give you revelation in order to help understand His Word. This movie was released in 1972, I was in my early teens when my father took me to see this at a local theater. I never forgot it because it was very dramatic at that time and for my age. When God began to use that movie experience to teach me Truth, it really opened my eyes to seeing this whole wide and narrow road in a different perspective. In this movie, there was a cruise ship that was out in the middle of the ocean when they were hit by a Tsunami. It happened so fast that the wall of water completely flipped the ship over where those who were still alive were walking on the ceilings and everything was upside down. Long story short, the top of the ship that was now underwater, and it was continually filling up with water whereas the bottom of the ship was floating on top of the water where there were still air pockets. There were two groups of people that the movie focused on. In the beginning, there was a huge group that had been in the main dining area and there was a preacher that was in that group. It was during Christmas and there was this huge, gigantic Christmas tree. They used the tree to prop up to a ledge where they could begin climbing towards the bottom of the ship in hopes of being rescued. Several men helped to get this giant tree to the ledge and then after one man was up there, he anchored it in a way where others could begin climbing. However, there were only few that chose to climb the tree while the majority thought it better for them to remain and wait to be rescued. I mean, there was no water coming in at that point, so they chose to remain even though they knew the ship was completely upside down. The preacher tried to tell them that they would all die if they stayed there but of course, we tend to go with the crowds, right? Once all of those who had chosen to climb the tree got to the ledge, all of a sudden water began to break through to the dining area. All at once, masses of people tried to climb the tree in a panic and the tree fell over and it was too late. So, at this point, you have the majority that died and the few journeying upwards in hopes of being saved. The people chose to believe what they majority believed, and only the few chose differently.

Besides this small group, there was also another group that was in a different area of the ship at the time of the Tsunami that were also trying to travel to the bottom of the ship in hopes to be rescued. However, neither group knew about the other. At one point, these two groups met. However, they were both moving upwards but going in different directions. So, we have this small group with the pastor leading them and this other group was a large group of people with another man leading them. The leader of the large group argued with the pastor that he was wrong, and the pastor stood his ground trying to convince them that they would die if they did not follow him. Now the reason was because there was this young boy who was in the group with the pastor that had actually spent much time with the crew of the ship. He was at an age where he asked many questions and the crew had shared many things with him. This young boy knew what end of the ship was actually thin enough that they could possibly be rescued in the event helicopters came to try and find any survivors. As it turned out, the majority believed they were right because it was the majority. The minority began questioning if they might be wrong because after all, there was a huge majority that believed they were right. However, the few decided to continue with the pastor. Of course, the story ends where the few were heading in the right direction and they were saved and the majority died. You see, this is how the human brain works. We would rather follow the crowd because if there is a huge number that believes one thing and just a few that believe differently, we tend to think that the majority must be right. However, God tries to tell us in His Word that only the few will be who make it to heaven. He also tells us that our wisdom is NOT His wisdom and our ways are not His ways. In other words, we do NOT think the way God thinks.

Matthew 7:13-14 (ESV) "Enter by the narrow gate. For the gate is wide and the way is easy that leads to destruction, and those who enter by it are many. [14]For the gate is narrow and the way is hard that leads to life, and those who find it are few."

Isaiah 55:8-9 (ESV) For my thoughts are not your thoughts, neither are your ways my ways, declares the LORD. ⁹For as the heavens are higher than the earth, so are my ways higher than your ways and my thoughts than your thoughts.

1 Corinthians 3:18-20 (ESV) Let no one deceive himself. If anyone among you thinks that he is wise in this age, let him become a fool that he may become wise. ¹⁹For the wisdom of this world is folly with God. For it is written, "He catches the wise in their craftiness," ²⁰and again "The Lord knows the thoughts of the wise, that they are futile."

Being reminded of this story, really woke me up. For one, I had never seen this movie but one time in my life, and God completely brought this whole movie back to my remembrance. If He does that, He is trying to give you some wisdom that will save your life. I began to really think about this. We, as people, always tend to go with the crowd regardless of the situation, but we also see this in the majority as they choose a church to attend. The mega-type churches must be leading the way to heaven more so than the small churches. The majority eat at this restaurant, it must be better. Have you ever just explored and gone into a run-down area of town to go eat in a small remote restaurant and discovered how great the food was? This is just another example. Of course, this does not mean that every church that is small or every remote restaurant in quaint areas are good, but we should beware of those who have gained popularity with huge growth because the Bible tells us that only the few will make it to heaven.

One more example that I want to share is how the majority choose a good book to read. I'm just going to talk about books on Christianity. There have been some huge mega-church pastors and huge evangelists who have become very wealthy because of the Christian community buying everything they have ever written. Once again, contrary to what the Word of God says, the majority believe that if they have grown a church to mega capacity, what they teach must be truth. The majority believe that if they can achieve just a little bit of what these mega-teachers have to say, they too will make it to heaven and also learn how to live this life to gain wealth and good health. Myself, I am not a known author and I could list many, many books out there written by others who are also unknown Christian authors. If you are not known, the people never seek to find your books either. Myself, when I began this journey away from the majority, God led me to seek all kinds of different topics to see what was written out there on certain things. In doing this, I found many of the *"not-known"* authors who were also traveling this same lonely road. In fact, there are many who do not even write books but have websites for people to read for *"free"* revelation that God has given them. Why write if no one buys your material? I know for myself, that I write because He called me to write. I do not write to become wealthy. I write and I give books away more so than they sell, as I have said. We are people who believe based on what the majority believe, but it all comes down to not seeking Him but seeking man. It all comes down to our time. We would rather follow someone else than seek God ourselves, but those mega-type preachers are never going to tell you that if YOU do not seek God yourself that you will NOT go to heaven. You cannot get to heaven without that relationship with Jesus Christ one on one.

Let me also say that after God had given me that insight into that movie, I thought it was very odd that the movie had actually used a pastor as being the right pathway. However, the pastor was just an analogy of Jesus Christ actually being the one that should be leading us, not a mere man which was something that He wanted me to see. Even so, the majority are so blinded by truth that in the movie, they actually chose a mere man instead of a pastor to follow which led them to their destruction. To clarify, Jesus wanted me to see that the pastor was an analogy of Him for this story but in real life, we should never be following a mere man and just because someone is labeled as a pastor, they are NOT Jesus Christ. A mere man is NOT who we should be following. When we follow a mere man regardless of what title they have given themselves, in the end, we will perish. God ordains those who are His ministers and just because someone claims to be a minister of the gospels, doesn't mean that they are such. If your pastor or priest doesn't preach hard core messages that the majority will never follow, they are not ordained by God. A good thing to do would be to read through your Bible at the actual messages Jesus gave and decide if that is what you are following.

My point to emphasize is that we are NOT to be following the majority but following the Truth. On the true pathway that leads to heaven, it will look like a country road. It is very important that we study to know what each pathway looks like. We should always be questioning the different voices that we hear. It is much harder to question when you are traveling with the crowd because we tend to believe that what the majority does must be right. However, that is man's way of thinking and we know that God's ways are not man's ways. *(Isaiah 55:8-9)*

As you begin your journey on the narrow pathway, it will seem as though you are traveling alone, and there will be at times a feeling of un-surety that perhaps you have missed it. This is especially true when you have those on the wide path continually telling you that you are wrong. We have to come to a place where we make a decision on who our God is. Do we follow people or do we follow God? It was a choice that every single one of Jesus' disciples had to make when they left all to follow Him. When your salvation is totally dependent on your walk alone, no one walking this out with you, you will strive to know God deeper and you will question every single thing. Remember, satan comes as a wolf in sheep clothing and Jesus tells us that many will be led astray. Jesus tells us that those who are His sheep will KNOW His voice and FOLLOW His voice.

John 10:27 (NKJV) My sheep hear My voice, and I know them, and they follow Me.

As sheep, we will question and eventually, we will step out to follow that one voice. Sheep will follow the One Master and the One voice that is NOT a pastor, priest, man or woman. Sheep will follow the voice of God through the Holy Spirit, as they strive to walk the pathway that leads to heaven. However, goats will never be satisfied and will always be looking for the best. Goats always believe that the grass is greener on the other side as was discussed in depth in chapter 3.

CHAPTER NINE
COLD ~ LUKEWARM ~ HOT

Matthew 7:13-14 (NKJV) ¹³"Enter by the narrow gate; for wide is the gate and broad is the way that leads to destruction, and there are many who go in by it. ¹⁴Because narrow is the gate and difficult is the way which leads to life, and there are few who find it.

As I have stated, few even find the narrow road as Jesus tells us in Scripture. I can only pray that those who are seeking Jesus Christ diligently make the choice to really search for this narrow road and that on their journey, they come to a place where they experience that road. What I mean by that is many times, there are those who get a real taste of Christianity but far too often, the distractions in their life out-weigh those brief encounters with what is real. These are the ones who will fall away from the truth without ever really experiencing God's goodness and purpose for their lives.

In this chapter, we are going to look at the three different types of Christians to bring light to the Scriptures and truth that will help those seeking to a deeper level understand the dangers of assuming that they are on the right pathway.

In the previous chapter, I have discussed the two pathways and two choices, but in this chapter because there are three types of people or three types of believers, the analogy I want to share is three types of road systems. We have discussed the interstate system and the country road as the two pathways but there are three road systems. The third road system is our highways. My focus in this chapter is to be able to bring to light the three types of *Christians* and to emphasize who is considered cold, lukewarm, and who is on fire for the Lord Jesus Christ.

Revelation 3:15-16 (ESV) "I know your works: you are neither cold nor hot. Would that you were either cold or hot! ¹⁶So, because you are lukewarm, and neither hot nor cold, I will spit you out of my mouth.

Exactly, what road systems do these three types of *Christians* travel? I think this is easy to see that those who are cold are traveling on the interstate system and those who are hot are on the country road, but who exactly is classified as cold and hot? Who would be classified as lukewarm? The Bible tells us that we must have eyes to see, and I believe part of being able to see truth is in actually visualizing many of these things. First, we should be able to understand that those who are cold are definitely unbelievers in Jesus Christ. However, I also believe there are many who claim to be Christians or at least believe they will go to heaven when they die that are right there with the rest of the world that doesn't know Jesus Christ at all! These are all cold, and they are all of this world even though there are many of those who say they believe in Jesus and think they are going to heaven. If you are one who spends a lot of your time studying the Scriptures, it is easy to also see those who are hot as they have made the choice to let go of this world and follow Jesus Christ! These would be looked at as the *"Jesus* freaks," those who are persecuted and hated by this world. However, among all who claim to be Christians, many would consider themselves as being hot even though their fruit says otherwise. We will look deeper into this later on, but for now we need to establish the three categories. Last are those who are lukewarm which I have stated in the previous chapter, they travel the same road as the world. Let me emphasize on this. Those who are lukewarm claim the title of being a Christian and even believe that they are really walking the lifestyle of a Christian, yet their walk is no different than that of this world. When I say that, don't assume that just because you have chosen to give up certain things in your life that you used to do means that you are on the right pathway that leads to heaven. If you were to look closely at those who are cold, many of those have also given up things in their lives as well, things that they may have done in their youth and have chosen to let go of. This does not make you a true Christian!

Those who are lukewarm have chosen to hold on to things in this world and are still conformed to this world, just like those who are cold. Those who are lukewarm still have the desires for the same things in this world, just as those who are cold. Those traveling the highway system are those who are lukewarm because they have chosen to compromise in their lifestyle as they try to hold on to as much of this world as they can. Many actually spend their time traveling back and forth from the highway to the interstate as they try to fit in with the world. The lukewarm that claim to be Christians, their lifestyles mimic the same lifestyles as the unbeliever and/or those who are cold. If your Christian walk is a compromise, you are classified as lukewarm by our Lord and Savior. Those who are lukewarm have formed a savior in an image that is easy to follow but it is not the God of the Bible.

In this chapter, we are going to examine all 3 categories in hopes that those who choose to read this book can begin to see who they are and where they fit into Christianity.

I remember as a child where it would become a game when you were trying to find something and someone else knew where it was. Instead of telling you, they would say, *"You are cold."* As you began to look around the room, that would change to, *"You are warm"* and then to *"You are hot!"* You knew when you were no longer cold and came to the place where you were warm, that you were closer to finding that which you were looking for. When you were finally told that you were hot, you knew that you were in the very vicinity of the item you were looking for. This is a very simple strategy, if you remain in the area where you are cold, it is only because you have no desire to find anything else. Being cold and staying in that place, you have no desire to find the prize or even play the game. Those that are cold have made up their mind that this is life, and this is where they have decided to remain. However, many times those that are cold will have others cross their path to share Jesus, and they make the decision to begin playing the game or they choose not to play at all. We were all cold at one time and those who have stepped out from that place made the decision to do something different, but that does not mean that they are still playing the game to actually find the prize.

You then have those who are lukewarm where they have become complacent in their walk with Jesus Christ. In other words, there are those who are lukewarm and are content where they have no desire to play the game anymore, and you have those who are lukewarm that believe they have found the prize, even though their walk is not one that is hot. Most who remain lukewarm believe that they are good and that they are close enough to the prize to win this game of eternal life.

Those who are actually hot, they know the prize is right there with them, but they also understand in order to remain in that vicinity, they must continue running as if their life depends on it because it does. Even though they may not can physically see Jesus Christ, they know He is right there with them. Paul tells us that he presses on toward that goal to win the prize.

Philippians 3:12-14 (NKJV) Not that I have already attained, or am already perfected; but I press on, that I may lay hold of that for which Christ Jesus has also laid hold of me. [13]Brothers, I do not count myself to have apprehended; but one thing I do, forgetting those things which are behind and reaching forward to those things which are ahead, [14]I press toward the goal for the prize of the upward call of God in Christ Jesus.

Cold vs. Lukewarm

First, we are going to look at those who are cold and those who are lukewarm together because they both fall into the same category of traveling the road which leads to hell. There are differences but there are many similarities. We could be classified as either cold or lukewarm dependent upon our lifestyles. Those who are lukewarm may be those who have gained very little knowledge of the Word of God or they may be those who have gained much knowledge of the Word of God. Those who are cold could also have knowledge of the Word of God. Either way, both of these are still conformed to this world.

Paul goes on to share with those who are walking the same walk he was walking, to continue thinking in like manner of what he was sharing. Let's continue reading in Philippians.

Philippians 3:15-19 (NKJV) Therefore let us, as many as are mature, have this mind; and if in anything you think otherwise, God will reveal even this to you. ¹⁶Nevertheless, to the degree that we have already attained, let us walk by the same rule, let us be of the same mind. ¹⁷Bretheren, join in following my example, and note those who so walk, as you have us for a pattern. ¹⁸For many walk, of whom I have told you often, and now tell you even weeping, that they are the enemies of the cross of Christ: ¹⁹whose end is destruction, whose god is their belly, and whose glory is in their shame – who set their mind on earthly things.

If you go through and read all of Philippians, Paul left all behind as he walked away from his previous life. He speaks of having suffered the loss of all things and counting them as rubbish, in order that he may gain Christ and be found in Him. Paul also speaks of having a righteousness that comes through faith in Christ. Sharing with other true believers of Jesus Christ, Paul encouraged them to continue on this race where they have gained maturity in thinking this way. How are we to think? We are to forget what lies behind and press forward for what lies ahead. We are to play the game where we continue to the place where we are no longer cold or lukewarm but hot. At this place, this is mature thinking and when our thinking is not right, God will let us know. There are many times in the walk of those who are striving and pressing forward, that the Holy Spirit will reveal truth to them where their thinking was not right. This is a walk that continues until the day you die and it is a walk by faith knowing that He will lead you, not a mere man! Paul warns us to keep our eyes on the examples of that right pathway. Paul was sharing with those who were also on the right pathway to keep their eyes on him, as he strived for that mark to win the prize. I never recommend anyone following anyone else. Paul is not here with us today, and there are many wolves out there trying to herd in the majority to follow them because they have another agenda. We must have a relationship with Jesus Christ, if we want to not be classified as the cold or lukewarm. We must seek Jesus Christ to know Him and by faith, we listen for His voice. His voice is there and I am amazed at how many people say that He never speaks to them. He probably doesn't because far too many are classified as either cold or warm, and they are completely complacent on where they are. They have quit playing the game, as they remain in an area of being warm following a pathway that looks like God, but it is NOT God! They have yet to be in the vicinity of being hot because they have compromised in their current status playing church. As Paul said, those who are not on this pathway, that would be the cold and the lukewarm, they are enemies of the Cross of Jesus Christ!

Before we go further, let me emphasize that the game of seeking until you are in the vicinity of being hot, is merely for an analogy to stir up those who are His true sheep. We should be stirred where we do not become complacent in our walk. We should continue from the place of being cold or lukewarm until we know we are living a life that is totally contrary to the Christianity of this world. True Christianity is NOT a game but rather it is real life, and if you are not at the place where you know you are on that narrow road, beware that your choice has been to remain on the same road that the majority are traveling.

Why would Christians remain in a place that is only lukewarm? First, the majority of the lukewarm probably believe they are on the right pathway because when we become complacent in our walk with Jesus Christ, we begin to die. The life of a Christian is one that is either always growing or it is dying. Another reason is that many have never really sought to find Jesus intimately, in order to grow to where they understand Scripture. Again, many may also be sitting under false teachings which has kept them conformed to this world, or they may even know the Truth and have chosen not to let go of this world. When you stand before Our Lord one day, your reasons for being cold or lukewarm are not going to matter because you will not be classified as a true Christian, and He will tell you to depart from Him. To know God is to have an intimate relationship with Jesus Christ. When our choices are to not pick up the Bible and spend time studying to know the truth, we have no one to blame. If we are blinded by the god of this world, we are on the same pathway as the world and are either cold or lukewarm.

2 Corinthians 4:4 (ESV) In their case the god of this world has blinded the minds of the unbelievers, to keep them from seeing the light of the gospel of the glory of Christ, who is the image of God.

You may say that you are not an unbeliever, so this does not apply to you. However, Jesus tells us that if we believe, there are certain things we will do. Many today are lukewarm and are conformed to this world. Their lifestyles are not of a true Christian. As a true Christian that really knows God, the Bible also tells us that we would keep His Word and if we do not keep His Word, we are not of God. In reality, if you claim to be a Christian but you have not let go of this world, you do not really know God, Jesus Christ, or the Holy Spirit intimately. You cannot know God by someone else's teachings. It must be a personal relationship where you have invested time in seeking Him.

John 8:47 (NKJV) He who is of God hears God's words; therefore you do not hear, because you are not of God.

John 8:54-55 (ESV) Jesus answered, "If I glorify myself, my glory is nothing. It is my Father who glorifies me, of whom you say 'He is our God.' ⁵⁵But you have not known him. I know him. If I were to say that I do not know him, I would be a liar like you, but I do know him and I keep his word.

We need to be careful here. When we spend all our time claiming to be a Christian but our knowledge has been gained through false teachings and there is no intimate relationship with Jesus Christ, we are nothing more than liars. We do not know the Father when we have never spent time to seek Jesus ourselves, and we either do not know the Word of God or we choose to not keep His Word. Either way, your end is not heaven unless you really know Him and to really know Him is to die to self. If we do not seek, we are NOT keeping His Word and the truth is NOT in us. If you are not at that place, your walk is no different than those in this world that do not even believe in God, those who have become satisfied with who they are and complacent with the world. Just know that being complacent is all about oneself, self-approving, self-satisfied, self-admiring. I discussed in chapter 8 many of those who are considered of this world, as you will see in 2 Timothy, once again.

2 Timothy 3:2-5 (ESV) For people will be lovers of self, lovers of money, proud, arrogant, abusive, disobedient to their parents, ungrateful, unholy, ³heartless, unappeasable, slanderous, without self-control, brutal, not loving good, ⁴treacherous, reckless, swollen with conceit, lovers of pleasure rather than lovers of God, ⁵having the appearance of godliness, but denying its power. Avoid such people.

What such people are we to avoid?

2 Timothy 3:6-8 (NKJV) For of this sort are those who creep into households and make captives of gullible women loaded down with sins, led away by various lusts, ⁷always learning and never able to come to the knowledge of the truth. ⁸Now as Jannes and Jambres resisted Moses, so do these also resist the truth: men of corrupt minds, disapproved concerning the faith.

The interstate system will be traveled by a huge majority, but it is mixed with the world and those Christians who are lukewarm as they travel back and forth trying to fit in with all. Many of these simply go through the motions of claiming to be a Christian by name only because they never do anything to learn of Him. They do not seek Him and those who actually go to church from time to time or even regularly, they play the part of a Christian for the timeframe they are in the church building but outside of that building, you cannot tell them apart from the world. They fit in with their surroundings every place they go. Therefore, many on this road system know nothing about God in truth even though they claim to be Christians. There is no difference in their life from those of this world. You can look at those that are conformed to this world and not even realize there are some of those who actually claim to be Christians because their walk is equivalent to the walk of those who have no desires to either know God or believe there is a God. They are all on the wide road which leads to hell.

As one who is conformed to this world, their walk fits into the standards set down by this world. In other words, they are in agreement with the way of life as the majority in this world who do not even claim to be a Christian. Their behavior is socially accepted among those they are in association with, they are definitely not persecuted as being *"Jesus freak,"* and they have the same traditions as set down from generation to generation which I will not get into in this book, even though most of the traditions of man were adapted by paganism. They fit into the crowd because their desires line up with that generation where they like the same standards, fashions, movies, etc. Moreover, their lifestyle follows the same paths as the majority where they run with the pack, swim with the stream, etc. They would dare not cause a ruckus and go against what the norm is.

In church history, a nonconformist was a Protestant who did not *"conform"* to the governance and usages of the established Church of England. Conformity is basically in compliance with the practices of the church of England which date back centuries. A great place to research how the different beliefs or denominations began to evolve is through Christianity.com.[1] I have the link in the references at the back of the book which discusses the Anglican Church, as well as the Catholic and moving forward. However, those following Jesus Christ broke all standards and caused disturbances every place they went. If you read in Acts 17, you will see that it was noted of Paul and Silas that every place they traveled, they had turned the world upside down with their teachings. During this timeframe Biblically, there were those who claimed to believe in God but did not accept Jesus, and they did everything humanly possible to put a stop to the teachings of Paul and Silas. However, the teachings of the Scriptures were never silenced to this day because there is a God and there is a Savior, Jesus Christ, who are still in control!

Let's stop here a minute. Moreover, most who claim to be Christians have a hard time being able to see that they fit in the category with those who are conformed to this world. This is because they have been blinded. Therefore, we need to ask ourselves, if we merely claim that we know God/Jesus but in reality, we never read or study Scripture, is this really seeking Him? If we do not seek Him, we can't find Him, and our walk in this life is not the walk of a true Christian but a walk that fits in with those who are cold and lukewarm. If you have never found Him intimately and your knowledge of Him is based off of your particular religion, you do not know Him. He said, there will be *"many"* (talking about those who claim to be Christians) that He says, *"Depart from Me for I never knew you."* (Matthew 7:21-23)

The Word of God tells us that there are many that do not know Jesus Christ and only few that are really traveling the narrow pathway. If you are on the interstate or highway, you may very well believe that Jesus is the Son of God and was sent as your Savior; however, you may very well have learned how to just play church. Many have no idea that this is what they are doing because they have become blinded from truth as I have shared.

If you are lukewarm, at some point, you decided that you wanted to be connected with a body of believers. Those who are lukewarm are those who decided to play the game at some point as I discussed earlier, and many of these believe that they are in the right circle and on the right pathway that leads to the prize. However, they have never learned how to play the game. It is not about playing to be close to finding the narrow pathway, but it is about playing to be ON the narrow pathway and close to the prize. This is the first step of gaining some truth, but if most of the knowledge you are gaining is false, you are not growing in a way that your lifestyle changes to be a true Christian. False knowledge will not save you and set your feet on the narrow pathway that leads to heaven. Let me say this, we can gain all kinds of knowledge, some true and some false, but if we are not living what is taught in the Word of God, we really do not believe. We are told in the Word of God that it is His commandment that we believe in Jesus. If we truly believe, we would also keep His commandment!

1 John 3:18-23 (NKJV) My little children, let us not love in word or in tongue, but in deed and in truth. ^{19}And by this we know that we are of the truth, and shall assure our hearts before Him. ^{20}For if our heart condemns us, God is greater than our heart, and knows all things. ^{21}Beloved, if our heart does not condemn us, we have confidence toward God. ^{22}And whatever we ask we receive from Him, because we keep His commandments and do those things that are pleasing in His sight. ^{23}And this is His commandment: that we should believe *on the name of His Son Jesus Christ and love one another, as He gave us commandment.*

To be on the correct pathway to heaven can only be obtained through the Holy Spirit.

Matthew 16:15-17 (NKJV) He said to them, "But who do you say that I am?" 16Simon Peter answered and said, "You are the Christ, the Son of the living God." 17Jesus answered and said to him, "Blessed are you, Simon Bar-Jonah, for flesh and blood has not revealed this to you, but My Father who is in heaven.

1 Corinthians 2:10-12 (NKJV) But God has revealed them to us through His Spirit. For the Spirit searches all things, yes, the deep things of God. 11For what man knows the things of a man except the spirit of man which is in him? Even so no one knows the things of God except the Spirit of God. 12Now we have received, not the spirit of the world, but the Spirit who is from God, that we might know the things that have been freely given to us by God.

Still, many who are lukewarm have never heard the voice of God. Their walk is totally based on whatever religion they have bought into, and there are many out there. I have heard many times over the years that there are those who are straddling the fence; however, there is no such thing as having one foot on the narrow road and one on the wide. You are either sold out for God or you're not. Now, you can be straddling the fence, but if you are, you have one foot on interstate and one on the highway. This doesn't really matter because you will still wind up in hell. However, to look at this in another view, you can be sitting on the fence. This is where you have begun to gain more truth but in gaining that, you begin to understand that in order to cross over that fence, it's going to cost you more than you realized. At this place, many are not really willing to give up certain desires that they have. They will sit on that fence looking at the other side trying to contemplate if they really want to cross over. They begin to realize that the more they understand, the more uneasiness they are feeling when they are not living according to true Biblical teachings. These feelings they are having is actually the Holy Spirit trying to lead them to the other side. However, there is always that other voice which is not God, yet they try to convince themselves that just maybe it is God. Hmmm... it would be so much easier if we just followed that other voice because the majority seem to be following it as well. The real scenario here is that we are not really sure that we want to do this *"Jesus"* thing after all. Understand, on the highway, you are going to gain false teachings but from time to time you are going to hear truth. Never think that God desires that you never hear the truth. On the contrary, He desires that none should perish, but the majority will still perish because they do not really want the truth which would require too much change in their life that they are not really ready to do. This is where you find yourself sitting on the fence. There was a song that I am only briefly familiar with about the highway that leads to hell. The title of this song is *"My Way or the Highway[2],"* sung by Relient K who were a Christian rock band formed in 1998. Pay attention to the lyrics.

Should I start this song off with a question?
Or should I say what's on my mind.
'Cause I'm not looking forward to leaving my friends all behind.
I didn't vote (though I'm not proud), cause I'm Canadian,
and I'm not allowed.
Give it a go or throw in the towel.
Stand all alone or swim through the crowd.
No one around to help you decide.
It's time to make up your mind.
It's time to make up your mind.
By the wayside we fell.
He said, "It's my way or the highway to hell."
Decision we make; life's an election.
Precision we take, seeking direction.
But there's so many lies.
Unsure where we can look.
But we've got a guide- a really thick handbook.
No one around to help you decide.
It's time to make up your mind.

It's time to make up your mind.
Are you with me or against me?
Noticed you're sitting on the fence.
We wondered why you're not cut and dry.
You got to choose our side and live, or their side and die.
Which hand holds your soul?
Do you want to guess one?
If it scares you to death, may that be your lesson.
It's your decision, make it the best one.
And should I end this song off with a question?

The Church Is Not Divided

Have you ever questioned why there are so many denominations? Have you ever thought for a moment that maybe what you are being taught may not be exactly right? I have asked so many questions over the years and it was in doing this that I learned there are no denominations out there that have everything right; however, there are those few churches out there that are striving to grow and learn based on truth. Then you have the majority of churches that may be teaching some things accurate but most of what they are teaching is out of context with the Word of God.

I can remember at one point in my walk where I became so frustrated with religion that I did not want to be associated with any name. In other words, I did not consider myself a Catholic, Baptist, Methodist, Non-denomination, etc. When asked what religion I was, my answer was that I was just a follower of Jesus Christ—a disciple! I remember one lady that I ministered to on a weekly basis was Catholic, even though she didn't attend services. After a few months of my coming to her home, she informed me that she appreciated me coming and sharing with her but I didn't need to keep coming. She continued to tell me that after I left each time, she would go get her *"Catholic Bible"* out to look up the Scriptures I had left to see if they were Biblical. She finished by telling me that what I had shared was in the Bible, but she had never heard the Scriptures I had left with her. She had been going through a hard time and was diagnosed with cancer, so I had been sharing Jesus and praying for her at her home. After informing me that she did not want me to continue coming and praying for her, she stated that she was born a Catholic and would die a Catholic. Wow, I thought to myself, first it was evident that she never read the Bible even though she owned one. Second, I knew that one day, she would stand before the Lord as He declared that He never knew her and her response would be something similar to this, *"But Lord, I am a Catholic, I should be in Heaven!"* This is what religion does to people. It separates us from a genuine relationship with our Creator because there are so many beliefs out there, but there is only one Bible and one Truth. Please note, by me using the Catholic religion in this story, by no means am I stating that all Catholics are not right with God. It just so happens that she was Catholic but never attended services. My walk with God has shown me that He has people in all walks that are truly His; however, my point is that a denomination will NOT save you! A priest or pastor will NOT save you! I have friends who are Catholic, Baptist, Methodist, Non-denomination, etc. I cannot say whether they are traveling the right pathway or not, for I am NOT God. My point in this story is to show that many put too much emphasis on where they choose to attend church or to seek God for that matter. A building will also NOT save you! It is only a personal relationship with Jesus Christ that will save you. Outside of that, you will perish. However, it is of utmost importance that you are in association with others who are truly walking the narrow road, as well as those who are gaining truth through His Word.

Let me just say, all those preaching watered-down messages in order to not offend and in order to grow their ministries, there will come a day when they will face terrible consequences, as they stand before Our Lord and Savior. There are times we believe that the church today is divided. I have heard this said many times and have even wondered this myself. However, I remember God showing me that His True Church is NOT divided. We always want to look at the church as being a building, but the Bible tells us that WE are the church. Those true followers of Jesus Christ are the church. His church will never be divided but because of those pastors who are not standing up and giving bold messages like Jesus Christ gave, there are so many out there that claim to be real Christians yet they are all divided in their beliefs, as there are so many different teachings. They are giving messages that the people want to hear but not what they need to hear. It is because of the multitudes of churches in America striving to gain the same riches as this world, that the people within these congregations are being led astray. Most of these churches are made up of goats not sheep, and the few sheep within these churches are starving to death because they are not being taught the true messages.

Many who are lukewarm may have gained some knowledge and even be in some type of leadership position. However, they may choose not to teach the whole truth for fear of losing their followings or losing their position among the people. As I found myself in this same position and my teachings began to line up with truth, as I was seeking Jesus Christ and pouring into His Word, other leaders began to sit up under my teachings. There were some who were true sheep and began to listen to what I was teaching and there were goats. It did not take long until the goats ran back to the pastors to make them aware of my teachings. I was threatened at that point that if I wanted to continue as a leader, I had to teach according to their methods not what the Bible taught. I was also warned that if I did not comply, I would lose my leadership position within that church. Of course, I walked away but how many true sheep today hear that which is true and shy away from standing up boldly for fear of losing their position. I'm not going to lie to you. I lost everything. I lost friends, family, church family, popularity, respect from others within that church group, etc. It was a hard time, but I made the choice that I wanted Jesus Christ not man! I did not want to be classified as the lukewarm.

We see many times that there are those who have great knowledge and they may even be on fire, but it is not a fire that is building up the Kingdom of Heaven. On the contrary, it is a fire that is building up a man's kingdom or even their own kingdom. Their messages may be hard core at times but if so, it is geared to control the flock where they continue to follow false teachings. The sad part is that there are some who truly want to follow Jesus Christ, but they have been blinded by the truth for listening to the messages that continue to keep them intact. The fault lies within themselves because they are seeking Jesus through a ministry not by studying themselves. As true sheep, we will become hungry and we will never feel full unless we are gaining true knowledge. However, if God knows that you are one of His, He will be speaking in that small quiet voice. I heard it many times as I sat under false teachings. When you come to the place where you begin to question, this is the place where you will do something about it. This is a great place to be as long as you do something—step out and begin reading and studying. However, many people are too lazy or too busy in this world to step out and really seek Jesus Christ. They never seem to have time to read and study on their own but place their whole salvation on that of a mere man. They are so distracted trying to store up their treasures in this world or distracted by the cares of this world, that they never step out to make a change.

Types of People

Let's look at what the Bible has to say about the different types of people in the parable of the sower.

Matthew 13:3-9 (NKJV) Then He spoke many things to them in parables, saying: "Behold, a sower went out to sow. ⁴And as he sowed, some seed fell by the wayside; and the birds came and devoured them. ⁵Some fell on stony places, where they did not have much earth, and they immediately sprang up because they had no depth of earth, ⁶But when the sun was up they were scorched, and because they had no root they withered away. ⁷And some fell among thorns, and the thorns sprang up and choked them. ⁸But others fell on good ground and yielded a crop: some a hundredfold, some sixty, some thirty. ⁹He who has ears to hear, let him hear!"

Now to hear Jesus explain the parable—

Matthew 13:18-23 (NKJV) "Therefore hear the parable of the sower: ¹⁹When anyone hears the word of the kingdom, and does not understand it, then the wicked one comes and snatches away what was sown in his heart. This is he who received seed by the wayside. ²⁰But he who received the seed on stony places, this is he who hears the word and immediately receives it with joy; ²¹yet he has no root in himself, but endures only for a while. For when tribulation or persecution arises because of the word, immediately he stumbles. ²²Now he who received seed among thorns is he who hears the word, but the cares of this world and the deceitfulness of riches choke the word, and he becomes unfruitful. ²³But he who received seed on the good ground is he who hears the word and understands it, who indeed bears fruit and produces: some a hundredfold, some sixty, some thirty."

To sum this up with those who are cold, lukewarm, and hot, let's look at each category. Those who hear the word and do not understand it. This is going to be a huge majority. Even those who have gone to church here and there, they may listen to what is being taught from the pulpit because the majority that teach today are teaching false messages that the people want to hear. These may even attend church on occasions such as Easter Sunday because they don't have to have ears to hear when it is not Biblical. However, let's assume that the majority in this first category hear the true gospel and do not understand it so that word is pretty much gone from their heart, as soon as it arrives. The evil one is satan and he is always there striving to keep any from really receiving the true word. Those in that first category are definitely categorized as being cold because they have no knowledge at all of the true gospels. We even have those who have heard so many false teachings, and they have realized that the church we see today is mainly comprised of false prophets and teachers which has made a bad name for true Christianity.

Romans 2:21-24 (NKJV) You, therefore, who teach another, do you not teach yourself? You who preach that a man should not steal, do you steal? 22You who say, "Do not commit adultery," do you commit adultery? You who abhor idols, do you rob temples? 23You who make your boast in the law, do you dishonor God through breaking the law? 24For "the name of God is blasphemed among the Gentiles because of you," as it is written.

Therefore, you have many who have stepped out of those circles only to blasphemy the church as a whole. So, there are those out there that see all religion or all walks with God as a joke, and they want no part of it. They begin to listen to the world that tells them that the Bible was written by man and no one should believe it. They begin to listen to those who want to tell them there is a God but you need to beware of listening to anyone who claims to be a Christian, mainly due to being led falsely and the church gaining a bad name. Some believe that you don't need the body of Christ, you can just walk this walk out alone with you and God. If your relationship is real, you can walk this walk with just you and God but not for ever because He wants us to be joined with other believers. He also wants us to share His Word to those that cross our paths.

We also have those who believe as long as they pray here and there but never read His Word that they are good. Beware what you listen to because satan is going to try everything to keep you where you are not connected to other believers, and we are to be joined together as ONE church. Being joined together as ONE church does not mean that you must meet in a building with the same group of people each week. We must go back to see what the first church looked like. Religion has a way of organizing everything according to a man's plan. All of these things give Christianity a bad name, and our witness on the streets has been affected because many do not want to hear or have anything to do with a church (building) or particular ministry. The true church of Jesus Christ is One but that does not mean they are one living in the same city, attending the same church building, etc. Look at the first church. God called them to go. Where did they go? They went wherever He led them. It was where they could walk or travel, and when they arrived at these places, they were joined by groups within that area and they would stay to assist with that ministry. Yes, this was the apostles and evangelists that traveled and connected with groups, and yes, we are not all given the title of being an apostle or evangelist. However, even within your own city or town, meeting with the same people week after week and never reaching out to share Jesus Christ in the streets, at the super market, in the parks, etc., is not true Christianity. We were never called to just sit on a pew week after week being fed. If you are being fed truth, true Christianity is what you do with that fruit. However, if the fruit is not growing in you, you have nothing to share except a false perception of Christianity.

Let me say, I have done street ministry for years. I also have been employed in a political entity for years where I have sat in board meetings with many who claim to be Christians, as they strive to figure out how to get rid of the homeless. They hate those who are homeless. People, wake up! The homeless are probably closer to being hot than most who live in their luxurious homes and have money in the bank. The homeless may be dirty on the outside but God looks on the inside and many who claim to be Christians are filthy on the inside!

Seed by the Wayside

To continue with the parable where satan immediately came and devoured the seeds that fell on the pathway, there are also those who believe that all who are good will go to heaven and you don't have to really do anything much to get there. These are still cold and still lost on interstate. To clarify, those who are cold either do not believe or they may believe but they have little to no knowledge and live out their lifestyles just as this world. Please know that even those who do not believe in God, most have heard at one time about the gospels and have rejected it. You cannot live in this world, especially in America, and have never heard about the gospels of Jesus Christ. You also have those who have false religions, other gods, and they are also in the category of being cold.

Seed on Stony Places

The second category in the parables, they hear the word, the truth and they receive it with joy but there is no root and they only endure for a while. The Scripture tells us that when tribulation or persecution comes, they fall away. This again is a huge majority. There is no root. Most people never pick up their Bible to study and there are some who do daily devotions which is a joke. You cannot read someone else's devotion that takes about 5 minutes a day and think this is growing! Once again, satan knows when there is someone out there that receives the truth with joy, and you can bet that tribulation and persecution are going to come. Once you are faced with problems or a crisis, you crumble under pressure because there is no growth and you just fall away—interstate system!

Seed Among Thorns

Then we have the third category where the seeds are planted among thorns which are the cares of this world, the riches, etc. Again, there is a huge majority that fall into this category as well. These are more than likely those who are playing church because this Scripture does not say they fall away, but it says they are unfruitful. This one says that the deceitfulness of riches chokes the word. To choke something means to constrict or to block. To elaborate, the true Word of God is blocked or constricted because this world still comes first in their life and there is not time to seek God when religion of man is much easier for their lifestyles. These are those who are lukewarm. This is a trap from satan where many are blinded by truth and cannot see this. Many of these have become complacent with where they are and believe that this is the true walk of a Christian. There are multitudes that flock into the mega churches today that fit in this category. There are also multitudes that flock into smaller churches, as many of the leaders of these churches all have the same agenda which is to grow in numbers. Mega churches did not begin as mega churches, but as small churches being led by a man whose desire was to rise up with great numbers in order to be known by this world. They believe that they are producing an enormous amount of fruit because they believe their fruit is in the numbers of followers in a particular movement. However, if that were true, then the Bible is false! Your fruit that you produce as a true believer and follower of Jesus Christ will never be about how many people you have following you. In fact, people should be following Jesus Christ not man. I have taught on this in chapter 4 but let me say, when we are following truth, our lifestyles will line up to be that of Jesus Christ. No, we will not be perfect until we leave these bodies, but our lifestyle will not be one that looks like this world. We will be set apart, and we will be persecuted because we are told this. We will also be hated by this world, as He was hated. I have touched on all of this in several chapters. My point is, once we are walking in truth, our lifestyles drastically change and our purpose in this life also changes where we are unashamed to go forth and share truth, even though we know that we are going to lose friends, acquaintances, family members, etc. Our fruit will be the fruit of the Holy Spirit within us, and we will also be producing fruit in other people as we stand up unashamed to go against all the false prophets and teachers leading the multitudes astray. We will never gain numbers, but we will have those few that actually break away from the multitudes because we dared to stand up and speak out what is true and what is false!

To elaborate on the fruit a little deeper, in Scripture Jesus gives a parable of the talents. You can read this in Matthew 25, but there is something we need to see here. We are all given talents. We are all gifted in certain areas. Our talents are not of our own doing, but they are given to us by God. One of my talents that was given to me was the ability to write. I have loved writing since I was a child. I also have the talent of speaking. I have been a public speaker for years. As a child and young adult, I never used my writing or speaking abilities in public because I never saw this gift until I found Jesus Christ. I wrote all the time growing up and even in college, but I didn't use this publicly. As a Christian, there was a certain amount of time that had to go by, as I grew into who God created me to be. I could have easily been like the servant who was given the talent and was afraid so he went and hid the talent. I was afraid; I was afraid to stand before people and speak. I was afraid for anyone to read my writings. However, God got a hold of me and placed me in situations that I could have run from and even thought of doing so, but instead, I rose to the occasion and began to allow Him to use me.

We all have talents that He has given us and these talents are to be used for His glory only, and they will produce fruit. The fruit may never be evident to us because the fruit is not to build a man's kingdom. However, there are many strangers over the years that I have ministered to on the streets and many that I have given my books to. I have no idea what seeds I have planted nor who has chosen to seek Jesus Christ for an intimate relationship because of my obedience. I may never see my fruit, but I know that I made the choice not to hide my talent and be afraid. I made the choice to use the talent that God has given me the only way I know how and that is writing, printing books, giving them away when the opportunity arises, and speaking to share what He has given me. Let me elaborate on one instance. I was in my car at a bank, in line to make a deposit. All of a sudden, a car drove up beside me. My first perception, it was a very nice and expensive car that had been transformed to look like something a drug dealer would have driven. The young man was listening to rap music blasting where everyone around could hear it. He did not want to turn his music down to put his deposit in the canister for the bank teller, so he jumped out of his car to stand beside it where he could hear his music and talk to the teller. Second perception, he had gold teeth and wore his jeans down to his thighs where his underwear was showing—drug dealer! Of course, these were my thoughts not something I was speaking outwardly; however, God knows what you are thinking, and we all have first impressions that may not be accurate! I turned up my *Christian music,* as I did not want to hear his music. God spoke to me and said, *"Stop judging this man and give him one of your books!"* I had some of my books laying in the front seat. I quickly felt ashamed and turned my music down and then rolled down my window. I called him over to my car and handed him a book, as I told him that God wanted him to have this book. I will never forget that moment. He embraced the book in his arms, as he held it to his heart and smiled at me saying, *"You are going to give me this book for free?"* I replied, *"Yes, God asked me to give you this book!"* He then replied, *"Thank you, thank you. I am going to read it!"* I have never seen this man since and probably never will. Could this man possibly be part of my fruit? As I stand before our Savior and He says, *"Well done,"* is it possible that I have fruit that I am not even aware of? Could this young man have possibly read the book and passed it on? Could the book have been passed on and passed on or maybe even eventually wound up in someone else's home where it was just lying around for months and months. After several months, is it possible that the book could have been picked up by someone else at just the right moment, as they may have been seeking Jesus for answers to their life? Somewhere through this process could one of those that read that book rise up powerful to go forth as a disciple of Jesus Christ? In doing so, could that person have become another

David Wilkerson who went unafraid into the streets of huge cities to share the true gospel for those who are the least of these? Look up David Wilkerson if you don't know who the least of these are. However, my point is that when we are obedient and we are seeking Jesus daily, we may be producing fruit and we don't even know of. To clarify one more thing, your fruit is NOT in numbers, but it is the fruit of the Spirit inside of you. When we have the fruit of the Spirit operating inside of us, God will send others across our path that are part of His plan. When they cross our path, we hear the voice of the Holy Spirit because the fruits of the Spirit are operating inside of us, if we belong to God. At that point, we are obedient as we follow that One Voice because as sheep, we know His voice. The voice I heard was to simply give the book to the stranger; however, God just wants a people who are willing to obey when He speaks. It is all His plan not our plan, and He gets the glory for any works we do because Jesus Christ is glorified through us!

John 17:10 (NKJV) And all Mine are Yours, and Yours are Mine, and I am glorified in them.

Let me add this before I continue: *(Fruits – love, joy, peace, patience, kindness, goodness, faithfulness, gentleness, self-control) Galatians 5:13-15* What fruits did I operate in when I obeyed the voice of the Holy Spirit? I operated in love, kindness, goodness, faithfulness, gentleness and self-control. What did my obedience create? It brought joy to me and it gave joy to the young man. It showed to the young man all nine of the fruits, all of them. What did it show to God from me? It showed him my faithfulness, which produced all those fruits within me. This is your fruit and when you operate in that fruit, it spills out upon those you are in contact with and it pleases your Father in Heaven—I promise you!

I spoke in depth in chapter 4 regarding John 17 which was the prayer that Jesus prayed to His Father for those that were His true sheep. Jesus was not praying for those of this world but only for those who have kept His Word, those walking the narrow pathway not the lukewarm. In verse 10 of John 17 on the previous page, we see that Jesus is glorified through those who are His true sheep, those who have made the decision to give this *"Jesus"* thing all they have. We will produce fruit but it will be to give Him the glory, not build up a man's kingdom where that man is glorified.

My fruit is not following me around like those who are lukewarm and on fire to build a man's kingdom, as they count the numbers sitting in their marvelous churches. My fruit is the fruit of the Holy Spirit, as I grow in His Word to become more like Jesus Christ. In producing the fruit of the Spirit, my lifestyle begins to look like that of Jesus Christ. I will touch lives but I may never know whose life I touched. That young man I spoke of above could have gone on to have chosen to let go of this world and become what Jesus called him to be. He could have gone on to be one that went into the street possibly to minister to those as David Wilkerson did. His actions could have led to many turning around their lives, and it began with my obedience. That is not for me to know. I'm just to take those talents and use them as He leads my life. I'm just to allow my small life to fit into His huge puzzle, as He is able to see how all of our lives fit together even though we may never see this.

Seed on Good Soil

Now, for the fourth category on the parable of the seeds, this would be those who hear the word and understand it. They are those who are on fire for the Lord, and they do bear fruit as I have discussed. This last category would be those who have chosen to step out and be bold. They have chosen to let go of this world, as they cross over to that narrow road that few will ever find. Those on this road are on fire for the Lord, and their life stands out from those in this world because they choose to live their life striving NOT to be conformed to this world but to live as Paul and Silas causing a stir wherever they go. These few are the ones who are persecuted, and they separate themselves from the majority that claim to be Christians. What I mean by that, they choose not to associate in the circles doing the same thing as the *"so-called"* Christians that look exactly like the world! They gain knowledge daily, as they pour into the Word of God and spend time in His presence. These do not play church, but they take the knowledge they gain and run with it boldly. They continue to allow the Holy Spirit access into their life, as He continues to change them daily where they go from glory to glory.

2 Corinthians 3:17-18 (NKJV) Now the Lord is the Spirit; and where the Spirit of the Lord is, there is liberty. ¹⁸But we all, with unveiled face, beholding as in a mirror the glory of the Lord, are being transformed into the same image from glory to glory, just as by the Spirit of the Lord.

True Christians are not like the children of Israel in the desert, as they joyfully walk through their storms in this life trusting God in all things, as He is still perfecting them. True Christians are always dividing the words that they hear and seeking Jesus Christ, as they hunger for more and more truth. They continually are letting go of this world as He is doing a great work in them, and they know their satisfaction will never come from anything in this world but from Jesus Christ. They do not crumble under persecution but trust Him and run to Him for every season and every storm knowing that there is always a reason they face certain situations. They endure as they patiently wait for tomorrow. They have grown to love the country road because their desires have changed where they delight in his presence, instead of surrounded by the distractions of this world. They yearn for His return. They delight in giving more than receiving. There is nothing they own in this world that they are not willing to walk away from. They understand this life costs them everything, but they will also gain so much more. They do not yearn for the riches of this world but for the riches of heaven. They are content with having nothing, as they are always excited for what lay ahead.

They see God as a big God able to do the impossible in their lives and in the lives of those they love.

Hated by This World

One more thing, I want to emphasize on why those who walk this walk will be hated by the world. A true Christian's walk bears the fruit of the Spirit. Let's look at that fruit again.

Galatians 5:16-26 (NKJV) I say then: Walk in the Spirit, and you shall not fulfill the lust of the flesh. [17]For the flesh lusts against the Spirit, and the Spirit against the flesh; and these are contrary to one another, so that you do not do the things that you wish. [18]But if you are led by the Spirit, you are not under the law. [19]Now the works of the flesh are evident, which are: adultery, fornication, uncleanness, lewdness, [20]idolatry, sorcery, hatred, contentions, jealousies, outbursts of wrath, selfish ambitions, dissentions, heresies, [21]envy, murders, drunkenness, revelries, and the like; of which I tell you beforehand, just as I also told you in time past, that those who practice such things will not inherit the kingdom of God. [22]But the fruit of the Spirit is love, joy, peace, longsuffering, kindness, goodness, faithfulness, [23]gentleness, self-control. Against such there is no law. [24]And those who are Christ's have crucified the flesh with its passions and desires. [25]If we live in the Spirit, let us also walk in the Spirit. [26]Let us not become conceited, provoking one another, envying one another.

John 15:19 (NKJV) If you were of the world, the world would love its own. Yet because you are not of the world, but I chose you out of the world, therefore the world hates you.

Why does Jesus tell us that if we belong to Him the world will hate us? In Galatians, we see that there are those who live to satisfy the flesh and those who walk by the Spirit. Where the Spirit is, there is life! If you are walking by the Spirit of God, your desires will NOT be to satisfy the flesh. If you are playing church, you will be living as the world and the world will love you. However, if your relationship with Jesus Christ is real, there will be evidence of the fruit of the Spirit in your life and the world will hate you. Those attributes are listed above. In verse 17, it clearly states that the lusts of the flesh are against the Spirit and the lusts of the Spirit are against the flesh. In other versions lusts is translated as desires, our desires can become lust in our lives where we will fall short. Light and darkness do not mix. Those playing church are living out their life to satisfy their desires, even if those desires may not seem so bad. You should not find a true Christian sitting in a bar watching sports and drinking beer with the guys. You should not find a true Christian wasting time and effort in this world idolizing sports, movie stars, those who are famous, etc. If there are some who claim to be Christians that are associating with those of this world, they are playing church. You will not find a woman who fears the Lord, associating with darkness. Light and dark do not mix. In fact, a woman who fears the Lord according to Proverbs 31, is one who recognizes that beauty is vain and does not waste her time or spend money foolishly to adorn her body to be like the women of this world. However, the attributes of a real Christian are love, joy, peace, patience, kindness, etc.

So, if real Christians walk in these fruits, why would the world hate them? Why do fake Christians hate them? The reason you will be hated by the world is because of the attributes of the flesh. Let me explain, those who live according to the flesh are all about self. All were born into sin and it is that sin that creates within us a self-righteousness. We grow up to learn how to satisfy every single aspect of our own desires. You have those in the world that have no desire to know Jesus who are living according to their own selfish desires daily, and then you also have many that claim to be Christians that have taken this Christianity to a level where they can still live out their lives enjoying their selfish desires. Many do not want to let go of self. So, why do they hate real Christianity? The reason is because when you come to a place where you make the decision to sell out for Jesus Christ and you give it every single thing you have, there is no self. Your life is no longer your own because it belongs to Jesus Christ. Those who are not sold out hate those who would dare come and try to teach them the true gospel because it would require that they give up self. It would require that they let go of areas of pleasure. People of this world spend their whole lives forming the person they desire to be, living the life they want to live, building up those idols in their lives, doing the good works in order to be seen and praised by man, feeling an accomplishment in things they have done and acquired, being increased by man, being served by man, and believing that their works are righteous enough to get them into heaven. The last thing they want is a true Christian trying to destroy their alter that they have created of themselves where there are many who worship them.

I have touched on this topic in chapter 8 as well as earlier chapters, but to emphasize this one more time, look at those mega churches, look at those Christian artists, look at those who bring in multitudes all in the name of Christianity who are all loved by this world. Joel Osteen was interviewed by Larry King and Oprah Winfrey for all the world to see. He is praised and glorified by many, but Jesus was never accepted by those in high places. Why is it that the world loves Joel Osteen but they did not love Jesus? The Christian artists are looked upon by the world, as they are in the social media just like other artists of this world. There is no difference. They are loved by the world, but Jesus was not, why is this?

Luke 20:46-47 (ESV) "Beware of the scribes, who like to walk around in long robes, and love greetings in the marketplaces and the best seats in the synagogues and the places of honor at feasts, 47who devour widows' houses and for a pretense make long prayers. They will receive the greater condemnation,"

The scribes were the religious leaders of that time. Today, we can interpret this to mean that Jesus warns His people to beware of those shepherds or teachers that want to be seen by man, praised by man; beware of those who seek for affection and applause by man; beware of those who want approval by man.

True Christianity

One more area to look at and that is to be able to see who you are. We look at an apple tree and we know it is an apple tree, how do we know? We know because it produces apples. Multitudes today claim that they are a Christian, how do we know if they are truly a Christian? It is by their fruit. There are all kinds of fruit out there, some which is bad fruit and some which is good fruit. A true Christian produces fruit which is good not bad. Your fruit will either produce life or death. I think all would agree that only good fruit produces life and bad fruit would produce death. If you are sitting up under false teachings, you have been programmed with that which is false. This means that what is in your heart is false. We have our eyes and ears that are the openings to our heart. If your choices in this world are to watch the filth of this world on your televisions, computers, telephones, etc., you are filling your heart with the filth of this world, and your heart is full of bad fruit. If you are listening to false messages, not seeking Jesus Christ yourself, that is what your heart is full of. If you are listening to the music of this world to include false artists that have their own agenda, your heart is full of bad fruit. What is in our heart will proceed out of our mouth and when we stand before Jesus Christ one day, He will look at all of us and the evidence will be clear. Our life will either be one that produced life or death. Our life will have either produced good or bad fruit.

At this point in this chapter, we should be able to see more clearly that our walk with God is totally dependent on how much we put into this. If we really desire to know Him and be a true Christian, we will stop being like the world and those who claim to be Christians when their walk looks no different than the world. Following Jesus Christ takes people who are willing to let go of everything that keeps them from drawing close to their Savior. As true Christians, Jesus also warns us to hold on to our fruit.

John 15:16 (NKJV) You did not choose Me, but I chose you and appointed you that you should go and bear fruit, and that your fruit should remain, that whatever you ask the Father in My name He may give you.

We are called as disciples to go and make more disciples. This is sharing our testimony with those that cross our path. However, in this day where there are so many religions and so many messages that do not line up with the Word of God, we must beware of what we are listening to. Jesus gives a picture of what we see today among those who stand up on those pulpits claiming to be men of God.

*Matthew 23:5-8 (NKJV) But all their works they do to be seen by men. They make their phylacteries broad and enlarge the borders of their garments. *^{6}*They love the best places at feasts, the best seats in the synagogues, *^{7}*greetings in the marketplaces, and to be called 'Rabbi, Rabbi.' *^{8}*But you, do not be called 'Rabbi'; for One is your Teacher, the Christ, and you are all bretheren.*

America is full of churches that lift up that man on the pulpit every single week as they call him by pastor or priest, etc. Jesus said none are to be called by anything but brother and if we do give them that title, they have become our teacher instead of Christ. These men love to be honored by all, as they stand up to be recognized by the community and many by the world. They want recognition by people based on what is seen outwardly but not within, as they wear their phylacteries made broad around their neck. In Biblical days, phylacteries were small black leather boxes that contained scrolls inscribed with verses from the Torah. As time went on, evidently those boxes became larger for appearance reasons.

Men wanted to be noticed by others of their status and greatness in the synagogues. Today, it has not changed as we see false churches with their many leaders being lifted up for all to see, as they fill the sanctuaries today. Elaborate buildings that are adorned with elegance for all to see the wealth of that particular church. The men who run such a program recognized by all, as being great men of God as they are called to lead God's people to salvation with their messages that tickle the ear and false doctrine that make Christianity look easy.

Matthew 23:13, 15, 25, 27-28 (NKJV) "But woe to you, scribes and Pharisees, hypocrites! For you shut the kingdom of heaven against men; for you neither go in yourselves, nor do you allow those who are entering to go in. 15Woe to you, scribes and Pharisees, hypocrites! For you travel land and sea to win one proselyte, and when he is won, you make him twice as much a son of hell as yourselves. 25"Woe to you, scribes and Pharisees, hypocrites! For you cleanse the outside of the cup and dish, but inside they are full of extortion and self-indulgence. 27"Woe to you, scribes and Pharisees, hypocrites! For you are like whitewashed tombs which indeed appear beautiful outwardly, but inside are full of dead men's bones and all uncleanness. 28Even so you also outwardly appear righteous to men, but inside you are full of hypocrisy and lawlessness.

Beware, those who are walking this walk out as lukewarm, that you see the signs. It is very dangerous today to claim to be a Christian and not know the Word of God. Jesus has a lot to say about religious leaders. In Biblical days, a proselyte was a person who was converted to believe in another's opinion or religion. These Scriptures should make us rise up to begin questioning what we are being taught or what we have been taught. Those religious leaders that are making other proselytes based off of their own beliefs are damned. Woe to those that are building up man's kingdoms for their own selfish reasons and leading multitudes astray. They shut the Kingdom of Heaven in people's faces, as they will never enter heaven nor allow others that are following them to enter as well. They do a very good job of making everything on the outside look good but God looks on the inside. They appear to be righteous on the outside but God sees the inside.

Before I go further, I need to emphasize a few other Scriptures. Let's look at Ephesians 4:11 before we go further.

Ephesians 4:11 (NKJV) And He Himself gave some to be apostles, some prophets, some evangelists, and some pastors and teachers.

If you look prior to verse 11, these listed here are all spiritual gifts. We are not told that these are titles. In fact, I covered in chapter 6 with Scripture that if we have the Holy Spirit living with us, we hear His voice and there is no need that any man should teach us. However, there are those who have the gift of being a prophet, evangelist, pastor and/or teacher. He never said it was a title. When we give man a title, they are increased. Man should never be increased, Jesus is increased. I have known many that are gifted as pastors and teachers that conduct services at a church building that are NOT called by a title, as such because they feel that it is wrong since it is their gift. Instead, they are either called by their given name or called brother *"so and so."* They also are the few. I have admired them so much because it is seldom seen. However, I believe it is clear in Scripture that we should not have a title. It is clear in Matthew that only ONE is our Teacher. We are given the gift to be able to teach or preach, but we do so as we are anointed by Him not by man. I am gifted in writing, no one calls me Author Jolene. Yes, that sounds funny but it really isn't funny. I am an author, but my name is just Jolene. I am not increased; He is increased because I can only write due to the gift that was given to me by my Savior. Without Him, I am nothing. We need to STOP increasing man because man is nothing without God!

To end this chapter, we need to beware of the fast-paced life on the highways or interstate systems, as they are filled with fun, lust, and every pleasure that fulfills our senses. Beware of the false teachers and artists today, as their purpose is to be increased to fulfill their own lusts at the expense of many sheep that are starving up under these false teachings. If you claim to be a Christian, yet these messages seem to be distant to you as you have never heard these teachings, it's not too late to begin seeking for that truth. There have been many times in my life where I would reflect on various songs that brought a sense of peace because of the words. Songs seem to have a way of bringing us comfort many times, and they are a form of art that portrays life—life and breath that has been given to us by our Creator. These songs many times portray our world on those back roads, such as the vast sceneries of mountains and rivers, all of which were created for our pleasures by our God. I will say, country roads do lead to that which was created by God naturally. When we seek that which He created, it is the closest we get to being able to experience heaven—heaven on this earth. When I experience that which God created naturally on earth, I am in awe of the majestic beauty of our world. We should have a song in our heart that portrays His magnificent world, one that brings tears to our eyes, as we think about traveling on the narrow pathway hand in hand with our Savior. We should be yearning for the day that He comes to take us home—the place we belong, which is in the presence of our Lord Jesus Christ. We should come to a place where we cry out for God's goodness where our thoughts immediately go back to those experiences that have shaped who we are in Christ. A song should always be in our heart, where we have no desire for the distractions of this world but for the goodness of God's mercy and grace. Halleluiah—praise God if you have experienced His goodness and that you hold on to that goodness where no one or nothing can lead you astray.

CHAPTER TEN
STORING TREASURES ON EARTH

1 Timothy 6:10 (NKJV) For the love of money is a root of all kinds of evil, for which some have strayed from the faith in their greediness, and pierced themselves through with many sorrows.

Probably the greatest stumbling block among those who claim to be Christians is the love of money or greed. Myself, I have thought about that Scripture many times and wondered just how many of us who claim to be Christians stand on the grounds that they do not LOVE money. Having money to be able to pay our bills and earning money by working hard is not loving money; therefore, if we can be assured what is in our heart is pure, we are safe, right? The problem with that is money is one thing in America that can be obtained fairly easy, in order to live a life that would be considered rich by the world's standards. If you have a job, live in a home, own a car, and have food on your table, you would be considered rich by the world's standards. We could go further and say that a vast majority in America even have mobile phones, computers, etc. Doing ministry on the streets, it amazed me of how many homeless people actually owned cell phones. However, you may not have extra money to go and do the things you dream of or buy the things you want to buy, but you are far better off than many countries today. Most Americans just take it for granted that they are truly blessed to not be on the streets; however, most people are never satisfied with what they have and always desire more. Those who are very fortunate to have all the necessities of life and the luxuries as well, continue to desire more and more of what money can buy. In America, we love having money and always desire more money because we love to spend, spend, spend on all those things we desire and then the majority who claim to be Christians, dare say that they do not love money! Yes, people in America love money!

If we go back to read what was written before the 10th verse in 1 Timothy 6, there is a bigger picture that instills something far greater on that of false teachers and also of true contentment.

1 Timothy 6:3-9 (ESV) If anyone teaches a different doctrine and does not agree with the sound words of our Lord Jesus Christ and the teaching that accords with godliness, ⁴he is puffed up with conceit and understands nothing. He has an unhealthy craving for controversy and for quarrels about words, which produce envy, dissension, slander, evil suspicions, ⁵and constant friction among people who are depraved in mind and deprived of the truth, imagining that godliness is a means of gain. ⁶But godliness with contentment is great gain, ⁷for we brought nothing into the world, and we cannot take anything out of the world. ⁸But if we have food and clothing, with these we will be content. ⁹But those who desire to be rich fall into temptation, into a snare, into many senseless and harmful desires that plunge people into ruin and destruction.

It's funny how this Scripture in 1 Timothy blends right in with those who are teaching false. Here, we are told that if we have only food and clothing, we should be content. We are also told those who desire to be rich fall into temptation. Let me clarify that statement, many may say they do not desire to be rich because in America, we believe those who are rich are those who live in huge homes, drive very expensive cars, go on extravagant vacations, the best of clothing, diamonds, etc. However, as I have stated, if you live in a home and own a car, you are pretty much considered rich in this world. Therefore, it is safe to say Biblically speaking, if we all desire to be rich as in having all those things we believe we need, we fall into the same temptation that brings people to ruin. With that established, it is the desire for the things in this world that bring us to destruction. A funny thing, when we gain things, it seems to bring us to the place that we want more and are never content. The Scripture teaches that just having food and clothing we should be content. I have shared of my experience of ministering on the streets, I have encountered some who have chosen to be on the streets in order to be that true minister to feed those living on the street the gospels of Jesus Christ. I have met many that are filthy on the outside but on the inside, there is something that stands out that you do not find in most people who attend church and live in nice homes. Of course, I am not telling anyone to go and sell all they have and follow Jesus because Jesus already said that. Does this mean that we are to sell all we have in order to make it to heaven? That depends on where your heart is. I believe when we are not seeking Jesus with our whole heart and living a life that stands out from the majority, that it may take drastic measures to ensure our salvation. However, we must definitely come to a place that nothing we own means anything to us. If we hear that voice tell us to sell something or give it away, we do not hesitate in our decisions because if we do, we have come to love stuff more than our Creator.

Most Christians today, want to claim that they buy the things they need, but they don't love money. Most would have to also agree that they buy the things they want and don't need. I'm not trying to be any different than anyone else, as I have spent much of my years buying and buying. I have also spent a good many years hearing His voice tell me to let go of many of those things I desired. I have on many occasions given away items that I loved or items that had become precious to me because of that voice. I think the question here is, are we like the young rich ruler that if Jesus were to say, *"Sell all you have and follow me,"* would we be willing to do so?

Matthew 19:16-22 (NKJV) Now behold, one came and said to Him, "Good Teacher, what good thing shall I do that I may have eternal life?" ^{17}So He said to him, "Why do you call me good? No one is good but One, that is God. But if you want to enter into life, keep the commandments." ^{18}He said to him, "Which ones? Jesus said, "'You shall not murder,' 'You shall not commit adultery,' 'You shall not steal,' 'You shall not bear false witness,' ^{19}'Honor your father and mother,' and, 'You *shall love your neighbor as yourself.'" ²⁰The young man said to Him, "All these things I have kept from my youth. What do I still lack?" ²¹Jesus said to him, "If you want to be perfect, go, sell what you have and give to the poor, and you will have treasure in heaven; and come, follow Me." ²²But when the young man heard that saying, he went away sorrowful, for he had great possessions.*

First, let me say that the reason Jesus told the young man to go and sell everything was because the young man claimed to have kept every commandment. When we live trying to keep the commandments, we will fail and if keeping the commandments was what would ensure our salvation, no one would be saved. We needed a Savior which was why Jesus came and died for our sins. No one is capable of keeping all the commandments or being perfect because if you study Scripture you would understand that to God, if we have ever hated someone, it is the same as murder. If we have ever had lustful thoughts, it is the same as adultery. The reason that Jesus told this young man to go and sell everything was because this man thought of himself as being perfect since he claimed that he had never broken a commandment. Remember, in the beginning Jesus let this young man know that there was only One who was good, but due to pride, this young man saw himself as being good. The point of this Scripture is NOT to make us believe that we must sell our homes and go live on the street; however, the point I am trying to make is that IF our possessions are so dear to us that we CANNOT give them away, we will NOT make it to heaven. Yes, there are going to be times that we will hear the voice of the Holy Spirit instructing us to get rid of something, and it is at those times we want to ignore that voice or believe that voice is NOT God. Believe me, satan does not want you to sell anything because it is our *"stuff"* that keeps us conformed to this world. The point is, there will be many that will NOT make heaven because of the cares and distractions of this world which includes the love for things. When we spend so much time, energy, and money on buying and buying and buying, it is not the lifestyle of a true Christian.

Luke 12:15 (NKJV) And he said to them, "Take heed and beware of covetousness, for one's life does not consist in the abundance of the things he possesses."

When we live like all of those who don't even claim to be Christians, we are no different. When our desires are for the things in this world, we are no different. You may say that you are not an evil person, but what is considered evil in the Word of God? Let's start with the Old Testament.

1 Kings 14:9 (NKJV) but you have done more evil than all who were before you, for you have gone and made for yourself other gods and molded images to provoke Me to anger, and have cast Me behind your back

This Scripture was intended for Jeroboam who was made leader over God's people who had turned from God and his lifestyle had become evil. However, these are the words of God to him but these words are for all of us who choose to live as Jeroboam did. Those who have other gods and idols are considered evil. When we love money, and we do love money when we are not content with having food and clothing only, our idol is money.

That Which is Evil

Whatever consumes your thoughts on a daily basis, has become your god and that is evil.

Isaiah 5:20 (NKJV) Woe to those who call evil good, and good evil; Who put darkness for light, and light for darkness; Who put bitter for sweet, and sweet for bitter!

Are we not living in a world that calls evil good and good evil? This generation has decided to change the rules, darkness is not a bad thing at all. It is good that we do not allow God in our schools anymore nor in our government. It is good that we murder babies that are in the womb and have no voice. It is good to keep up with the norm and force the beliefs of those who are evil on those who are striving to live by the Word of God by agreeing to same sex marriage. Those who live by these things are evil, but so are those who do nothing to oppose them. You are just as much to blame when you stay silent. God gave us a voice to speak up for what is good and right in His sight. The Christian population has stayed silent for so long that all of these things have happened before our eyes and now there are groups that are trying to stop many of this, but those groups are just the few striving to come against what the world perceives as normal. We stay complacent in our own little world's instead of standing up for what is right and speaking truth! This is evil.

Isaiah 32:6 (NKJV) For the foolish person will speak foolishness, And his heart will work iniquity: To practice ungodliness, To utter error against the LORD, To keep the hungry unsatisfied, And he will cause the drink of the thirsty to fail.

If you practice ungodliness and you spread false messages concerning the Word of God, your words are foolish and what is in your heart is evil. This Scripture is geared towards those who stand up in the name of Jesus with false teachings. This is so prevalent in America as there are multitudes of churches that do NOT teach truth, and you have multitudes within those congregations that are hungry and thirsty for truth but are being filled with lies. Woe to those ministers of death, as they are leading the multitudes astray.

What does the New Testament have to say about pursuing righteousness?

2 Timothy 2:22 (NKJV) Flee also youthful lusts; but pursue righteousness, faith, love, peace with those who call on the Lord out of a pure heart.

It talks about fleeing youthful lusts, why? When we are young, we are more foolish because we have not gained the wisdom needed to live differently. When we are young, we have many desires which are the same thing as lusts. That is why it is important to realize that as we mature in the Lord, we are to pursue righteousness where we flee from those lusts which we can contribute to our youth. It is not just righteousness that we should be pursuing, but also faith, love and peace. If we are not pursuing righteousness, faith, love and peace, we are pursuing evil. It's black and white, there is never a middle ground. You cannot serve two gods, you will either love the one and hate the other or serve the one and not the other. Is your heart pure when you call upon the Lord?

John 3:20 (NKJV) For everyone practicing evil hates the light and does not come to the light, lest his deeds should be exposed.

What are the evil things? If we are not living by the commandments, if we are not producing the fruits as noted in Galatians 5, anything beyond that would be things which are evil. When our lifestyles are that which is evil, we hate the light. When we teach false messages, we are evil and hate the light. When we live as this world lives, loving the same things as this world, our lifestyles are evil and we hate the light. No wonder Jesus will spit those who are lukewarm out of His mouth. God is light and He is love, without the light and without love, your life is evil. When your life is minus God and minus love, you hate God because He is light and He is love! Once again as discussed in the previous chapter, what is in your heart is what will come out of your mouth. If you are filling it with this world, you have no good in you and your mouth speaks and shares evil with all those who sit in your presence.

Mark 7:21-23 (ESV) For from within, out of the heart of man, come evil thoughts, sexual immorality, theft, murder, adultery, 22coveting, wickedness, deceit, sensuality, envy, slander, pride, foolishness. ²³All these evil things come from within and they defile a person."

What does all of this have to do with us buying and buying and striving to have more and more. This is all about hoarding, simply put, when we live out this life striving to gain all of this world, whether it be in material wealth, status, popularity, fame and fortune—we are naked and poor according to God. We have nothing and we will leave this world in which we served the god of this world to live forever in hell.

Revelation 3:15-17 (ESV) "I know your works: you are neither cold nor hot. Would that you were either cold or hot! ¹⁶So, because you are lukewarm, and neither hot nor cold, I will spit you out of my mouth. ¹⁷For you say, I am rich, I have prospered, and I need nothing, not realizing that you are wretched, pitiable, poor, blind, and naked.

There was a time when God was head over the family. This was in an era where divorce was not as prevalent as we see it today. This was at a time when families stayed together and prayed together. It was a time when families taught their children godly principles, and they raised them to be polite and to help other people. There was a time when families helped others and were neighborly. However, even in those days, you had people who had gained great wealth or many who lived above the standards in those days. Like today, those who were wealthy, many believed they were Christians but this was not apparent in their actions just as it is not apparent today.

I want to share a story with you from a television show that was filmed many years ago. As I watched this, I was amazed at how there are so many people in this world who are very wealthy and yet, they do not give what they no longer want because they are so concerned with making that little bit of money off of something than to give it away for free. This lady was a widow as her husband had died. However, she was very wealthy for that timeframe but today, she probably would have been considered middle class. Becoming tired of her current china, she decided to order a brilliant china set all the way from France. When it came in, she stored her other china away unsure what to do with it. One day, there was this family who lived by Scriptures who ate off of plates that were made from wood or tin, as they were considered poor by the world's standards. However, this family had each other, a small log home built by their own hands and they pretty much lived off the land. One of the children happen to see the china that was stored and wanted so much to earn the money to buy the set, so she could give it to her mother. This woman seeing that this little girl wanted so much to give this as a gift to her mother, did not offer to give her the dishes but rather made a deal with the father to work for her to pay for the china. Yes, that is how people in those days paid for things many times, but the point here is that the woman did not need the money and the woman didn't want the china anymore. It was sitting in her home in a box taking up space but instead of just giving it away to bless that family, she wanted to make a profit. This is selfishness and greed.

When God gets a hold of you on your perspective of storing up treasures, you will find yourself giving and giving and giving. I have had so many things over the years that I have stored away just in case I needed them again. The time came when God taught me to just give it away. I have had people try to pay me for things and I refused to take the money. I'm not talking about giving away your junk but things that you could make a profit. I have given away many things that I could have made a fairly good profit. I have even had people ask me why I didn't have a garage sale to make some extra money instead of just giving things away. There was a time I did do garage sales for extra money, but God showed me not to waste my time on trying to make a dollar when I could bless someone who needed what I had. Why on earth do we hoard when our neighbors may very well need something we have? As the years continue, I find myself striving to downsize. I am by no means where I need to be but my point is that I hear His voice, and His voice is much more important than storing up stuff that could be given to someone in need. We have to come to the place where we clean house. This will first begin on the inside of our heart and then will overflow to the outside where things we have accumulated mean nothing to us.

Civilization

There is a true story that I want to share. This is the story of Juana Maria. When I first heard this story, God spoke to me because there is something far greater to see. In this life, we have acquired so many things and have so many choices. We live among communities where there are so many people that our lives are full of choices, distractions, all those things that choke out the Word of God. What if we lived someplace very remote where we had nothing but what God created? What if we were someplace where there were no people, just God?

Juana Maria is better known to history as the Lone Woman of San Nicolas Island. In fact, her name is not even Juana Maria. This was the name given to her because she was the last surviving member of her tribe, the Nicoleño. She had lived alone on San Nicolas Island off the coast of California from 1835 until her rescue in 1853. The Channel Islands were inhabited by two distinct ethnic groups who occupied the archipelago. One group was the Chumash who lived on the Northern Channel Islands and the second group was the Tongva, Juana's tribe, who lived on the Southern Islands. In the early 1540s, Portuguese conquistador Juan Rodriguez Cabrillo explored the California coast and claimed it on behalf of Spain. In 1814, a party of Native Alaskan otter hunters massacred most of the islanders after accusing them of killing a Native Alaskan hunter. There was speculation that the Franciscan padres of the California missions requested that the remaining Nicoleños be removed from the island, there is no documentary evidence to back that claim. However, in 1835, the schooner Peor es Nada, commanded by Charles

Hubbard, left southern California to remove the remaining people living on San Nicolas. Upon arriving at the island, Hubbard's party gathered the Indians on the beach and brought them aboard. Juana Maria was not among them by the time a strong storm arose. When the crew realized the imminent danger of being wrecked by the surf and rocks, they panicked and sailed toward the mainland, leaving her behind. There are different accounts as to the discovery of the *"lone woman,"* with various offers made to find her and bring her to America. However, George Nidever, a Santa Barbara fur trapper, launched several expeditions of his own to try to find her. It was on his third attempt in 1853, that one of his men discovered human footprints on the beach and pieces of seal blubber which had been left out to dry. Further investigation led to the discovery of Juana Maria. She was living on the island in a crude hut partially constructed of whale bones and was dressed in a skirt made of greenish cormorant feathers. It was also believed that she lived in a nearby cave. Juana Maria was taken to Santa Barbara Mission, but was unable to communicate with anyone. Juana Maria was reportedly fascinated and ecstatic upon arrival, marveling at the sight of so many things she had never seen. She was described as being a woman of medium height, thick and to be about 50 years old but was strong and active. It was believed that she spent somewhere between 18 to 20 years alone on the island. She existed on shell fish and the fat of the seal. It was seven weeks after her arrival into civilization that Juana Maria died of dysentery. After years of very little nutrient-laden food, her new diet had caused a severe and ultimately fatal illness. To read about her yourself, you can just google her name as there are many historical stories written about her.

What can we learn from this story? It was not that the new diet was unhealthy, in the 1800s there were no grocery stores lined with processed-foods. The new diet was not what her body was accustomed to, yet she lived remotely and lived off of the land without civilization. When I first heard this story, I was amazed of how quickly she died once brought into the crowds. Juana had nothing in the material sense, yet she survived with everything she had naturally being very healthy when she was found.

I first want to discuss civilization. When we look at the two choices in our lives and the two pathways that are offered, the majority will never pick the pathway that leads away from civilization and away from the choices and distractions. Let me clarify, on the island where they found Juana, she lived and was healthy. It was also noted that she seemed to be a very happy person as she was always smiling. Brought into civilization, there are so many choices. There are choices of what to wear, how to fix our hair, what to eat, where to go, where to live, what kind of car to own, where to go for entertainment, what church to attend, and I could go on and on. The point is, are we really happy inside? Are we really thriving inside? Is there really meaning to our lives when our choice is to follow civilization or rather the crowds? There are probably only a few that would choose to live outside of civilization, and we know this because the Bible clearly states that it will only be few that make the decision to choose life instead of death. To clarify, life is with God and death is outside of God. In our lives, we continually make choices every single day. Our life is full of choices. I'm not saying that we have to go find a deserted island and live on it, but that's not a bad idea, especially if it ensures our salvation. If you will remember Scripture, it was John who was exiled on the island of Patmos that I will touch on more in depth further on. However, the point to this story of Juana is to be able to see that outside of civilization, if you are walking with Jesus Christ, you can still live and live well. Juana Maria lived outside of civilization, she lived and breathed, she had health and she had no wealth! I'm not going to get into this deeply, but I want to make the statement that sickness and disease are brought on by man's sinful nature. Juana Maria was very healthy until she came into civilization. Yes, it was the diet of different foods that made her sick, but it was being brought into civilization that ultimately, killed her. Did Juana Maria know God? No one knows this but if we look at this in a spiritual sense, when we live outside of Jesus Christ, we are already dead—spiritually dead! The lifestyles in America are pretty much geared around all the distractions and choices of what to buy, what to eat, where to go, etc. Our lives are consumed as we live among all the distractions that separate us from Jesus Christ and we may be living in the natural sense, but we are not alive!

Let's tie this story in with a few other stories that I want to share. I remember hearing about a man from the United States who was in another country, and he was put into prison. This is not an isolated story, as we hear about these situations more and more. However, this man was in isolation for 45 days without seeing anyone. During this timeframe of being completely alone, he began to cry out to Jesus Christ, and he found Him. This radically changed his life where he lived to share his story because this situation changed who he had once been to who he was today. There is a similar story of a missionary who had been put into prison in another country for his Christian beliefs. This man spent years in confinement without any contact with other people until the United States was able to make a deal for him to be released. Those going into missions in a foreign country where they hate the name of Jesus Christ, are going forth by faith that God will lead them. However, there may be times that some of these missionaries are captured and imprisoned as is this story. Upon his return to the United States, he was asked what it was like for all those years in confinement. His reply was that it was a long vacation with Jesus Christ. If our lives were minus all of the distractions and all those things we tend to accumulate, our focus in this life would be on drawing closer to Jesus Christ instead of allowing the enemy to fill us with the greed and lust of this world.

The final story I want to share is that of John in the Bible, the last remaining member of the Twelve Disciples. He was the disciple that Jesus not only loved deeply but while hanging on the Cross, He told John to take care of Mary, His mother. In his later years of life, John was exiled to the island called Patmos as a result of anti-Christian persecution under the Roman Emperor Domitian. On this island, separated by others, was where John began having visions that were written into the Book of Revelation. The Book of Revelation is one of the most important books for us to be able to have a glimpse of heaven and hell. It seems that when God separates us from this world, all the things in this world, that He is able to do a mighty work with our lives from the inside out. When our time is filled with His Words, the Word of God, those Words continue to radically change who we are on the inside and that transformation begins changing us on the outside. It is only through our outward person that we will go and do those things we are called to do, but it begins with the inside which is our heart. It is imperative as a true Christian to live and breathe the Word of God which only will happen, as our choices are to not allow this world to penetrate through our eyes and ears. Our choices of what we choose to read, watch, and hear.

How does all of this tie into storing treasures on earth? This my friend, is true Christianity. Our lifestyles should be one where if we truly have that conversion and Jesus lives with us day in and day out, we need nothing else! This is life, true life! Why do we desire those things of this world when we already have everything we need, if we just cry out to Our God for His mercy and grace upon our lives and allow Him to lead us on a long vacation with Him forever and ever!

CHAPTER ELEVEN
THE CROOKED ROAD

The highways which I will refer to as the crooked road, by far are the most dangerous of all road systems as a Christian. The highways have been discussed in great detail in other chapters but because of the hidden dangers to the Christian, I believe this road needs to be reviewed to greater clarity as it pertains to the Bible. As we have discussed, there are three road systems and three scenarios. According to the Word of God, there are those who are cold, warm and hot. Only one pathway leads to heaven while the other two, lead to hell. In reality, there are only two roads like the Scriptures tell us but there are three kinds of people. The analogy on the road systems are to help us be able to see what road we are traveling in this life, as it pertains to a life with Jesus Christ? This analogy may help us to understand or see the scenario clearer. Your choices are one of the two pathways which lead to hell, the interstate system and the highways, or the country road which leads to heaven. The interstate is where those travel because it is such a breeze, as they fly down this road system at high speeds getting to their destinations much quicker all the while staying conformed with the world. This system if full of all kinds of people to include the world, and it keeps those who travel conformed to this world and blinded by truth. We also have learned that the country roads are where few will travel, and then we have the highways which are going to be referred to as the crooked roads. The highway system was built prior to the interstate. The highway system can also be a fast-paced system like that of the interstate, but the highway is where those who are lukewarm normally travel.

Like I said, the highway system can also be fast-paced but there are many stops in between your destination unlike that of interstate. Traveling on highways, it is the pathway that leads to all other pathways. You can go in the direction of the interstates and you can also go in the direction of the lonely country roads. The highway system is the equivalent to the crooked road as it winds around mountains, rivers, canyons, etc. While traveling on the interstate system, there are all kinds of distractions that lead you to the highways. Once on the highways, as one who considers themselves a Christian, they can still fulfill their lusts for this life or they can detour onto the country road if they are able to find it. Think about it visually, highways are crooked roads. They wind and turn here and there and lead in many directions. God, through the Holy Spirit, is always trying to get the attention of those who are His. First, He is trying to get you off the fastest paced lifestyles in order that you can find the narrow road. The majority of Christians spend more time on the crooked road than any other road. This is where they can play church.

We are told in Scripture that He would rather we be cold than lukewarm. The problem here is that the majority who claim to be Christians are lukewarm due to hearing some watered-down message that promises them salvation, which is totally contrary to the Word of God. They believe the messages being taught by the false men and women who claim to be ordained by God today, and therefore, they leave the interstate system and get on the highway which is where the majority of *"so-called"* Christians remain until they die.

In order to get on the little country road in the natural, it would seem that we must first get on the highway system. As I was studying this, my thoughts went back to those first disciples that really left all to follow Jesus Christ. I could not see in their walk where they seemed to be lukewarm except for Judas. When I was contemplating what God was trying to show me, I was able to see something more spectacular. First, I can truthfully say there have been times in my walk with God where I was on fire and times when I was just lukewarm. These times were based on what I was listening to and what I was reading. The openings to our heart are either through our ears to hear or our eyes to see. When our choices are to continue filling ourselves with the things of this world, our heart will be full of things that are NOT God and things that will lead us straight to hell. If we are going back and forth to learning of Him and still trying to hold on to those things in this world that we love, we are traveling the highway system where we are lukewarm, and He will spit us out of His mouth. I know that many of us are so stubborn that we are determined to do things our way, and our way is not always the right way. It is at these times that God allows our sin to play itself out to its fully developed form. He will allow your sin to grow, unchecked, until it causes devastating consequences for you and your family.

James 1:15 (NKJV) Then, when desire has conceived, it gives birth to sin; and sin, when it is full-grown, brings forth death.

In this life, we have a mix of people. There are those who hear the gospels and immediately believe because they have accepted the Holy Spirit, and they become on fire for the Lord supernaturally. They never went from the interstate system to the highway but through the supernatural, they left the interstate and found themselves on the country road amazed at the supernatural transformation of their lives. There are also those who spend much of their time going from interstate to highway and back again because they are trying to hold on to the world and Jesus at the same time. Then you have those who completely get off of interstate but they remain on the highways for various reasons, never finding that country road.

Regardless, if you have had an encounter where you went supernaturally to the country road or if you spent time on the highway where you eventually found the truth and got it right, the point is, we must continually seek Him where we can gain the knowledge to really know Him. We were never meant to remain on the highway where we are just lukewarm. We were never meant to base our salvation on what someone else has told us but to seek Him ourselves until we find Him. Please know that if you have decided to get off of the fast-paced lifestyle where you find yourself on the highway system, the crooked road, this is NOT salvation. Remember, the highway system can also be a fast-paced lifestyle, and satan will do everything he can to keep you busy and conformed. This road does not ensure your salvation. If you are on the highway and trying to find the country road, it does not take years. Salvation is NOT a process that takes years. If you are traveling to a location in the natural and that location is located in the middle of nowhere, it does not take you years to get there unless your focus has become on the distractions all around you, and you have chosen to enjoy those things you encounter on your journey. To be more explicit, if you were to make the decision to travel to a remote location in this world where you had to travel by car, plane, boat, etc. in order to get to that remote location, any place on earth would not take years unless you became distracted or chose to enjoy the different places you encountered and only then your journey could take years. However, any journey from interstate to highway to the country road could take a few hours, few days, or weeks depending on where you are currently.

The Overflow from the Heart

My point that I want to make is that if your seeking God and finding Him was genuine, it should not take you long to be on fire for the Lord, at least it should not take you years. What do I mean when I say you should be on fire for the Lord? When we have so much Jesus in us because we cannot get enough of His Word, as we are always hungering for more and more, it will spill out of us. If we hunger for more of Him and continually seek Him, He is going to fill us. As we begin to be filled with more of Him daily, there is only so much that you can put in and it is going to overflow. The overflow will pour out of you. It will spill out in your conversations. In being around other people, it does not take long until what is really on the inside of you will begin to spill out. Think about it this way, if your love in this life is sports, you will spend a great quality of time watching and listening to sports and then when you get around other people, that is what you will be inclined to talk about because that has become your god. In the same sense, when you let go of all those idols you once had and you use your time wisely to pour into the Word of God and seek Him, when in conversation with other people, that will begin to spill out of you as well. You will find yourself continually sharing Jesus. It becomes your life. It becomes who you are. I know this because I have walked it many times. I have been at nothing but church social events and that is all that would spill out of me but, I could be standing in groups where the conversations were any and everything but no conversation of Jesus Christ. The reason—most *"so-called"* Christians never spend any time studying His Word or even praying. Therefore, what is inside of them is determined by what they have chosen to serve as their god. So, if you are at a place in your life where you need a Savior and you are seeking Him not to fix your life but to change your life for His good, finding Him should be real. On the other hand, if you are looking for a god to fit into your schedule because you have no desire to give up your life, and you only want a god to be what you think he should be, it will be a counterfeit god. However, if we are really in a place where we want what is real, we will find Him and it won't take years. The problem is that the majority get on that crooked road to become a Christian and they remain there. In fact, we are told that the majority never even **find** the narrow road. The majority of counterfeit Christians play church going back and forth from the interstate to the highway. This is NOT Christianity, but the problem is that those playing the game of church seldom ever find the lonely country road and believe the highway is safe. They may get a taste of Christianity on that highway, but they also know that they are not far from getting back on the interstate system. Their choice is to remain close to the world, so that they can continue to enjoy their sin all the while playing church and believing they are safe.

Let me say, I have heard of those encounters where people found Jesus Christ and immediately, they walked away from everything and sold out completely. However, I cannot say that my encounter happened that way. First of all, I began going to church because I was engaged to marry someone whose family was very involved with the church. He could not marry me unless I went through their ritual of accepting Jesus into my heart. I went through the motions and did what was required but it meant nothing. However, as I spent time going to church and going through the motions, I began to seek Him because of questions I had in my life. Basically, my life at the point where I went through the motions, I did leave the fast-paced lifestyle of the interstates but remained on the highway for some time. The highway system was where I claimed to be a Christian, but I was not walking a life that would lead to salvation. Let me clarify, we must be very careful of man's religion because salvation is heartfelt not felt in one's mind by reasoning. Now, let me clarify that. Your heart will deceive you as we are told in the Word of God, but your walk with Jesus must be heartfelt. How is that? Your mind must be renewed to the mind of Christ which is also Biblical. If we are not filling our mind with His Word, our mind will listen to the reasonings from many various religions out there which are not necessarily true. On the other hand, if we are renewing our mind by studying, reading and seeking Him, we will begin to think like Jesus thinks. Once our thoughts line up with his thoughts, our encounter with Jesus will be heartfelt.

We are not saved by doing some ritual that is not even Biblical. There is nothing in the Bible that tells us to ask Jesus to come into our heart. Jesus is sitting at the right hand of God in heavenly places. *(Ephesians 1:20)* Jesus tells us that it was better that He go because One greater would come which is the Holy Spirit. The Holy Spirit is the One that comes to clean up our lives and this is the voice we hear. Yes, they are all one and the same, but without the Holy Spirit in our lives, the voice we choose to follow is NOT the voice of the true God. In John below, Jesus made this clear.

John 16:5-11 (NKJV) "But now I go away to Him who sent Me, and none of you asks Me, 'Where are You going?' ⁶But because I have said these things to you, sorrow has filled your heart. ⁷Nevertheless I tell you the truth. It is to your advantage that I go away; for if I do not go away, the Helper will not come to you; but if I depart, I will send Him to you. ⁸And when He has come, He will convict the world of sin, and of righteousness, and of judgment: ⁹of sin, because they do not believe in Me; ¹⁰of righteousness, because I go to My Father and you see Me no more; ¹¹of judgment, because the ruler of this world is judged.

On the crooked road, there are many who go to church regularly, and they have based their relationship with God on what they have learned by man. This is playing church, even though, they believe they are living a life as a Christian. The Bible is our judge and when we do not study, we perish on this crooked road. You may say that your walk with the Lord is genuine, but I will show you that it is not genuine if you are still holding on to areas in this life! Playing church is where you act spiritual when you are around other church members, but God looks at what you do in private. This includes ministers of the Bible.

Matthew 6:3-4 (NKJV) But when you do a charitable deed, do not let your left hand know what your right hand is doing, ⁴that your charitable deed may be in secret; and your Father who sees in secret will Himself reward you openly.

John 6:57-58 (NKJV) As the living Father sent Me, and I live because of the Father, so he who feeds on Me will live because of Me. ⁵⁸This is the bread which came down from heaven—not as your fathers ate the manna, and are dead. He who eats this bread will live forever."

Like I said, if you are not spending time in the Word of God, pouring into His Words of life where that is what is in your heart and that is what comes out of your mouth, you will not live forever with Jesus Christ. Jesus is the bread of life. *(John 6:35)* When we are not seeking Him but instead, we are filling ourselves with so much of this world, our god becomes the god of this world.

Associations

Let's examine what we do in our private time outside of the church crowd. Is your lifestyle one where you are okay to have anything on your television in your home? Do you think it is okay to talk any way and laugh at any jokes when you are around those outside of your Christian circle of friends? Do you spend countless hours on the computers, television, cell phones, playing video games, and yet call yourself a Christian? In your private time, do you engage in offensive materials such as pornography? Outside of your circle of *"so-called"* Christians, do you associate with darkness? What I mean by darkness, do you associate with those in this world that fit into the category of Sodom and Gomorrah? Such as those who live contrary to the Word of God. This would be living a double life where you have two circles of friends. You have those you spend time with playing church and then those you spend time with outside of church. Your friends outside of church live in darkness where they have given themselves over to enjoying the pleasures of the flesh—sex, adultery, homosexuality, spending money foolishly, loving the world and the things in the world, etc. In other words, pleasures of the flesh would be anything that satisfies your flesh.

Galatians 5:16 (NKJV) I say then: Walk in the Spirit, and you shall not fulfill the lusts of the flesh.

Other Scriptures say desires of the flesh instead of lusts of the flesh. Basically, this means that when we spend hours fulfilling our own desires that have nothing to do with the advancement of God's purpose, we are fulfilling the lusts of the flesh. This is a double life where you are on the highway system and considered lukewarm. This is where you see nothing wrong with associating with those on the interstate system merely going back and forth depending upon your particular choices for that day. You are a counterfeit Christian when you try to fit in with those who are cold in this world, those who do not believe in God, those who do not believe Jesus Christ is Lord, or those who believe in other gods.

You may say that you only associate with those who go to church, but let me tell you a story I heard once. There was this Christian family, and they allowed this man to come live in their home. He lived there for years. He sat in a corner of their living room, and he had a filthy mouth where he spoke all kinds of lewd things. He spoke about pornography, sexual immorality, and He even made fun of Christianity and used the Lord's name in vain. This family accepted that because they regularly took their family to church and lived as most who claim to be Christians. You may say that you would never allow a person of such into your home, but the majority of Christians see nothing wrong with doing this every single day, as they allow their televisions to be turned on to allow everything I just described. You may say this is not the same thing; however, if your choice is to allow filth and immorality into your home, this is exactly the same thing. Ask yourself, if you knew Jesus Christ was coming to your home for dinner, would you have your television turned on to showcase the ugliness that portrays most American homes on a daily basis? This is the world we live in, and the majority of Christians today have compromised to be just like the world. The Bible warns us of the days we live in, and we just accept this as Christians believing that we can live a double life. Would churches today during services ever play a movie that showcases what we play in our homes? Most churches would not, but then there's the *emerging churches* that are growing in great numbers today that would and do allow the world in because their desires are for those who are unbelievers. However, those churches that still teach from the Bible would not allow anything and everything that is in our social media today to be broadcast during their services. The sad part is that even though there are still some churches that would not allow such, the majority of people today to include many pastors do go home and showcase these things in their living rooms every single day. Does this hurt your walk with Jesus? Absolutely, you be the judge.

Mark 7:20-23 (ESV) And he said, "<u>What comes out of a person is what defiles him.</u> ²¹<u>For within, out of the heart of man</u>, come evil thoughts, sexual immorality, theft, murder, adultery, ²²coveting, wickedness, deceit, sensuality, envy, slander, pride, foolishness. ²³All these things come from within, and they defile a person."

You be the judge, but you better judge yourself harshly. None of us are perfect, but what we choose to surround ourselves with and what we choose to read and listen to comes through our eyes and ears and goes into our heart. What is in your heart will come out and if you do not agree with that, you do not agree with the Word of God. This is not my words but His Words!

Revelation 21:6-10 (ESV) And he said to me, "It is done! I am the Alpha and the Omega, the beginning and the end. <u>To the thirsty</u> I will give from the spring of the water of life without payment. ⁷The one who conquers will have this heritage, and <u>I will be his God and he will be my son</u>. ⁸But as for the cowardly, the faithless, the detestable, as for murderers, the sexually immoral, sorcerers, idolaters, and all liars, their portion will be in the lake that burns with fire and sulfur, which is the second death." ⁵<u>Put to death therefore what is earthly in you</u>: sexual immorality, impurity, passion, evil desire, and covetousness, which is idolatry. ⁶On account of these the wrath of God is coming. ⁷In these you too once walked, when you were living in them. ⁸But now you must put them all away: anger, wrath, malice, slander, and obscene talk from your mouth. ⁹Do not lie to one another, seeing that you have put off the old self with its practices ¹⁰and have put on the new self, which is being renewed in knowledge after the image of its creator.

First, making note of the items I underlined, those who are thirsty are those who run to God to satisfy that thirst. We only satisfy that thirst, as we seek Him diligently. We seek Him by prayer and studying in order that we can live an upright life. He is God to those who are thirsty, not to this world as you can see when you continue to read from that point. These are strong words but that is so we walk in a manner worthy of serving Him. We walk in a manner in which our life depends on it because it does. We are to put to death everything that is earthly. There is NO mention in the Bible that we are to seek the inventions of man to a degree that televisions and computers become filled in our heart. What is in a man will come out of his heart. I hope that you serving the inventions of this day work out for you when you stand before Him, but I fear for your life because not seeking Him daily, will not produce the lifestyle that it takes to make it to heaven.

Colossians 3:1-10 (NKJV) If then you were raised with Christ, seek those things which are above, where Christ is, sitting at the right hand of God. ²Set your mind on things above, not on things on the earth. ³For you died, and your life is hidden with Christ in God. ⁴When Christ who is our life appears, then you also will appear with Him in glory. ⁵Therefore put to death your members which are on the earth: fornication, uncleanness, passion, evil desire, and covetousness, which is idolatry. ⁶Because of these things the wrath of God is coming upon the sons of disobedience, ⁷in which you yourselves once walked when you lived in them. ⁸But now you yourselves are to put off all these: anger, wrath, malice, blasphemy, filthy language out of your mouth. ⁹Do not lie to one another, since you have put off the old man with his deeds, ¹⁰and have put on the new man who is renewed in knowledge according to the image of Him who created him.

This Scripture does not say that those whose life portrays a life lived out full of the substance in this world will appear with Him in glory one day. Every single day, our choices determine who we are and if we are living a lifestyle that portrays Jesus Christ. Our associations should be those who are striving to have a lifestyle that pleases our Lord. We should be associating with those who are of liked mind, those whose walk and their lifestyle is that of a true Christian. You may say that Jesus hung out with those who were of this world, but it was because He knew their heart. Let's look at some examples.

Luke 19:1-10 (ESV) He entered Jericho and was passing through. ²And behold, there was a man named Zacchaeus. He was a chief tax collector and was rich. ³And he was <u>seeking</u> to see who Jesus was, but on account of the crowd he could not, because he was small in stature. ⁴So he ran on ahead and climbed up into a sycamore tree to see him, for he was about to pass that way. ⁵And when Jesus came to the place, he looked up and said to him, "Zacchaeus, hurry and come down, for I must stay at your house today." ⁶So he hurried and came down and <u>received</u> him joyfully. ⁷And when they saw it, they all grumbled, "He has gone in to be the guest of a man who is a sinner." ⁸And Zacchaeus stood and said to the Lord, "Behold, Lord, the half of my goods I give to the poor. And if I have defrauded anyone of anything, I restore it fourfold." ⁹And Jesus said to him, "Today salvation has come to this house, since he also is a son of Abraham. ¹⁰For the Son of Man came to seek and to save the lost."

Jesus knows our true heart and what our intentions are, and He came to restore and to save those who are His. First, Zacchaeus was seeking. Jesus knows when we are truly seeking Him. Zacchaeus was NOT seeking Him for riches, popularity, and fame because he was a man of wealth as the Scripture states. He was also evidently well-known among the crowd for they spoke against him. It was also evident, that those in the crowd believed Zacchaeus to be a sinner and believed that they were not. Remember, Jesus tells us that He came for those who needed a physician not for those who were well. In other words, Jesus came for those who knew they were sinners and needed Him, but He did not come for those who thought themselves righteous. Zacchaeus had everything he needed in the natural but that was not enough. There was something missing in his life and evidently, he had heard of Jesus and just wanted to be able to look upon Him as He walked by. We see that Jesus already knew what was in Zacchaeus' heart, and He addressed Him to come down. Zacchaeus received Him with joy, and Zacchaeus was changed due to his encounter with Christ. How do we know this? We know this because Zacchaeus gave half of everything to the poor, and he restored to all those he had defrauded. Zacchaeus made things right because Jesus radically changed his life. I want to point a few things out here. First, notice that Jesus did not tell Zacchaeus to go and sell everything like he told the rich young ruler. Jesus did not have to tell him that because He knew that Zacchaeus' heart was right. It is not about selling all you have; it is about lining your heart up with Scripture where you hear the voice of the Holy Spirit. Once we are in right standing with God, we will hear that voice and follow that voice that pertains to our own life. Zacchaeus' life was to make things right with those who were poor and those he had defrauded. The second thing to note, is that a true Christian will have a conversion that will be seen on the outside once God gets a hold of them on the inside. However, you have the hypocrites that can only remember who people were at one time because they cannot even see their own sin. We are all sinners and we all come short of His glory as Paul tells us. *(Romans 3:23)* In Biblical days, there were those who thought they were right with God, and they judged others harshly. These were the Pharisees. They did not believe Jesus' words because they thought themselves to be holy men. They judged Jesus harshly because of His associations.

Mark 2:16-17 (NKJV) And when the scribes and Pharisees saw Him eating with the tax collectors and sinners, they said to His disciples, "How is it that He eats and drinks with tax collectors and sinners?" ¹⁷When Jesus heard it, He said to them, "Those who are well have no need of a physician, but those who are sick. I did not come to call the righteous, but sinners, to repentance."

You see the Pharisees were those who thought they knew the voice of God and thought they lived righteously. Jesus spoke these words knowing that there are NONE that are righteous but yet, many believe they are in right standing with God. Jesus associated with sinners because they knew they needed a Savior. He did not come for those who thought they were righteous, why? The reason is because those who think they are living a life that is in right standing with God, are NOT seeking for the truth. Jesus came and died on the cross for all those who know they are sinners and need a Savior. Why would you seek a doctor when you believe you are well?

Jesus' associations were with sinners but are we not all sinners? His choices of who He associated with had to do with what was on the inside of someone and that is the same today. It does not matter what your spiritual state is at the moment but who you desire to be. Your choices to either run to God or away from God will determine who exactly you are to Jesus Christ.

God knows our heart individually. He knows that man or woman, who in their private time they are broken because of their lifestyle. It is in our brokenness that we can find Him and come to know Him. However, there are many in their brokenness that run away from God instead of to Him. It is those who run from Him that reject Him. Yes, we are to be a light in this world and the salt of the earth, but Jesus rejected many of those who lived a sinful life because they had no desire to really know of Him. In our brokenness, we are given chances to seek but not everyone seeks. In the same sense, not everyone knows God nor will everyone seek Him to know Him. It is those that have rejected Jesus that He will also turn from them at some point.

Matthew 7:21 (NKJV) "Not everyone who says to Me, 'Lord, Lord,' shall enter the kingdom of heaven, but he who does the will of My Father in heaven.

John 6:26 (ESV) Jesus answered them, "Truly, truly, I say to you, you are seeking me, not because you saw the signs, but because you ate your fill of the loaves.

John 3:18-21 (NKJV) "He who believes in Him is not condemned; but he who does not believe is condemned already, because he has not believed in the name of the only begotten Son of God. [19]And this is the condemnation, that the light has come into the world, and men loved darkness rather than light, because their deeds were evil. [20]For everyone practicing evil hates the light and does not come to the light, lest his deeds should be exposed. [21]But he who does the truth comes to the light, that his deeds may be clearly seen, that they have been done in God."

Our associations in this life are important. Jesus associated with sinners because we are all sinners, but He walked away from those who were not His. He walked away from those who chose not to seek Him. He walked away from those who chose not to do His Father's will. He walked away from those who did seek Him but did so for personal gain. He walked away from those who outwardly were sinners but He also walked away from those who played church but in their private time they loved darkness. You see light and darkness will never be in association together. When the sun comes up, the darkness fades away. When darkness comes upon us, the light leaves. A counterfeit Christian always has a scripture in their defense for associating and being a friend to the world. Beware, many use Scriptures out of context and if you are not called to be a friend to those in the world, you are stepping into dangerous waters. Those who became His disciples, they left all behind to follow Him. Likewise, those who chose to hold onto areas of this world, left nothing behind and did NOT follow Him.

Luke 14:33 (NKJV) So likewise, whoever of you does not forsake all that he has cannot be My disciple.

If you want to defend why you associate with those who are NOT considered Christians Biblically, then you better look at your life because He will never call you to do so unless your life first looks like the lives of His disciples. Have you given all and left all behind? In the street ministry I was involved in for years, I met those who had left everything to actually live on the street to be a minister to those on the streets which I discussed in chapter 10. They have exactly what it takes to be a light among the darkness because they chose to go into the world as He tells us, but they left all behind to do so.

Living a Double Life

John 17:14 (NKJV) I have given them Your word; and the world has hated them because they are not of the world, just as I am not of the world.

As Jesus prayed this prayer to His Father regarding those who belong to Him, we are able to see IF our Christian walk is real, we are in this world but not of this world. However, we cannot go into the world to minister true Christianity when we are a counterfeit Christian. He will not call you to go unless you have let go of the things that are keeping you from finding that narrow road. Let's not look at the prostitute, drug addict, homosexuals, thieves, and murderers for a minute—let's look at you. Christians tend to think they are okay when they do not fit into one of those categories above. However, God has called those who belong to Him into the ministry once they have left all behind. Let me clarify, being in the ministry merely means that if you are a true Christian, your lifestyle will go forth as a disciple sharing Jesus Christ and ministering to those who He sends across your path. Being in the ministry does not necessarily give you a title nor a building for you to teach. However, the important thing to see is that He has not called us to sit around and play video games for hours each day; He has not called us to spend countless hours in front of a television each day; He has not called us to spend hours and hours surfing the internet each day; He has not called us to focus on building a life of security; He has not called us to strive for the riches in this world; He has not called us to strive to gain power through our own ambition; He has not called us to focus on gaining the wisdom of this world. If you fit into any of those categories, you more than likely are following the wrong voice. Perhaps you are following a pastor, priest, etc., but you may also be following your own voice that desires this world more than you realize. This my friend is living a double life and the danger is that most in this world on this pathway will never realize this until it is too late.

Matthew 7:21-23 (NKJV) "Not everyone who says to Me, 'Lord, Lord,' shall enter the kingdom of heaven, but he who does the will of My Father in heaven. 22Many will say to Me in that day, 'Lord, Lord, have we not prophesied in Your name, cast out demons in Your name, and done many wonders in Your name?' 23And then I will declare to them, 'I never knew you; depart from Me, you who practice lawlessness!'

How exactly can we live this double life and think we are safe? This is because we have bought into believing what we hear from most pulpits today which are merely watered-down messages to give the people what they want to hear. The majority of people want a savior that is easy to follow because most people are not going to follow something that requires too much of them. Yes, they are okay with throwing some money out here and there to help build up a man's empire, and they are okay with giving some of their time for the cause. However, if a pastor started preaching hard core Biblical messages that were truth, the congregation would suddenly be faced with the reality of what a real Christian is, and then the majority would leave to find another church.

As I have said, those who are lukewarm do have some truth and maybe even quite a bit of truth, but the truth they do have is not enough to awaken them where they make the choice to cross over to that narrow pathway. However, even if they were to hear truth and many have heard from time to time outside of those church walls, but they have been blinded and really do not want the kind of Christianity that requires change. Just like the young rich ruler, he desired to really follow Jesus until he realized that it meant giving up things that he could not give up. Do you know why he could not give up his things to follow Jesus? It was because our things become our god. It is because we look at the true God as being a small god. We cannot really understand just how big God really is. Somehow, we talk ourselves into believing what the majority believes, thinking that in the end because we were not really a BAD person, that He will have mercy and grace on our lives. After all, it is spoken from the pulpits of hell every single week in the majority of the churches that our God will give grace to those who sin because He knows we are unable to be perfect. This gives us the license to continue living in our sin. I hope this works out for you in the end because it did not work out for the young rich ruler.

John 12:40 (NKJV) "He has blinded their eyes and hardened their hearts, Lest they should see with their eyes, Lest they should understand with their hearts and turn, So that I should heal them."

When we turn from our sin, we are healed. The great Physician comes to those who turn because they know they need a Savior.

John 9:39-41 (NKJV) And Jesus said, "For judgment I have come into this world, that those who do not see may see, and that those who see may be made blind." ⁴⁰Then some of the Pharisees who were with Him heard these words, and said to Him, "Are we blind also?" ⁴¹Jesus said to them, "If you were blind, you would have no sin; but now you say, 'We see.' Therefore your sin remains.

Do you understand that Jesus opens the eyes of those who seek Him because they know they are sinners and need a Savior—they need the great Physician. Yet, those who think they already do see because they have chosen to believe in following a ministry that teaches falsely, these are blinded by the truth! These believe they are righteous. They believe their religion teaches truth, yet they never seek for a Savior that will bring them to a place where there is NO guilt because of the lifestyle choices. When we are continually pouring into the Word of God, our choices continue to allow the Holy Spirit access to clean up our lives. Our lifestyle becomes one of intimacy with Jesus Christ, and it is by hearing that we believe and seeing that we are able to walk in faith alone knowing that He has opened our eyes to see what the majority will never see. There is no longer guilt because our lives are so filled with His Word that what is on the inside of us pours out continually. This my friend is walking in the desires of the Spirit not the desires of the flesh.

Psalm 146:8 (NKJV) The Lord opens the eyes of the blind; The Lord raises those who are bowed down; The Lord loves the righteous.

The Lord loves the righteous but He hates the sinner.

Psalm 5:4-6 (NKJV) For you are not a God who takes pleasure in wickedness, Nor shall evil dwell with You. ⁵The boastful shall not stand in Your sight; You hate all workers of iniquity. ⁶You shall destroy those who speak falsehood; The LORD abhors the bloodthirsty and deceitful man.

If you study, the Scriptures show us a God that loves and a God that hates. So many times, we hear people say that God hates the sin but loves the sinner. This is NOT Biblical. God is a God who hates. I've shown this in chapter 8, as well. He loves the righteous but He hates the sinner. Study the Old Testament and you will see that God sent His people many times to kill those who were not His which also included their children. We all know the story of Sodom and Gomorrah as well, but there are many other stories where He sent His people to destroy others. However, we are all sinners and saved by grace, yet this does not give us a license to continue in sin. Those who are counterfeit Christians will use the Scriptures to continue living their own lifestyles which do not line up with that of a true Christian. So, as true Christians, are we to hate also?

Psalm 119:127-128 (NKJV) Therefore I love Your commandments More than gold, yes, than fine gold! 128Therefore all Your precepts concerning all things I consider to be right; I hate every false way.

Psalm 119:163 (NKJV) I hate and abhor lying, But I love Your law.

How do we love and hate also? I know that we can love people and hate the sin because evidently as children of God, we should hate murder, we should hate abortion, we should hate deception and dishonesty. However, should we love those who willingly make the choices to hurt other people for their own selfish reasons? I'm not talking about forgiveness here because everyone can be forgiven; I'm just talking about how we should feel towards others that make the choices to live outside of God's laws. Jesus associated with the sinners, but it was the sinners who made a choice to follow Him because their desire was NOT to remain in their sin. His associations were with those who desired to be forgiven and once forgiven, they turned from the world and to Him in order that their lifestyles became changed from that of this world. Jesus on the other hand, chose to NOT associate with those who willingly chose to live a lifestyle that was contrary to the Word of God. We see Him walk away from them and when He was confronted by them, His responses were always speaking that which was true, even though, it was not the response they wanted to hear. By Jesus' responses, it was evident that He had no desire to be in association with them. I'm sure this would fall into the category spoken of when the Scriptures teach us that God hates the sinner. Jesus did not have to say that but His actions very well showed that He had no desire to be in association with those who were evil. There is a huge difference in those who sin but they hear God's

Word, and they desire to know truth. We have all been there but because of our desire to KNOW Him, we make that choice to let go of this world and to follow Him. At this place is where we pour into Him and real growth begins. So, our hatred is NOT portrayed in saying or doing evil against someone because that would put us in the same category, but our hatred is portrayed in that we choose to NOT be in association with those who willingly have chosen NOT to let go of this world.

Those on the crooked road live a double life believing that God understands that these are strong holds in their lives. These may be strong holds but when you accept a lie believing that this is just who you are, God will give you over to that lifestyle. You are playing with fire when your life is divided. You are playing with fire when you are not willing to give up those friends and acquaintances that pull you into their lifestyles.

Psalm 119:113 (NKJV) I hate the double-minded, But I love Your law.

We cannot live a double life because the end result is that God classifies you as being a lukewarm Christian, and there is a lot to say about the lifestyles of those in that category. Those who are lukewarm have basically placed God in a small box and have never contemplated just how real hell is. I know because I have been there where I would hear that small voice and ignore that voice because I did not want to give up something in my life. When I did walk away, that was hard as well because I wasn't sure I wanted to give up my place and status that I had acquired within the large church as a leader. Thankfully, I didn't completely stop listening and my heart did not grow cold.

Lukewarm, I Will Spit You Out of My Mouth

However, being a lukewarm Christian is not where you want to be when Jesus comes back. Yes, those who are cold will also go to hell but whoa to those who are lukewarm. It's not that the punishment for the lukewarm is any greater than that for the cold, since both will go to hell. However, there are some points to make about those who are lukewarm that may rather be cold in the end. Before I touch on this, let's first read this Scripture in order that we understand why the lukewarm are referenced in a way where Jesus would rather that we be cold.

Revelation 3:15-16 (ESV) "I know your works: you are neither cold nor hot. Would that you were either cold or hot! ¹⁶So, because you are lukewarm, and neither hot nor cold, I will spit you out of My mouth.

To look at the church spoken of in this Scripture in Revelation, it was Laodicea. Laodicea lacked their own water supply. For water, they had to import it either from the city of Colossae where there were cold mountain springs of water and suitable for drinking or from the north in Hierapolis, where there were hot springs that were suitable for therapeutic and healing baths. On the other hand, Laodicea was renowned for its dirty, lukewarm water in which visitors almost immediately spit out after tasting. Both the hot and cold water were considered good and useful, whereas the lukewarm was of no use. This Scripture refers to being of good use. As a Christian, if you are merely lukewarm, you are of no use to God. Lukewarm Christians spend their time living as this world and if anything, they present a picture to the world of false Christianity and therefore, they defile the true Biblical teachings. He would rather we be cold because at least, being cold you are not sharing false messages that are leading the majority away from true Christianity. The water analogy showed that there was good in both cold and hot water but the lukewarm had absolutely no use. As a Christian, it is much easier for those who are going forth as true ministers of the Word of God and penetrating the truth into those who are cold than the lukewarm. If you were cold and had not been taught false teachings, you would by far be more receptive to the truth than those who are lukewarm. This is why Jesus tells us that it would be better if you were cold. Those that are lukewarm fall into a very dangerous place because they have been taught Scripture out of context, and it is hard to convince them that they are following the wrong voice. I know because I have been there as well. I have been in the place where I would hear true Biblical teachings, but I would immediately walk away because I had been trained to believe what was coming from the pulpit where I had chosen to sit and refused to listen to anyone else. It took me hearing and hearing again and again before I began to search Scriptures for myself. Even in searching the Scriptures, it took me quite some time before my eyes were opened to truth. Today, there are very few of those that I was acquaintances with that have walked away because those who are lukewarm believe they are following truth.

The good news is that if God is not finished with you yet. He will allow you to go through the necessary storms in order to awaken you to seek Him diligently. You may be weary because your life is continually not going in the direction you desire, and your struggles have become exhausting. I have touched on the trials that we would experience many times on the interstate system which is God's way of allowing storms in our lives to awaken us so that we make choices that lead us to the narrow pathway. We will see these trials or storms on both the interstate and the highway systems. However, not to sugar coat anything, even for those who do find the narrow pathway, there will still be storms in their lives as well. We are told that there will be trouble in this life as a follower of Jesus Christ no matter what pathway we are traveling. However, many times those storms are just to keep those who are His in check with Jesus Christ. In any case, we know on all walks of life that it is not a bed of roses, pain comes in all forms; however, depending on what road system you are on will determine how you walk through the storms. Many, when faced with hardships, turn to seeking the Lord and many just bury themselves deeper and deeper into the distractions trying to numb the pain. I never believe in chance but always believe things happen for a reason, especially if you are striving to find a God you do not know or to understand to a greater level. We serve an awesome God that desires none should perish, even though, He knows the outcome will be that the majority will perish. I by far would much rather face a storm knowing that my relationship with Him is strong and intact instead of facing a storm when I know I am living a double life. On the crooked road, many times there are road signs that warn of danger, but we tend to look away and continue traveling on farther and farther. It is at these times that the trials come because our choices were to continue on the crooked road and not seek God.

The majority who label themselves as a Christian and know enough of the Word to play the game are not ready to give up this world. How do you think this is going to work out in the end for you? Do you really believe that our God is going to look at you and your life when you stand before Him and say, *"Well, I see that you spent your life calling yourself a Christian, yet—you spent approximately 56 hours a week sleeping, 2 hours a week in church, 2 hours a week doing good works, 14 hours a week watching television, 27 hours a week talking on your cell phone or texting, 12 hours a week surfing the web, 1 hour a week with your daily devotion, 14 hours a week eating, 40 hours a week at your job, but I totally understand that life is hard; therefore, I'm going to say well done my son, you have made it to heaven."* You do the math, it is your life; however, if you really believe that is the God you serve, you do not know Him. He desires that we seek Him. He desires that we know Him. He desires that we walk with Him just like the disciples walked with Jesus daily. Let's add this up, the 2 hours a week in church plus the 2 hours a week doing good works and the 1 hour a week in your daily devotion comes to 5 hours a week. If you only spent 5 hours a week doing your job, would you really know your job? Do you think your employer would say, *"I see that you only worked 5 hours this week, well done!"* Or, if you only spent 5 hours a week with your family, how long do you think your marriage would work? Do you honestly think that 5 hours a week is going to impact your children to grow up to be real Christians or counterfeit Christians? Do you believe 5 hours a week will impact your children to grow up to be godly parents or to be parents who seldom spend anytime training a child in the way they should go, so that they do not stand before their Savior one day as He tells them to depart from Him? Your children will follow in your footsteps. They will become the type of parent that you are unless someone who chose to let go of this world happens across their path to teach them what you failed to. Hopefully, they listen or they will spend eternity in hell with their earthly parents.

You know the sad part is that hell is real and it is forever. Hell is suffering and being in pain forever. The worst part of being in hell for those who spent their lives as a lukewarm Christian is going to be living for eternity separated from Jesus Christ because at that point, they will understand that they had the chance to really know Him. You are going to realize that you had the chance to be in heaven with Jesus Christ for eternity, but you chose the things in this world over eternity. You are going to remember those times you heard that small quiet voice when you were sitting up under false teachings, and you chose to ignore that voice over and over again because your desire was for the things in this world. You are going to remember at some point that you didn't hear that voice anymore because He will not call you forever. You are also going to realize that you will never hear that voice again and not only will you never hear it, you will also realize that you can cry out all you want to for His forgiveness, but He will never hear you again. You can pray and you can call upon His name but it is over. You are going to know that you had the chance to spend eternity in heaven with a Savior that died for any who would accept Him. You are going to realize that you traded eternity in heaven away for all the possessions you acquired on this earth and you traded it away for your status, for popularity, and for money. You are going to spend eternity in hell remembering that you could have had heaven but your choice was to enjoy fleeting pleasures for a short time. All of this sounds pretty dismal, but that is not all. There is one more thing that those who are sent to hell will spend eternity suffering over, and that is for those who had children. As a parent, if you did not do your part to live and breathe real Christianity to your children, more than likely they will be spending eternity beside you in hell. This will be another area of regret as you cannot turn the clock back and change anything. You will spend eternity living in darkness suffering, as your children will also be suffering beside you.

Let me say, God does not send anyone to hell, we send ourselves there as we make the choice to never seek Him. We will never seek Jesus Christ out of fear for hell but out of the true desire to really know Him. It will only be those who have developed that deep intimate relationship with Jesus Christ that will desire to let go of this life and live for Him. When things in this world become our god, we cannot have both. Living in hell is living in darkness because we are outside of the light and God is light. Jesus cried out on the cross, *"My Father, why have you forsaken me," (Matthew 27:46)* because He was able to feel what those outside of the light feel. Jesus was able to feel what it was like to not be able to cry out to His Father and hear His voice. Jesus was able to know what it feels like for the Father to be absent from Him. All those who have never really heard His voice, live every single day outside of His presence. There is no love for Jesus Christ/God when you have never experienced being in His presence. Hell will be living in darkness forever and ever without the Father's presence in your life. Those who truly love Him are willing to let go of anything that would separate them from His presence. It's time for those who are His that are living outside of His presence today to rise up and seek Him diligently, so that they are in communion with Him. It is only by this means that we can save others. We are useless and have no good fruit when our lives do not portray to those we love and to complete strangers how great our God really is.

Sacrifice Our Life for Others

There is a story that I have written about in one of my books that I am going to share here as well. I'm not going to go into deep detail but enough for you to get my point. Years ago, I was at a place that God placed me, and it became evident why I was there, as the night went on. A young man had approached me and began talking to me. After a short-time, he began to share a tragedy that had happened in his life a few months prior. It was evident that this young man was in a lot of pain, and it was also evident that God needed me at that moment to share with him but also God needed to teach me something. The story was that his younger brother was drowning when they were at a lake, and his father jumped in naturally to save his son. The father did save the boy, but the father was unable to make it back to shore and he drowned. A lot of pain was in that family; however, what I want to share is that there is not a parent out there that would not sacrifice their own life to save the life of one of their children. However, this is saving the child from a natural death. On the other hand, there are very few parents willing to save their own children from a spiritual death. Why is this? The reason is that we are a selfish people and unwilling to let go of the things in this world that are all passing away to even save our own children. It amazes me when I see the countless mothers out there that are so addicted to social media that they seldom spend any one on one time with their children. There are fathers out there that are not fathers to their own children. They have no problem in being the sperm bank but are vacant in the lives of their biological children because they are unwilling to rise up to be what God called them to be. Children today are being taught by what they read and listen to on social media because it has become our babysitters, so that parents can live out their own selfish lives fulfilling the lusts of the flesh in whatever capacity that might be—music, movies, video games, and lusts of the flesh to include pornography, fashions, motorcycles, automobiles, sports, higher education, hair styles, cosmetics, etc. Look at your own life and the things you love and are unwilling to give up, these are the lusts of the flesh. Those things become your god. Lukewarm Christians fit into these categories which are no different than the world. Lukewarm Christians have made their place in this world and are unwilling to be different than the world.

Let me say, this generation of people are being molded to fit into a society that is doomed for hell. There are churches on every corner to make us feel like America is a godly country, but America is the home to the most fake Christians in this world. You may disagree but other countries do not play church like America does except those countries that have been heavily influenced by American Christianity. We have countries that are cold because they do not believe, and we have countries that do believe and do not live like Americans striving for the riches of this world. America is considered rich but whoa to those who claim to be Christians and desire the riches of this world. America has bought into a persona of what a Christian should look like, but you cannot find that type of Christian in the Word of God. This generation of children are being raised to be conformed to this world, just like their parents who do not have time for them. This generation of parents are all about themselves. You can see this when you start paying attention to the mothers in public or in their own homes, as they seldom put their cell phones down. My people perish from lack of knowledge and discipline.

Hosea 4:6a (NKJV) My people are destroyed for lack of knowledge.

Job 36:12 (NKJV) But if they do not obey, They shall perish by the sword, And they shall die without knowledge.

Proverbs 5:23 (ESV) He dies for lack of discipline, and because of his great folly he is led astray.

Our lives have to be disciplined. If we are not disciplined, we will not do those things which produce life instead of death. It is funny how we are disciplined in areas that satisfy our flesh but not in those areas that produce life to our spirit. Feeding our flesh is so much easier than feeding our spirit; however, as long as we cater to our flesh, our lives will only be filled with those things which are darkness to God. How much knowledge are you gaining each week through the Word of God to be able to penetrate that knowledge into your children? What is teaching our children today? Is it the television and social media? Is it the musicians and movie stars? Are they being taught what is real or what is false? Are they being taught how to be a disciple of Jesus Christ or how to be a counterfeit Christian? Are they being taught that life is hard as a true Christian? Are they being taught that they will be hated and persecuted if they live according to Biblical standards? Are they being taught that it is okay to be different and stand out as a Christian? Are they being taught that they only live in this world and are not of this world? Are they being taught that their choices in this life are crucial in making it to heaven? Ask yourself, in the end, how is this going to work out for your children? How is this going to work out for the little people that you claim you love but are unwilling to let go of this life that is leading the majority to hell? You are traveling that highway system even though you have some truth, and you are making the choice to lead your own children to hell with you. In the end, He says, *"Depart from me because I do not know you."* How is your life currently working for you? Be your own judge based on Scripture, where do you believe that your children will spend eternity? Remember, if you are wrong, you will live for eternity in hell watching your own children suffer side by side with you! Perhaps, you do not have children, but I'm sure there are people out there that you love and your life could be an example to them as well.

As we draw closer to Jesus Christ, we learn of Him. In learning of Him, we begin to learn God's ways and His thoughts. I can remember the breakthrough myself many years ago as it was like a lightbulb going off in my mind. My way of thinking began to line up with His way of thinking in different areas. I finally understood that God's ways were not our ways. His thoughts were not our thoughts.

Isaiah 55:8 (NKJV) "For My thoughts are not your thoughts, Nor are your ways My ways," says the LORD.

Living in the Desert

We often encounter hardships and trials because He is trying to get our attention and remove things within our heart that need to be removed and add those things necessary that we need in order to walk this walk and find that narrow road, where we can grow and become more Christ-like. As we allow the Holy Spirit access into our lives, we should count it all joy for hardships to come as they bring us closer to Jesus Christ. When we gain this knowledge, we can accept the troubles in our lives knowing that God does everything for our good, even though we may not know what His final plan is, but we can count it all joy because we are being led by our Lord Jesus Christ. Who do you want leading you in this life? Do you really want to be the one guiding your steps or do you want an all mighty God who loves you taking the wheel? I remember years ago hearing the song, *Jesus Take the Wheel*. Let me tell you, when that song came out, I was in a dark place in my life having decided to steer my own course all the while trying to keep Jesus in the back seat. I was a lukewarm Christian because I chose to associate with the world all over again. It was a very dark time in my Christian walk where I made a lot of bad choices. I can remember the pain I felt when I heard that song. I can remember crying and crying because I did NOT want to be the one leading my life, but it was so hard finding my way back to where I could get my life on track again. We must come to a place where we make the decision to let Him take the wheel. We must come to the place where we let Him lead our life and accept the necessary storms into our life, in order that He can continue to do the work within us that needs to be done for our own good. Christians really need to study His Word as it was given to us, so we can walk through this life with His wisdom. We should avidly study in order that our walk becomes pleasing to Him, where we do not fall into the same trap as the children of Israel in the desert. We have examples all through the Bible for our own good if we would just study.

Let's look a bit deeper at the children of Israel and their walk in that desert place. They were not satisfied, even though God had brought them out of slavery. The children of Israel were lukewarm in their walk with God. Those who are on that lukewarm road are in slavery in the spiritual sense, as they are blinded by truth. It is no different than the children of Israel. There is only one light, one truth and if our choices are to be like this world, we are in bondage from the truth.

John 8:31-32, 34 (ESV) So Jesus said to the Jews who had believed him, "If you abide in my word, you are truly my disciples, ^{32}and you will know the truth, and the truth will set you free." ^{34}Jesus answered them, "Truly, truly, I say to you, everyone who practices sin is a slave to sin.

Everything may seem good just like it did to the children of Israel because they were having a moment of time in their sin, while Moses had gone to the top of the mountain to spend time in the presence of God, in order to hear His voice clearly without the distractions. Moses' focus was on being in God's presence and in His perfect will. Moses' focus was being able to accomplish what he set out to do which was to lead God's people to the promised land. Our promised land is heaven, and there are ministers of the Word of God that have chosen to step out from the majority and seek God on the narrow pathway, in order that they hear His Word. In gaining truth, these ministers bring it back to the people in hopes that some hear and receive where they are spared from the same fate as the children of Israel. Those few that have stepped out to bring truth to a world full of lukewarm Christians are standing at the top of a mountain looking down on our world as it is currently, and they see that same vision that Moses saw as he began descending from the mountain. The multitudes below are running around doing their own thing living out this life, as they please. They are busy fulfilling their lusts of the flesh and being conformed to this world. They have constructed idols that they have bowed down to serve. This is what the lukewarm population looks like. They all have idols just as they did when Moses came down to give them wisdom from God. Are we rejecting that wisdom today, as they did in Biblical days? You be the judge.

We can live in this world day by day to satisfy our flesh but when times get tough, that is when those who claim to be Christians, the lukewarm, run to a church for prayer in order that God intervenes and saves them from their trouble. This is the children of Israel. You also have those who hide up under a ministry and they label it Christianity, but it has their own personal mark all over it. It has their agenda, their preferences, their choices, their lifestyles, etc. Jesus is NOT the one leading them, but their own selfish desires and motives are leading them. This is also the children of Israel. When we remain in those places that God has not called us to, He will allow us to fall. God will allow us to be blinded because of our own disobedience.

The outcome of our choices will eventually go in a direction that we were not expecting or produce a storm in our lives that brings great pain, then who will we be blaming? Many blame God at these times. How about those people who have lost a loved one to some kind of tragedy, who do they blame? Many times, they blame God. The children of Israel were never satisfied; they constantly blamed God for taking them out of slavery into a desert area where they had freedom, but they did not like the lifestyle. The children of Israel did not want to embrace the storms even though they would have subsided eventually, if they had just had faith in God and trusted Him with their life. Yet, so many times we think that we know what is best for our lives not God. This again is putting God in a box and seeing Him as a small God not a big God. If we really studied Scripture, we would be able to learn more about God's ways and understand why there must be trouble. When we understand that the trouble comes for a reason, we can then learn to walk through that particular storm all the while trusting our Savoir, as He walks with us. There are always things in our lives that need to be removed and things added. God is continually doing a work in us but when we fight His methods, we gain nothing except eternity in hell. We remain on that highway that leads to hell because our choices have been to only give God so much and to only allow Him access to a small portion of our lives. We are not willing to let go of who we are, what we have, etc. in order to allow a big God to completely transform who we are from the inside out.

Philippians 2:12-13 (NKJV) Therefore, my beloved, as you have always obeyed, not as in my presence only, but now much more in my absence, work out your own salvation with fear and trembling; 13for it is God who works in you both to will and to do for His good pleasure.

1 Thessalonians 2:13 (NKJV) For this reason we also thank God without ceasing, because when you received the word of God which you heard from us, you welcomed it not as the word of men, but as it is in truth, the word of God, which also effectively works in you who believe.

When the Knocking Stops

As we travel on those crooked pathways, if we will turn our attention to our Creator and seek Him, we may be able to see the detour signs as He tries to warn us to get off of that crooked road. It does not matter where you are on that crooked road, God always has a detour that will lead you to the narrow road but it takes turning to Him, turning away from your sin and letting go of this life.

Proverbs 1:23-31 (NKJV) Turn at my rebuke; Surely I will pour out my spirit to you; I will make my words known to you.

²⁴Because I have called and you refused, I have stretched out my hand and no one regarded, ²⁵Because you disdained all my counsel, and would have none of my rebuke, ²⁶I also will laugh at your calamity; I will mock when your terror comes, ²⁷When your terror comes like a storm, And your destruction comes like a whirlwind, When distress and anguish come upon you. ²⁸"Then they will call on me, but I will not answer; They will seek me diligently, but will not find me. ²⁹Because they hated knowledge And did not choose the fear of the LORD, ³⁰They would have none of my counsel And despised my every rebuke. ³¹Therefore they shall eat the fruit of their own way, And be filled to the full with their own fancies.

We want to believe that God is always there if we call out to Him; however, Jesus Christ stands at that door and knocks but He will not knock forever. There comes a time when the knocking stops. Those who are lukewarm and continue to base their salvation from what is taught on the pulpit every single week are treading in deep water as they have chosen to make a mere man into their god. When we spend all of our time pouring into this world and not into the WORD of GOD, eventually my friend, the knocking will stop!

Revelation 3:20 (NKJV) Behold, I stand at the door and knock. If anyone hears My voice and opens the door, I will come to him and dine with him, and he with Me.

In this Scripture, Jesus was speaking to the church of Laodicea, which were those who were considered the lukewarm. He has NOT given up on those who are lukewarm, but He is knocking and this is a heartfelt knock. Many have felt this knock and rejected it. I heard this knock many, many times in my life. There were times I rejected the knock and other times, when that knocking put me on my knees, as I cried out to God for forgiveness. Jesus calls us my friend, and He calls us by knocking on the door to our conscience due to our choices in this life that are leading the majority to hell. The great dangers in this day are the many choices to religion; however, there is only one clear pathway. Wolves are on every corner striving to gather up the lost sheep and lead them astray. This is Scripture being fulfilled daily, as there are many false shepherds leading them on the wide pathway to hell. Ask yourselves today, who is feeding you? Are you seeking Jesus Christ intimately one on one, pouring into His Word, or are you allowing a mere man to lead your steps in the direction of his teachings?

Jeremiah 50:6 (NKJV) "My people have been lost sheep. Their shepherds have led them astray; They have turned them away on the mountains. They have gone from mountain to hill; They have forgotten their resting place.

The time is coming where Jesus will return for His sheep. The state of those who claim to be Christians is very sad today, as we look at this world and cannot tell the Christians from the non-Christians. We see a sleeping church today that does not have eyes to see nor ears to hear. The church today is none other than a cult of religion that has caused a scattering of the sheep by the modern-day Pharisees. The majority of *"so-called"* Christians live by religious rules and man-made interpretations of the Word of God, distorting the true Gospel of Jesus Christ.

Hosea 10:12 (NKJV) Sow for yourselves righteousness; Reap in mercy; Break up your fallow ground, For it is time to seek the LORD, Till He comes and rains righteousness on you.

In this day and age, the knocking is there because sin is rampant. The knocking is our warning, are you listening? The knocking is our salvation, are you listening? The knocking is getting louder and louder, but the majority are so caught up in their own lives that they continue to tune out that sound. They continue to live day in and day out, as if their wickedness is not really that wicked. They continue to live day in and day out, as if their choices for this world are not really choosing evil over good. How long will His people ignore His ways?

How long will His people be blinded by truth, and how long until the knocking stops?

1 John 2:16 (ESV) For all that is in the world—the desires of the flesh and the desires of the eyes and pride of life—is not from the Father but is from the world.

There was a time in America, where the preaching lined up with the Word of God, but that time is no more. Today, there are the few compared to the multitudes that actually stand up to teach Biblical, sound doctrine. Those wolves who stand on the pulpits of the majority of churches today teach heresies, as they blasphemy the Holy Spirit. Their religious doctrine is accursed by God and those who choose to continue following a man instead of God will be damned with them.

2 Timothy 3:12-13 (NKJV) Yes, and all who desire to live godly in Christ Jesus will suffer persecution. 13But evil men and imposters grow worse and worse, deceiving and being deceived.

There was a time when America did not have all the distractions that we see today; America did not have the lifestyles that we see today. Our choices daily do not honor God. The result of all the new technology has had a great cost to the American family, as we see the reality of broken homes, fatherless children, drug addicted youth and adults, sexually addicted men and women, sensuality and conformity to the lifestyles that are portrayed by Hollywood, as these idols have infiltrated within the majority of homes beginning with the parents and passed down to the children. satan has been brought into the majority of homes, as those who claim to be Christians are blinded by the truth. The majority believe that internet and cable television is harmless and are blinded to the effect that it has on them and their children. The modern-day churches have conformed to be like the world, in order to continue to grow and live like their idols as well. These churches operate in the flesh, as they are powerless to the true gospel of Jesus Christ. How did we get to this place? If you go back to a different timeframe, this was NOT Christianity. How then did we get to this place? This my friend is all Biblical as we are told in the end times, sin will be rampant. How did this evil spread so fast among the people? It spread by all the technology that we live by daily, and it has become our god! The majority who read this will be nothing more than the rich young ruler, as Jesus told him to go and sell everything. I have touched on this story, but let me say, what that young ruler felt in his heart was the feeling of really wanting to serve Jesus Christ, but he knew that he could NOT let go of that part of this world. The majority who read this already know that they cannot let go of this part of their life.

Let me say, I have technology but IT DOES NOT CONTROL me! There are some things I choose to NOT have, one of those is cable television. I choose what I allow on my television. I choose to be disciplined. I use the internet to research and study His Word. I choose what I will read. I choose places that I will go. All of these things are discipline, but it is allowing the Holy Spirit to lead and guide your steps and to hear that knocking on your heart when you are out of place. Do NOT ignore that knocking because as you ignore that sound, you will step further and further into sin and compromise more and more. Remember, one day the knocking will stop! There are times when our distractions in this life are so loud that we cannot hear that knocking, but it is there. There are times when our televisions are too loud or our music is too loud, and we cannot hear that knocking. I'm sure most of us can say there was a time in our lives that someone came and knocked at the door to our homes and we really did not want company, or we did not know the person at the door. What did we do? We ignored the knock and what happened? Eventually, the person went away. My friend, a day will come when the knocking stops because we have chosen to ignore that knock, and He will NOT knock forever.

Romans 1:28 (ESV) And since they did not see fit to acknowledge God, God gave them up to a debased mind to do what ought not to be done.

We do not acknowledge God when we do not open that door. How do we know if we are not opening the door? Our lives will be filled with the sin of this world. Read further into Romans chapter 1 and you will see the list of the characteristics of all those who chose NOT to open the door and allow Him access into their lives, in order that He could clean up the filth on the inside.

Romans 13:11-14 (NKJV) And do this, knowing the time, that now it is high time to awake out of sleep; for now our salvation is nearer than when we first believed. [12]The night is far spent, the day is at hand. Therefore let us cast off the works of darkness, and let us put on the armor of light. [13]Let us walk properly, as in the day, not in revelry and drunkenness, not in lewdness and lust, not in strife and envy. [14]But put on the Lord Jesus Christ, and make no provision for the flesh, to fulfill its lusts.

Luke 13:25-27 (ESV) When once the master of the house has risen and shut the door, and you begin to stand outside and to knock at the door, saying, 'Lord, open to us,' then he will answer you, 'I do not know where you come from.' [26]Then you will begin to say, 'We ate and drank in your presence, and you taught in our streets.' [27]But he will say, 'I tell you, I do not know where you come from. Depart from me, all you workers of evil!'

We may be lost as a goose on that crooked road, even though we are surrounded by the majority and there are distractions on every corner; however, if we would just stop and get on our knees to cry out to Him, this is the beginning to know Him and hear His voice. Our choice is the highway or His way. Making the decision in our heart begins with humbling ourselves and turning to Him, so that we become real and not some counterfeit Christian. This is the beginning to turning from a life that leads to hell to the Truth. We do a complete 360°, turning around from our old ways to allowing Him access, as He begins to transform us into the image of Jesus Christ. As it is, we are the image of the world. It takes true repentance to bring about that change and a willingness to let go, as the Holy Spirit cleans up our lives.

Revelation 3:3 (ESV) Remember, then, what you received and heard. Keep it, and repent. If you will not wake up, I will come like a thief, and you will not know at what hour I will come against you.

Revelation 3:19 (NKJV) As many as I love, I rebuke and chasten. Therefore be zealous and repent.

Acts 3:19 (NKJV) Repent therefore and be converted, that your sins may be blotted out, so that times of refreshing may come from the presence of the Lord.

2 Corinthians 7:9-10 (NKJV) Now I rejoice, not that you were made sorry, but that your sorrow led to repentance. For you were made sorry in a godly manner, that you might suffer loss from us in nothing. [10]For godly sorrow produces repentance leading to salvation, not to be regretted; but the sorrow of the world produces death.

A word of encouragement, you may currently be traveling on that road which zigzags here and there, but the good news is that you do not have to remain on that road. If you are in the midst of a place where you cannot seem to find God, the good news is that you recognize you need to find Him. Once you know this, you need to continue to cry out to Him alone for forgiveness—true repentance. You need to cry out to Him for direction, so that you can find that narrow pathway that leads to heaven. We cannot redo the things we have done and are ashamed of, but once we make that commitment to make it right and strive to walk out this life on the narrow road, we can leave a mark for those we love with the time we have left. It does not matter how young we are or how old we are, God's plan has always been to use those who diligently seek Him in order to share truth with those who are lost and don't even know it. It's all about loving like Jesus loves and the willingness to continue this journey no matter how hard it gets.

CHAPTER TWELVE
CROSSING OVER

If you have come this far in this book, hopefully, your desire is to surrender where your journey begins to take you to the place where you find that narrow pathway. In crossing over, we must surrender our lives daily to Jesus Christ and allow the Holy Spirit access into our whole being. This happens as we begin to let go of areas in our lives and replace wasted time in this world with time in the Word of God or doing His will. This takes discipline and prayer. It takes a commitment to Our Lord Jesus Christ that you have come to the place of surrender, and you are ready for that next journey.

There may actually be many out there that desire to find that country road, but finding it can be a struggle. When we have experienced the pleasures of sin, it is very hard to let go of those strong holds in our lives completely, where we can actually hear the true voice of God that will lead us to the narrow road. Even though, we may know what is right and what is wrong, because of experiencing the pleasures of sin, it is hard to let go of this life as we know it but not impossible. If we look at David, the Bible tells us that he was a man after God's own heart. David loved God dearly, but he had weaknesses that he struggled with overcoming. If you have not read the story in its entirety, I challenge you to do so. Most of David's life is covered in 1st and 2nd Samuel.

To begin with, let's review the highlights of this man's life. David was the youngest of the seven sons of Jesse. Some of David's ancestors were Jacob, Judah, Boaz, and Ruth. Throughout the years, the great traditions of this gallant family were maintained by the house of Jesse, David's father. The noble traits of all his great and well-known ancestors were bestowed upon David. The prophet Samuel, hearing from God, was told to go to Bethlehem where he would find the future king among one of the sons of Jesse. Samuel was to anoint one as king to replace Saul. When Samuel was presented with the 6 oldest sons of Jesse, he knew none of them were the one who was to be anointed as king. Jesse, then called for his youngest son who was tending the sheep and when presented to Samuel, he knew by divine revelation that David was the chosen one. At that time, Samuel anointed him as the future king of Israel.

Moving forward in the story, Saul, being stricken with an evil spirit, had fallen into a deep melancholy and not knowing that David had been anointed as the future king, he summoned for him to play music on his harp. It was at this timeframe that King Saul was battling the Philistines, which were their longtime enemies of Israel. This was where David encountered Goliath, a Philistine giant who shouted out to the crowds of Saul's army as the Philistines stood on one side of a mountain and Israel on the other side. Goliath was about 10' tall and he was clad in armor made of bronze from head to toe, with a javelin that slung between his shoulders and a spear made of iron. Taunting the Israelites, he shouted for a man to come forth to fight and whoever would win that fight, the loser would serve the other. This greatly frightened the Israelites, for there was not a man brave enough to go forth to fight Goliath. For forty days, Goliath came and stood on that mountain shouting out to the Israelites but none would go forth. David, going back and forth from the king to his father's house to tend the sheep each day, had gone to take his brothers who were fighting in this battle with the Philistines, provisions. Hearing the words spoken by Goliath, David inquired about this man who would defy the armies of the living God. In leaving, David went to Saul to let him know that he would go against this Philistine. Saul, stating that David was merely a youth, could not fight such a man. In 1 Samuel 17, we see his response.

1 Samuel 17:37 (ESV) And David said, "The Lord who delivered me from the paw of the lion and from the paw of the bear will deliver me from the hand of this Philistine." And Saul said to David, "Go, and the LORD be with you!"

Up to this point, we see a very young man of God who had walked with the Lord for many years. As the story goes, we know that David went forth for Israel, and God allowed Goliath to fall to the ground with merely a stone and a slingshot. What **we** are uncapable of doing, God is more than capable. From this point in David's life, he became part of Saul's family, marrying his youngest daughter, fighting wars for Saul, etc. God blessed David's life tremendously and eventually, he became king of Israel.

Many times, in our lives, we desire for more of this world and to be elevated to a place where our name becomes known. In Old Testament times, we see many of God's chosen elevated to a high calling but New Testament times, we have a greater calling and riches have a way of bringing people to an end. Old Testament times, being elevated by God also came at a cost, as was the case with David. Yes, he was a man after God's own heart but he also was human and had weaknesses which cost him severely.

David's trouble began due to his polygamy of having eight wives. Polygamy was common in those days; however, it was not consistent with Scripture as we can see all the way back to Genesis. God had prescribed marriage to be between one man and one woman. When we go forth and decide to even divorce and take up another spouse and have multiple children by different women or men, this brings a flaw to the model which was set down by God for a reason. We can see today the result of so many children who have one parent absent, and these children suffer the consequences which becomes a pattern. In America, we have made it so easy to take off the old and put on the new. In David's timeframe, you didn't have to take off the old, you just merely took in more wives to add to your collection. David's lust for women eventually led him to commit adultery with Bethsheba who was married to Uriah, a man who was a leader in David's army. When Bethsheba became pregnant, David pretty much construed a plan to have Uriah murdered. Besides these issues, it was evident in the lives of some of David's sons who had sexual sins as well. One of his sons raped his sister and another one murdered the one who raped her. David was grieved by these instances, but he chose not to do the right thing by disciplining his sons when they were wrong. When we make the choice to walk away from living our life according to Scripture, there are always consequences. David's lifestyle portrays times where he walked closely with God and had favor, and there were times when he missed the mark and had to pay the consequences. Our lives are no different. David's sins cost him greatly, for he had a daughter who was raped, lost one son who was murdered by another son, and eventually that son was killed as well. Other costs to David's sin was paying the price for committing adultery with Bethsheba, as their son who was the result of sin died as an infant. David, being a man after God's own heart, committed one sin after another but he still loved God. When I look at David's life, I see so much of my own. Yes, we are all capable of committing much sin and we do and I have. However, if we belong to God, we will go through many trials and storms in order to get it right. God knows those who are his and if you are one of His, your life will be a hard road. You will face circumstances you never thought possible. You will make wrong choices followed by the right choices. You will feel like a failure at times but relieved on other occasions, as you know you made right choices. However, when we miss the mark, we will always face consequences to our choices, but if our heart is right with God, he will not forsake us. Let me make this clear. It is through true repentance that we are forgiven and restored back to God. True repentance is salvation through faith. Without faith, believing on the true gospels of Jesus Christ, we will NOT be saved. Without true repentance, we will NOT be saved. True repentance is turning completely from that sin and continuing your walk with God, even though, you will still have to pay the consequences to your sin.

Choices

As I said, desiring riches and fame in this world, can lead you to a place where you really don't want to go. The result of our choices daily will determine our pathway. David at one time was traveling a righteous pathway that led to God but as he was given more by God, he began to day dream about his desires, even though they were not godly. Many times, in our walk with God, He blesses us financially or places us in a higher role which gives us authority over others. In those high places, if we do not stay in check with God by seeking Him diligently, we may slip. I'm not going to say fall because we are told that even though we may stumble, He will not let us fall.

Psalm 37:23-24 (NIV) The LORD makes firm the steps of the one who delights in him; 24though he may stumble, he will not fall, for the LORD upholds him with his hand.

However, this Scripture pertains to those who are His. If you are not in a true relationship with Jesus Christ, you will fall. When we find ourselves faced with temptations, we should always run to God instead of away from Him. It is when our choices become doing what we desire instead of seeking God that we stumble. When David began to fantasize over another man's wife, he should have run to God.

Let's look at a few scenarios. First, let's assume that you have found and experienced the narrow road. Like David, if you find yourself slipping onto the highway system striving to stay on the narrow road, but you keep getting deeper and deeper into your sin, you must get alone with God and begin diligently seeking Jesus Christ for strength. We try to do things in ourselves and run from God instead of to God because of shame, but that is what satan wants us to do. We cannot overcome sin in ourselves, and we cannot take away our fleshly desires without His strength. Running to God no matter how ashamed we feel is the only way to overcome and gain the strength we need to get back to the country road.

Another scenario is that perhaps your life has grown cold, where you began meditating on your desires until you found yourself fulfilling those desires. You have then gone full force into the highway system, even though, you have continued to hear His voice. This can be a very dangerous place because we have studied in chapter 11 that eventually, the knocking will stop. Eventually, you will no longer hear His voice. The other danger here is that none of us are guaranteed tomorrow. People die suddenly every single day and then it is too late to make things right with God.

The last scenario I want to emphasize is one where you are reading this book right now, and you know you are on the highway system living in sin and have never experienced the country road. I pray that you are reading this book because you desire to really know Him. Maybe your experience of Christianity has to this point been based on some watered-down message, which is prevalent in most of the churches today. You are cold or lukewarm, but you are not hot because you are basically lost where there is not wisdom and knowledge based on the true Word of God. You are living buried deep in sin. The good news is the *Good News*. Jesus died that none should perish but all should find Him. You have the choice to detour. Yes, get off the interstate or highway as fast as you can. Seek Him diligently and allow the Holy Spirit into your life. How do you do this? The same way that the disciples of yesterday did this. It is not some man-made prayer or ritual. It is where you begin to diligently seek Him. Today, we have access to Bibles in America. You get a Bible and you begin to read the New Testament—you cry out and you pray for His wisdom and knowledge, and you DO NOT STOP! You continue daily seeking and praying, and He will come to you. Warning, satan will also send all kinds of distractions to try and keep you conformed to this world. Don't give up, continue and continue. It does not matter how many times you feel that you are on a zig zag pattern because you probably are. Do not go with the flow but go against the flow until you learn of Him and find Him which will lead you to that country road. He will begin His clean up in your life where there will be many, many choices. Choose Him and choose Him and continue to choose Him. Let go of everything you can let go of, as He molds and makes you into His image.

Let me emphasize something here that is important before I continue on sharing about David. I said above, *"Do NOT go with the flow!"* Think of a river, the majority who claim to be Christians are flowing down stream with the world because it is much easier than going against the current. Remember, the Bible tells us that it is only the few that really make it to heaven. It is only the few that dare go against the crowds. The Bible also tells us that our ways and our thoughts are NOT God's ways nor thoughts. I have already covered this in Scripture. With all of this in mind, you have to begin to think out of the box. You cannot think like the crowds or you will be taking the easy road which is downstream with the current. The Bible also tells us that the wide road is easy and the narrow road is hard. Going against the current in a river is very hard, my friend. My life following Jesus Christ has had much heartache and pain. The *"so-called'* Christian community have been quick to tell me that I must be doing something wrong, but the Bible tells me that my walk will be a hard road to travel, nothing easy about it. Be ready for a hard road because this world is NOT your heaven, unless you want this world to be the only heaven you will ever see. With all of this said, think out of the box. I never buy a Bible that has man's philosophies and opinions in it. These mega-church leaders are quick to cash in on having their own study bible out there, so that they can steer your thoughts and beliefs to follow them not Jesus Christ. However, there are some good study Bible's out there but until you know which preachers are real and which are wolves, stay clear of what you choose to study. Another thought, also be wise what version of the Bible you choose. It is much better going with one of the older versions such as KJV, NKJV, and one of my favorites is the ESV. Newer versions continue to be made that are gradually changing the wording which is not real noticeable yet, but eventually these newer versions will become the norm for our society, where the gradual changes will become more evident but not to those who are not disciplined in their study time with God and His Word. At some point, investing in the *Strong's Concordance* is a must since you can look up words in the Greek and Hebrew to get the actual meaning, since these were the original translations of the Bible.

One more thing to consider about David, I have heard many justify their sin through his story, but we better be very careful there. There are always consequences to our sin and David was no exception. Even though, God loved him dearly, sin has consequences. As if losing his first-born son by Bethsheba was not enough, if you continue to read the story you will see that David almost lost his throne and his kingdom was never again the same. David paid a huge price for his sin, but he learned from that sin and accepted the consequences by God. Once we have tasted the country road, there may be times like David that we step back onto the zig zag of the highway system. However, like David, we accept the consequences to our sin and make things right again. Did David continue to go back and forth from the narrow road to being lukewarm? The Scriptures lead us to believe that once David had come to terms with his sin against God and accepted the consequences, he was ready to continue his walk with God remaining on the narrow road and striving to fulfill his duty to God. David lost a lot, but he didn't lose God.

The narrow road is not an easy road to follow. There are many times that I miss it and take a detour but thankfully, I hear that voice calling me to get back on track. It's very painful at times and very hard, but Jesus told us that this walk would be a hard walk. He never called us to a life that would feel good to our flesh because it will always be about disciplining our flesh.

Storms

The good news is that even though the narrow road will sometimes be treacherous and we will find ourselves in the midst of a storm, God never ever meant for us to remain in those storms. As we grow closer to Him, we will learn of Him. In knowing Him deeper, we will eventually understand that storms come and go in our lives for reasons. Storms are meant to shake things up a bit.

As we look at storms in the natural, we can actually come to a place where we realize there is meaning in the storms. Think about a fierce storm in the natural that you may have encountered. Many times, storms can take things away but they can also add things. I taught a lesson many years ago and have written about one such storm. This particular storm happened in 1883. It began with a volcanic eruption that sunk two thirds of the Krakatau Island located in the Indonesian province of Lampung. Tens of thousands of lives were lost as there were also tsunamis that followed this eruption. The massive amount of material deposited by this natural disaster dramatically altered the ocean floor surrounding the island and significantly increased the land mass of its neighboring islands. In 1927, there was another eruption that once again took away land mass from the Island of Krakatau and created another smaller island that they called Anak Krakatau which meant *child of Krakatau*. If you would like to read about these natural disasters, you can google Krakatau eruption of 1883 and Krakatau eruption of 1927. There are several accounts written on both of these. Please note, the spelling is frequently noted as Krakatoa, but the correct spelling is Krakatau.

A natural storm helps us to be able to understand spiritual storms. In a spiritual storm when we are going through a tough time, we seldom stop to think that just maybe God is doing a work in our lives and the outcome will all be worth it. For the natural disaster, because of the storms or eruptions, there were things taken away and things added. The neighboring islands gained more land mass and Krakatau had less land mass. In 1927, a whole new island was created and named as the child of the original island. Looking at this in a spiritual sense, we come to the Lord to change our lives and we really get more than we bargained for but not understanding how God works, we murmur and complain because we fail to comprehend. In our storms, God is merely removing things that need to be removed and adding things that need to be added. God sometimes will remove things in the natural and sometimes even things spiritually that are not of Him. He also adds things that need to be added. As God is doing a work in us, when we submit to Him and just trust Him, it will not take 40 years like it did the Israelites. When we trust the work that He is doing in us, one day we will awaken and realize that we are a child of God just as Anak Krakatau is a child of Krakatau.

Storms are His way of making us more like Him. He knows what we need more than we do, and the Holy Spirit was sent to us as a helper to begin this cleanup process in our lives. As we submit to the Holy Spirit and allow the necessary changes within our lives, we will begin to see how to walk through the storms knowing that we were never meant to remain in them. All storms are for a season and go much quicker when we stop fighting the changes necessary with our lives. As we walk through the fires unblemished, through the waters without being drowned, and through all that the enemy throws our way without being shaken, the Holy Spirit will build a whole new spiritual being, and we will be called a *child of God.*

CHAPTER THIRTEEN
LIVING OUTSIDE OF CHRIST

There may be many out there that desire to find that narrow road but they remain on the outside of that road because of their choices. The narrow road is a hard road to travel and it cannot be done without His wisdom and His guidance on a daily basis. It cannot be done without His love and His passion.

Living outside of Jesus Christ, you will never be able to gain the passion to really know Him intimately. When we are passionate towards someone or something, this is an emotion that is very strong and cannot be contained, as it will spill over onto all those we come in contact with. It's like being filled to overflowing with the Scriptures in our heart because of the massive amount of time we spend seeking Him. Would it not be awesome to daily be so full of the Word of God that we live out this walk with so much passion that our lives radically change the lives of those that are in constant contact with us? This is the walk of Jesus Christ. Jesus was full of passion as He was the Word made flesh, and He overflowed with those very words that radically transformed the lives of those who were fortunate to know Him personally. When we have this same kind of passion inside of us, we will go forth and seek first the Kingdom of Heaven.

Matthew 6:33 (NKJV) But seek first the kingdom of God and His righteousness, and all these things shall be added to you.

Several years back, I visited Eureka Springs in Arkansas and took my granddaughter to see the Passion Play, which is performed on the side of a mountain with amazing men and women who portray the walk of Jesus on this earth all the way to the Cross. You cannot sit there and watch this play without feeling the emotion and passion towards Our Creator. God, in all of His majesty, He did not need to save man but He desired to save man. His love for mankind is pretty amazing that He would suffer for all who would turn to Him. This is passion for mankind and without having that kind of passion, you will never ever be able to walk the narrow pathway that leads to heaven. Without this kind of passion, your walk will merely look like the walk of this world which is outside of Jesus Christ. We have passion for following Jesus Christ not because we feel forced to follow Him or because of fear that we will go to hell, but we have passion because we have come to know Him. Passion and intimacy go hand in hand. You cannot have one without the other. If you are married or have ever been married, there was passion that led you to that altar and in the same sense, there will be passion that leads you to the Cross.

We cannot make ourselves fall in love with Jesus, but we can seek and seek and seek until we find Him. Truly finding Jesus Christ is the only way that you will fall in love with Him. When you fall in love with someone, you desire to spend time with that person. It's the same thing. I hear people all the time say that they have a hard time disciplining themselves to spend time in the Word of God or in prayer—time spent with Him. Yes, we must be disciplined, but we will never find it easy to spend time with someone that we are not in love with. It is about true love, the God-kind of love. God is love and outside of Him it is merely the world kind of love. We seek Him because we love Him. Let me say, seldom will anyone fall in love with someone else when they do not know them. There are some who may say that they fell in love with their spouse the moment they saw them, but that is merely falling in love based on the outward person. Real love in a marriage has nothing to do with looks, but it has everything to do with falling in love with that person for who they are on the inside. If we marry for the wrong reasons based on looks, money, etc., we know nothing about true love. Marrying someone should be based on spending time with that person prior to making those vows, in order that you connect with who they are on the inside. It is not different with Jesus Christ. You cannot fall in love with Him without spending intimate time with Him. The majority of those who claim to be Christians do not even know Him. Your relationship with Jesus is about the time that you choose to spend with Him one on one. Your relationship with Jesus will not be based off of what a man or woman on the pulpit shares about Him on a weekly basis. Your marriage would never last very long if you live in a home with your spouse but you never ever communicate. You would be strangers in your own home and that is what leads many to the divorce court. Relationships suffer today due to people living for this world not for the world to come. Our lives have been programmed to strive for a good life here on earth, as we let go of the promises in the Word of God. Our passions have turned for the things in this world, and there is no room for Jesus Christ. As long as we are surrounded by the things in this world, the temptations are so strong that it is impossible to walk out this walk in Christ by ourselves. However, that is why Jesus tells us that nothing is impossible through Him.

Mark 10:27 (NKJV) But Jesus looked at them and said, "With men it is impossible, but not with God; for with God all things are possible."

There is not a Christian out there that will ever be able to walk this walk in themselves. This is why we must seek Him daily, so that He leads us. We need His strength and His wisdom. We need to look to Him for all things and have the willingness to let go of those things we try to hold on to that will not save us. The material wealth in this world will be the death of most who call themselves Christians because it is hard to let go of this world and the things in this world.

Colossians 3:1-2 (NKJV) If then you were raised with Christ, seek those things which are above, where Christ is, sitting at the right hand of God. ²Set your mind on things above, not on things of the earth.

When your heart is right because you have truly found real Christianity and your walk is genuine with the Lord, there will be a change within where those things you once cherished in this world, no longer have value.

Proverbs 11:28 (ESV) Whoever trusts in his riches will fall, but the righteous will flourish like a green leaf.

Matthew 16:26 (NKJV) For what is it profit to a man if he gains the whole world, and loses his own soul?

Luke 8:14 (ESV) And as for what fell among the thorns, they are those who hear, but as they go on their way they are choked by the cares and riches and pleasures of life, and their fruit does not mature.

Esteeming the Riches of God

A really good story to read about is the one of Moses. I'm not going to go deep into this story, but we can learn from this man's walk. You can read the full story in the Old Testament, the books of Exodus, Leviticus, Numbers, and Deuteronomy. However, I want to make mention of the Scripture in Hebrews.

Hebrews 11:23-29 (NKJV) By faith Moses, when he was born, was hidden three months by his parents, because they saw he was a beautiful child; and they were not afraid of the king's command. ²⁴By faith Moses, when he became of age, refused to be called the son of Pharaoh's daughter, ²⁵choosing rather to suffer affliction with the people of God than to enjoy the passing pleasures of sin, ²⁶<u>esteeming the reproach of Christ greater riches than the treasures in Egypt; for he looked to the reward.</u> ²⁷By faith he forsook Egypt, not fearing the wrath of the king; for he endured as seeing Him who is invisible. ²⁸By faith he kept the Passover and the sprinkling of blood, lest he who destroyed the firstborn should touch them. ²⁹By faith they passed through the Red Sea as by dry land, whereas the Egyptians, attempting to do so, were drowned.

Moses had the world at his hand. He was considered the daughter of Pharaoh because she had raised him. He had all the riches and anything he desired but for some reason, he chose to walk away from all of it. Moses walked away because he *esteemed* the riches of God to be greater than the riches of man. In other words, Moses had an encounter with God to believe that He was God. In Moses' heart, he knew that there were far greater riches awaiting those who would dare walk away from the riches of this world to follow the voice inside. Evidently, Moses heard that voice and knew it to be so real, that he chose not the riches of this world but the world to come. We can learn a lot about this man because he had everything that money could buy in those days, but he chose instead to leave all behind and follow that which was invisible to the natural eye.

We need to be thankful for what we do have and desire those things above not what is here to tempt us. As Jesus stands at the door knocking, the majority are so caught up with the distractions in this world that many who call themselves Christians never hear that knock. Perhaps some of them do hear and their response sounds something like this, *"Okay, I'm going to start back praying tomorrow,"* or maybe they are saying, *"Yes, Lord I hear you and will begin reading my Bible again starting tomorrow."* The said truth is that most continue to put it off and put it off, hearing His voice but there will always be tomorrow and tomorrow never comes.

Revelation 3:20-22 (AMP) 20 Behold, I stand at the door and knock; if anyone hears and listens to and heeds My voice and opens the door, I will come in to him and will eat with him, and he [will eat] with Me. 21 He who overcomes (is victorious), I will grant him to sit beside Me on My throne, as I Myself overcame (was victorious) and sat down beside My Father on His throne. 22 He who is able to hear, let him listen to and heed what the [Holy] Spirit says to the assemblies (churches).

In ourselves, we will NEVER be able to be disciplined to do what it takes to run this race to the finish line. This is a warning to the church; we are the church if we are His people. There may be times in your life where you cry out to Him and the door does not open. When we are busy with the things of this world, distracted with the things of this world, we may cry out to Him in our pain, but we hear nothing because we have not been listening to His calling. We may not hear His calling because we are only listening to hear what we want to hear. The majority, many times they already think they know God when they really do not know Him. We should never just speculate that we know Him and know His ways because we are not God. Just like the Pharisees, they too thought they knew God and that is why they rejected Jesus. Their perception of who God was did not line up with the teachings of Jesus. In reality, they never wanted a God that would require them to change their lives and to give up their idols. We see this same thing with the majority today who think they know God.

People do not want to let go of those things in this life that distract them. They want to believe that they do know God and do know who Jesus is, but their god fits into their own personal life that they have strived to create in themselves. Yes, I know myself what those distractions are in my own life, as I too have had to make some hard choices but it has been worth it. I have heard His voice many times, and there are times I chose not to listen and then other times, I made the choice to listen and obey. When I choose not to listen, there is normally a consequence to my disobedience where I have to run back to Him for forgiveness. I also have to accept the consequence for not listening.

My People are Destroyed for Lack of Knowledge

In my own life, God has allowed so many storms because His desire was that I was able to see through those storms and understand. In any natural storm that affects our lives, we have a hard time being able to see. Over the years, I have lived in several states and have driven through many storms to include snow storms. I have had to pull over many times in my travels because the storms would be so fierce that I could not see physically. Many times, there are those who are faced with natural storms that choose to continue on their route even though the roads are treacherous. Many times, those who strive to continue in a storm instead of listening to that inner voice, they perish. I have read many stories and watched many true accounts that were made into movies of disasters that happened because there were those who would continue when it was NOT safe.

Traveling here and there in this world outside of Jesus Christ can be treacherous. When we ignore that inner voice and we make up our own mind that we are going to follow in the path that we choose, it can be perilous. Two scenarios to consider, one is a natural storm which could be an earthquake, hurricane, tornado or any other type of natural disaster that causes damage and hardship in our lives, and two would be those physical storms that suddenly bring affliction to ourselves or someone we are close to. This first scenario, we may encounter a natural disaster where the outcome causes something tragic to happen. Most people have a hard time understanding why God would allow this to happen, especially when they believe that they know God and believe that they are following Jesus Christ. For the second scenario, those who face physical storms in their lives where there may be a terminal illness or situation similar, most question why God would allow these things to happen, especially when they feel that they are following the right pathway. I believe what people fail to see is that there are many hidden treasures in the Word of God. We are told in His Word to seek Him. We are told that there would be hardships. We are told that the road to heaven is a hard pathway, nothing easy about it. We are told that only few will even find it. We are told that God's people perish from lack of knowledge in several different Scriptures which I am going to emphasize on these.

Hosea 4:6 (NKJV) My people are destroyed for lack of knowledge. Because you have rejected knowledge, I also will reject you from being priest for Me; Because you have forgotten the law of your God, I also will forget your children.

In this Scripture, God was speaking to Hosea who was a priest. God's purpose was to enlighten Hosea about rejecting knowledge. When we reject knowledge, God's knowledge, are the consequences not the same for us? Remember, knowledge is reading and studying the Scriptures to really know and understand God, so that we come to understand why we face hardships or storms in our lives. There are always reasons, but we murmur and complain instead of seeking our God for answers and understanding.

Job 36:12 (NKJV) But if they do not obey, They shall perish by the sword, And they shall die without knowledge.

If you read in Job from the beginning in 36:1, you will be able to see that Elihu was much younger than the three friends of Job who had come to give wisdom to Job, even though their words were foolishness and not wisdom from God. Elihu had sat and listened for some time, out of respect for those who were older and possibly wiser. However, once the three men had shared much of their worldly wisdom, Elihu spoke up to share to Job what he saw which were words of wisdom. In verse 12 above, these words apply to all who would seek God. He was giving wisdom on who God is. Our God will walk with anyone who seeks Him diligently and spends the time to know Him. The Scriptures go back once again to listening and obeying. We are not seeking Him or striving to gain His knowledge when we choose not to read and study Scriptures. I will say this, but this is something I continue to say in my books, you cannot come to know Him through the teachings of someone else. Knowing Him is personal, one on one. If we claim to be Christians but we never study the Word of God, we are merely counterfeit Christians that will never find that narrow road. We will perish.

Proverbs 5:21-23 (ESV) ²¹For a man's ways are before the eyes of the LORD, and he ponders all his paths. The iniquities of the wicked ensnare him, and he is held fast in the cords of his sin. He dies for lack of discipline, and because of his great folly he is led astray.

This Scripture does not say we perish from lack of knowledge but from lack of discipline which is vital to gaining knowledge. God's eyes continually see the paths we choose to take which are wicked, and our choices hold us in captivity where we eventually die in our sin due to lack of discipline. Where should we be disciplined? If you are a parent, then you would admit that you desire that your children are disciplined in doing the things you expect and not doing that which you forbid. Of course, as parents, we also know that our own children do not always adhere to what we tell them. This is where they are disciplined by us because we desire that the end result to be that they grow up to do well. We also discipline them and expect them to live according to our rules set down because we love them deeply and want to protect them from bad things happening. When our children step out and disobey us to do whatever they want, many times this places them in a situation that is dangerous and there are many young people all over the world that die due to not going by the rules. One example, would be drinking and driving which can results in an accident. God is no different, other than, His love for us far out ways our love. The majority of those who claim to be Christians do not have the discipline, and therefore, they have not gained the knowledge. We are deceived by the many lies we hear in this world and especially in the many churches that teach false messages, in order to snare the people, all the while leading them down the pathway that leads to hell. This my friend, is lack of knowledge and to change this, we must discipline ourselves to seek that knowledge.

Let me clarify something here, we are all created in His image and those who claim to be Christians, do so because they also claim to believe in God. You may believe that God's people could be referring to just the Jews, or you may believe this could also be referring to all those who claim to be Christians, as well. However you choose to look at this, the point I want to make is that just because someone thinks they are going to heaven does not mean that they will go there. His people perish from lack of knowledge. We perish because we do not know the truth. Knowledge is knowing. Knowledge comes by reading, studying and listening. When we try to walk through this life as a counterfeit Christian based on someone else's beliefs, we will perish. We cannot gain knowledge if we are not reading and studying ourselves. Yes, God is an awesome God and he also sends others across our path that we should pause and listen. However, if we are not reading and studying ourselves, we will never know if what we are listening to is true or false. We must be disciplined to studying the Word of God.

2 Timothy 2:15 (KJV) Study to shew thyself approved unto God, a workman that needeth not to be ashamed, rightly dividing the word of truth.

We should be studying that we know truth! We will never know God if we never spend time in the Word of God. As Timothy tells us, we should be rightly dividing the Word of Truth. How do you divide the Word of Truth? You do it with your sword. The sword divides, it is sharp and it cuts through dividing that which is NOT God from that which is God! We are told to put on the whole armor of God, this is part of our gear, and the sword which is the Word of God! Our sword rightly divides the truth. Without studying the Word of God, there is No truth in us.

Ephesians 6:17 (ESV) and take the helmet of salvation, and the sword of the Spirit, which is the word of God.

Our sword is the Word of God! If you do not read and study His Word, you are not equipped for battle, meaning that you are not going to win in the end! The Word of God divides that which is true from that which is false, but if we are so busy in this world trying to live like the world, we will be fighting on the wrong side. You cannot fight the battle to save your soul when you have no clue what a true Christian is supposed to look like.

Heb 4:12-13 (NKJV) For the word of God is living and powerful, and sharper than any two-edged sword, piercing even to the division of soul and spirit, and of joints and marrow, and is a discerner of the thoughts and intents of the heart. [13]And there is no creature hidden from His sight, but all things are naked and open to the eyes of Him to whom we must give account.

It is His Word that divides everything. It divides what is true and what is false. It divides what is sin and what is not. It divides the true Christians from the false Christians. It divides those living in this world from those living in Christ. Are you living outside of Jesus Christ today? Do your choices in this world paint a picture of one who is outside of Jesus Christ or one that lives within the perimeters of the gospels of Jesus Christ?

I cannot sit in a sermon listening to a pastor giving a message without my mind dividing every single thing that man is saying. Let me say, if you spend enough time in Scripture and seeking God, when you sit and listen to a message, you will have Scriptures flowing through your mind as you are listening to what is being said. This is discernment which is the ability to judge well. We are to be able to discern all messages if we are truly seeking Truth! There are times that I can discern that which is false and other times, where I may not always agree but it may be an area that is not life or death. At those times, I go back to study the Scripture to discern what is truth. None of us know the Scriptures like Jesus because He is the beginning and the end; He was the Word made flesh for us.

John 1:1,14 (ESV) In the beginning was the Word, and the Word was with God, and the Word was God. [14]And the Word became flesh and dwelt among us, and we have seen his glory, glory as of the only son from the Father, full of grace and truth.

Revelation 22:13 (NKJV) "I am the Alpha and the Omega, the Beginning and the End, the First and the Last."

There is only One God, and He enlightens us to the truth and brings the Scriptures alive to us so that we understand and see the truth! I'm sure that once those who belong to Him make it to heaven, they will be able to see the truth of His Word fully. Until that time, we should be able to divide those messages to discern truth from that which is false, life from death. There are many times I see something differently from what is being spoken; however, it may not be something that is going to affect my journey on that narrow road. We were all created to be different, and we all learn at different paces, and see from different perspectives. However, there are times I have heard messages that are false teachings that the listeners following such will be led away from that narrow road, instead of securing their walk with Jesus Christ. It is at those times, I know I have no business being connected to that movement because it is one of the many that people run to in order to hear a message that makes them *"feel good"* instead of a message that awakens them to truth. True Biblical teachings will never feel good to our flesh, but this is where we choose to live by the spirit or by the flesh.

Seek First His Kingdom

If we are spending time in the Word of God, we are gaining the necessary knowledge needed to know how to walk this walk out and find that narrow road. We should always be seeking God above anything else in our lives.

Matthew 6:31-33 (NKJV) [31]Therefore do not worry, saying, 'What shall we eat?' or 'What shall we drink?' or 'What shall we wear?' [32]For after all these things the Gentiles seek. For your heavenly Father knows that you need all these things.

³³But seek first the kingdom of God and His righteousness, and all these things shall be added to you.

We should also be seeking God because our desires are to know Him not because we think that by serving the Lord of Lords and King of Kings, He will bless us with earthly treasures. This is taken out of context today and is one thing that leads the masses away from the truth. People want to serve a god that gives them the desires of their heart, not to serve a god that desires they walk away from the riches in this world, in order to give everything to Him. If your heart is right with God, your desires will not be for the riches of this world. It is only at the place where our heart is truly genuine that God can use us, in order to spread the true gospel to the world. Think about it like this, if you gain the riches of this world which are the desires of your heart, your heart is wicked and there is NO truth in you. Do you really want to be like this world or do you desire to be like Jesus Christ? Jesus had no desire for the riches of this world and if you focus on His walk while on this earth, it was not a walk of riches. However, it was a walk of the riches of God, but those riches are not what can be seen with our physical eyes only our spiritual eyes.

Matthew 6:19-21 (NKJV) ¹⁹"Do not lay up for yourselves treasures on earth, where moth and rust destroy and where thieves break in and steal; ²⁰but lay up for yourselves treasures in heaven, where neither moth nor rust destroys and where thieves do not break in and steal. ²¹For where your treasure is, there your heart will be also.

I always refer back to the two books of the Bible. There is a huge movement in the *"so-called"* churches that draw in the multitudes because the teachings are all about serving a great god that wants to bless them with riches of this world. Yet, we do not see that in the New Testament and the church is born out of the New Testament. Spurgeon said it best when he noted that the Old Testament promise was one of prosperity but the New Testament promise is one of tribulation.[1] The

New Testament gains Jesus Christ who is a Savior for those who desire to leave all and give up all to serve and follow Him.

Luke 14:26-27 (NKJV) "If anyone comes to Me and does not hate his father and mother, wife and children, brothers and sisters, yes, and his own life also, he cannot be My disciple. ²⁷And whoever does not bear his cross and come after Me cannot be My disciple.

First, let me say that Jesus also said that He came not to bring peace but division among man.

Luke 12:51-53 (NKJV) Do you suppose that I came to give peace on earth? I tell you, not at all, but rather division. ⁵²For from now on five in one house will be divided: three against two, and two against three. ⁵³Father will be divided against son and son against father, mother against daughter and daughter against mother, mother-in-law against her daughter-in-law and daughter-in-law against her mother-in-law."

We always think a life with Christ is filled with peace, but we must study Scripture in its entirety in order to get the bigger picture. The division happens in our lives when there are those who are striving to live a life with Christ and those who will not let go of this world. Our families are divided, governments are divided, countries are divided because there are always going to be those that make the choice to live as the world. However, those who truly belong to Christ are NOT of this world. The only way we live in peace is when we choose to live according to His ways not man's ways, but we will still experience the divisions of those we know as they will not be in agreement with us. Peace brings us back to the fruit of the Spirit since it is one of the characteristics of one who walks in His Spirit. We are called to live in peace with everyone, but that does not mean everyone will live in peace with us.

Hebrew 12:14 (NKJV) Pursue peace with all people, and holiness, without which no one will see the Lord.

Again, in 1 Peter, we are told to turn from evil. We cannot turn from evil if we try to hold on to this world. It is only as we turn from evil that we find that peace and we pursue it.

1 Peter 3:11 (NKJV) Let him turn away from evil and do good; Let him seek peace and pursue it.

Finally, it is the peace of God that guards our hearts and our minds where we can live out our days fulfilled, not with the riches and things this world has to offer but greater things that are unseen.

Philippians 4:6-7 (NKJV) Be anxious for nothing, but in everything by prayer and supplication, with thanksgiving, let your requests be made known to God; 7and the peace of God, which surpasses all understanding, will guard your heart and minds through Christ Jesus.

Yes, today we are divided by our beliefs and divided by religions and divided by different gods. Whom shall you choose because everyone chooses a god? When you say you have no god, in reality, you worship satan as your god or you worship this world and the pleasures within this world. However, if you are of this world, you are still bowing down to satan. We either belong to Christ and the world to come or we belong to satan and this world. Remember Jesus' response when He was told that His mother and brother were there to see Him? He replied that His mother, brothers and sisters were those with Him, following Him.

Mark 3:31-35 (NKJV) Then His brothers and His mother came, and standing outside they sent to Him, calling Him. 32And a multitude was sitting around Him; and they said to Him, "Look, Your mother and Your brothers are outside seeking You." 33But He answered them, saying, "Who is My mother, or My brothers?" 34And He looked around in a circle at those who sat about Him, and said, "Here are My mother and My brothers! *³⁵For whoever does the will of God is My brother and My sister and mother."*

In the same sense, when we are truly following Him and have let go of this world as we are commanded, our love will be first for Him and then for those who are truly our brothers and sisters in Christ. We will walk away from those who do not believe, even if they are relations to us in the natural. Above, in Luke 14, we are told to *hate* those of our relations, mother, father, etc. In the Greek, that word hate is miseo. Miseo means to detest, to persecute, to love-less, and to hate. We are told that if we do not hate all to include our own life, we cannot be His disciples. What we need to understand is that if there is anything in this world, any person in this world that we love more than God, we cannot be disciples of Jesus Christ. This includes hating our own life because the life we live outside of Him is contrary to His Word. In other words, we completely die to self that there is nothing or no one that takes precedence over our lives. This would include that we would die for the sake of the Gospels of Jesus Christ. When you look at the lives of those first disciples, you see that they gave up everything in their lives in order to follow and imitate Jesus Christ.

Man's Heart is Deceitful

I will say that if you reason with your mind, as it is renewed to the Word of God instead of reasoning with your heart which can deceive you, you will be able to see the true gospel as it unfolds in the Scriptures. I remember when I walked away from the majority, it was because I had started questioning what we call the church today. I questioned because the church we see in the Bible did not look like what we call the church in this day and time. It only took me stepping out to start seeking this difference, and my eyes began to see so much more than I would have ever dreamed, if I had not stepped away. Many times, we can perceive in our heart that we are following Jesus when we are not.

Jeremiah 17:9-10 (ESV) The heart is deceitful above all things, and desperately sick; who can understand it? ¹⁰*"I the LORD search the heart and test the mind, to give every man according to his ways, according to the fruit of his deeds."*

If you truly study and are led by the knowledge you gain in your mind through Scripture, you will be able to see that it makes sense that our walk should look like the walk of the first disciples. They were continually chastened by our Lord because His desire was to set them apart from this world. Once set apart from the world, their focus in walking as a true follower of Jesus Christ gave glory only to Him. By this, I mean that there were no riches set aside for those first disciples. Yet, lukewarm Christians follow a certain false ministry because their true desires in their heart are for the riches of this world, in whatever category they choose to class this according to the Bible. Of course, this is taught out of context! Whether the riches mean money in the bank, big homes and nice cars, to include all the luxuries the rich enjoy in America, or their riches may mean a life of security where they have just enough of everything that they desire to be happy. The New Testament does not teach anywhere of Christians gaining treasures in this world regardless of their value, but rather it teaches that they leave all behind to follow Him.

Matthew 24:37-39 (NKJV) [37] *But as the days of Noah were, so also will the coming of the Son of Man be.* [38] *For as in the days before the flood, they were eating and drinking, marrying and giving in marriage, until the day that Noah entered the ark,* [39] *and did not know until the flood came and took them all away, so also will the coming of the Son of Man be.*

This means that the majority will be living this life to its fullest, eating, drinking, marrying, enjoying life. This includes all who live just like this world, to include the counterfeit Christians. Yet, we are told to not store our treasures here on earth. *(Matthew 6:19-24)*

God has great plans for those who choose to step out and follow on a pathway where there is little evidence of the world being infiltrated into their lives. The word here is evidence. What evidence is stacked against you? When we stand before Jesus Christ one day, as our judge, He will determine if you are guilty or innocent. The evidence will either be in your favor, or it will condemn you to a life of hell. What evidence is stacked against your life today? Is there evidence that you fit in with this world, or is there evidence that you are alien to this world? It will take letting go of this life, if your heartfelt desire is to live eternity with Jesus Christ because you love Him over every single thing in this world! It takes making choices that the majority will never make. It takes studying and reading where you give your life for His purpose, not for your own desires.

Romans 8:1-4 (NLT) Life in the Spirit ¹So now there is no condemnation for those who belong to Christ Jesus. ² And because you belong to him, the power of the life-giving Spirit has freed you from the power of sin that leads to death. ³ The law of Moses was unable to save us because of the weakness of our sinful nature. So God did what the law could not do. He sent his own Son in a body like the bodies we sinners have. And in that body God declared an end to sin's control over us by giving his Son as a sacrifice for our sins. ⁴ He did this so that the just requirement of the law would be fully satisfied for us, who no longer follow our sinful nature but instead follow the Spirit.

We choose to follow in the steps of Jesus Christ not in our sinful nature. Jesus is at the door knocking for those who truly seek Him. If we allow the distractions of this world access into our lives, we may never hear that knock.

I have always been a people watcher where I sometimes sit in places observing those in this world. If you step out of your comfort zone and begin to really gain knowledge from the Word of God, go to a crowded place and just sit down to observe the people of this world. It is amazing how you begin to have a different perspective once you have begun to gain truth. In watching people, you see those pouring the music of this world into their soul; you see this generation watching the perversions through the entertainment in Movies and Hollywood in general; you see this generation filling themselves with so much darkness which fills their minds and their hearts; you see this generation striving for the riches, striving to satisfy their earthly bodies, striving to gain success, striving to gain the wisdom of this world; you see this generation looking up and admiring all those in this world who have achieved greatness whether that be in riches or fame; you see this generation bowing down to all their idols; you see this generation striving to satisfy all the desires of their flesh; you see this generations serving the god of this world in all capacities; you see this generation so blinded by the truth that they do not know God; you see this wicked generation living it up for today unconcerned about what tomorrow could bring. I was in the work place for many years, around people daily who claimed to be Christians. It has always amazed me of how many in the work place claim to be Christians, yet outside of the church building, the filth comes flowing out of their mouth because it is in their heart. They seem to be good people from the world standpoint because they are educated by the standards of this world, they hold high places in business, make good money, give to the church, married with a family, attend church services regularly, living as this world lives because there is no difference among them.

These lukewarm Christians fit in perfectly among the world and their numbers are great! According to the standards of God, what it takes to be a real Christian, they will never make it to heaven unless they stop playing church and get real. These counterfeit Christians enjoy many of the same pleasures of this world, which the god of this world has to offer. They have not sacrificed their life to be worthy to serve Jesus Christ.

Consider Your Ways

A vision that God gave me one day as I was sitting and looking out at the many people, what I saw were crowds of people but no one was going in the right direction. All the people were going in different directions, looking in different directions as they were scattered about not concerned with where they were headed and not considering where they were or considering their ways. This is a picture of the church today, we are told as in the days of Noah, it will be the same when Jesus comes back. Do we not consider our ways? Do we not think about just maybe the road we are traveling ends at a destination unexpected?

Haggai 1:5-6 (ESV) Now, therefore, thus says the LORD of hosts: Consider your ways. ⁶You have sown much, and harvested little. You eat, but you never have enough; you drink, but you never have your fill. You clothe yourselves, but no one is warm. And he who earns wages does so to put them into a bag with holes.

I believe that many who are blinded in this world choose to remain at that place putting their trust in the false teachers that are out there by the multitudes. I believe it is easier for them to do that instead of facing reality. In traveling with the crowds, we tend to think that since we are not alone, just maybe it will not be all that bad. Just maybe Jesus will look at our good deeds and not how we spent the majority of our time trying to fit into this world. Most people do not really want to find the narrow pathway, if truth be known as I have said. Most want to believe that they are already on that narrow pathway. Most will never stop to think about what that pathway actually looks like. Most will never study the Scriptures to unfold the many truths that are hidden and not preached from the majority of the pulpits in America.

There are also many who believe that God with all of His mercy will understand that as Christians in these earthly bodies, it is impossible to live in this life sinless. There is a great distinction about living a life for Christ and living a life for your own desires. As true Christians, we will never be perfect but our lifestyles will change. True conversion is a changing experience. True conversion is like a lightbulb going off where you all of a sudden do not have the same desires you once had. Real Christianity is seen in those whose minds change, whose desires change where their life begins to look to Jesus daily to lead them out of sin and into a walk that most will not go. This pathway is not filled with the distractions of this world. This pathway is not about gaining anything in this world. This pathway is not self-motivated. This pathway is not about gaining your place in this world. Real Christians are okay with being separated from the world for His good. Real Christians hear His voice and are okay with letting go of things in their life that are hindering their walk with Jesus Christ. Those who struggle and are unable to walk this walk have become a slave to sin, but real Christians seek Him to overcome.

John 8:34 (ESV) Jesus answered them, "Truly, truly, I say to you, everyone who practices sin is a slave to sin.

In chapter 11, I touched on being a slave to sin but what exactly does that mean? If you are in bondage to sin, this is living outside of Christ. The opposite of bondage is freedom. As Americans, we have freedoms that other countries do not have; however, most of us live each day never even thinking about what it would be like living in a country that had no freedoms. We live each day as if everything is pretty good; other than, the normal problems that we may face. In America, we have many privileges that we also take for granted. Most of us can eat when we want, sleep when we want, go where we want to go, etc. We have our luxuries such as a home with running water, air-conditioning, heat, electricity, cars, jobs, money in the bank, etc. We can buy books that we want to read, clothes that we want to wear, etc. Life in America is pretty great because of the freedoms, but in reality, all of these free choices have captured the majority of people today as they are blinded by the truth.

There is only one truth and that is the Bible. God's Word is truth. Even today, in a court of law, you must swear that you are telling the truth. I'm not sure that the Bible is still used in all courts of law today, but the Bible was the origin in the judicial system when it evolved. However, today, I do not believe that swearing is going to make that person who is in trouble be truthful. It is only having a true relationship with Jesus Christ that one would tell the truth, even if the outcome was not in their favor. However, are we really free? Not according to the Bible, we are not! Being a slave to sin is bondage in the spiritual sense and is far worse than being in bondage in the natural. The laws were first created by God, and it is His laws that are the ultimate deciding factor on the outcome for your life. You may live a pretty good life here on earth, but it is short-lived compared to eternity. You will face the judge of all judges on your final day, and your judgment on where you spend eternity will depend on your relationship with Jesus Christ. I could say that eternity for you would be decided based on the sin in your life, but most would come back and say that we are all sinners and no one would make it to heaven. You are absolutely right! However, Jesus dying on the Cross did not give us a license to sin. On the contrary, He sent the Holy Spirit to live with those who would seek Him, and it is through this spiritual aspect that we are able to overcome the sin. This does not mean that we will NEVER sin, but it does mean that our lifestyles will be totally different than the majority who claim to be Christians. As Jesus tells us in the above Scripture, whoever practices sin is a slave to sin.

Romans 6:22-23 (ESV) But now that you have been set free from sin and have become slaves of God, the fruit you get leads to sanctification and its end, eternal life. 23For the wages of sin is death, but the free gift of God is eternal life in Christ Jesus our Lord.

Overcoming Sin

So, how exactly do we overcome sin in our lives where we live out our lives being pleasing to God? Those who sin are a slave to sin, but those who overcome are free but they become slaves of God. The good news is that they who are slaves of God are full of the fruit of the Spirit, which leads to sanctification and eternal life in heaven. We overcome as we seek Him. I cannot say this enough, you will NEVER overcome the sin in your life if you are trying to do this in yourself, and you will never walk away from sin if your lifestyle spends very little time putting anything of God into it because your desires are full of this world. We cannot serve both God and the things in this world! *(Matthew 6:21)*

I remember hearing once, to think about just *"one"* thing that you desire which consumes most of your thoughts daily and/or your time. Is it a sport, perhaps your children or spouse, someone you love, video games, your job, music, or anything else that you think about on a daily basis? Be sure to include anything that consumes your time such as your computer or cell phone. You see, whatever things or person that consumes your time and thoughts becomes your idols. I have ministered to so many people who claim that they never have time to pray or read their Bible much less study the Word of God. It is NOT that we do not have time, it is because this generation has replaced those things which should be priority with things of this world that will lead them straight to hell. Living outside of Jesus Christ is living your lifestyle just like the majority of the world who are all dying and going to hell. It comes down to people saying that they believe in God because they believe there is a God, but they do not really believe in God as in knowing Him.

Do you ever wonder why we live in a world like we do? Do you ever think about how this world has advanced so fast in such a short time? If we look back in time, the first car was invented in 1885 and just look at what the cars look like today. In 1879 was when Thomas Edison invented the light bulb. Indoor plumbing started showing up in other parts of the world in 1829 but it was not until 1930 when indoor plumbing began arriving in America. The blow-dryer for hair was invented in the early 1900s but in America, it was in the 1960s when you began seeing the hand-held blow dryers, and they were not everywhere until in the 1970s. I remember growing up that we were not able to get the hand-held models until in the 70s. Home computers did not hit the market where homes could afford them until the 1980s. Mobile phones were not affordable for the majority of people until the mid to late 90s. I don't have to go any further because since that timeframe, the world as we know it has entered a different era where everything has exploded! What I mean by that, is technology is so far advanced in such a short time and continues, that it is hard to keep up with buying the latest and most advanced of anything technical. All these new advancements also continue to be more accessible and affordable for the majority of Americans, but at what cost are all of these luxuries?

Our lives have been made easier with washing machines, dryers, all the kitchen gadgets and all the latest in technology, but at what cost are all of these things? It is a huge cost because if you are honest, there are things that have captured your desires. Our desires are no longer for the simple things in life but for the inventions of man. We are warned in the Bible about loving this world. If your lifestyle is one where you enjoy spending countless hours each week enjoying the luxuries and entertainment of this world, the cost of all of these things will result in your spiritual death because you cannot serve this world and Jesus Christ too! The answer to the question, what does a slave to sin look like? You can look at all of those living in this world programmed to the entertainment and luxuries of this world, as they are conformed to this world. This is why the Scriptures tell us, *"As in the days of Noah,"* because we are in those days!

If your desire is to truly follow Jesus Christ, it takes letting go of the things in this world and pouring into Him. If you discipline yourself to spend time and time and time in His Word as you study and seek, you will be filled. It is in the fullness of Him that when you sin, immediately, you turn from that sin and ask for forgiveness. This all is determined by what is in your heart. If you have so much of Him in your heart because your choices are to fill your eyes and ears with good and not evil, that is what your heart will be full of. As He flows through your being, you will not be able to commit the sins you once could. When you miss it, out of a grieving heart, you run right back to Him. In time, your choices are to walk away again and again from the lifestyle you once had.

Life of Holiness

Living outside of Jesus Christ is a lifestyle of sin instead of holiness. To be in fellowship with Jesus Christ leads to a lifestyle change where the evidence is a life of holiness. When you are called to this lifestyle, you are set apart. The word holy means to consecrate. Let's break this apart, the word consecrate means to make or declare sacred or to dedicate to the service of a deity. Consecrate also means to set apart. God calls us to a life of holiness where we are set apart from this world. Basically, we are separated from those things that displease God. When we live outside of Jesus Christ in our lives, in reality, we are living in the midst of the very things that displease God. When we make the choice to let go of the desires of this world and submit to the lifestyle of Jesus Christ, we are set apart from this world and dedicated to the service of following in the footsteps of Our Creator. You better bet that when you are walking according to Scripture and following Jesus Christ, not some man-made religion, that your service will be a divine nature as your desires are to fulfill His will not your own.

Leviticus 20:26 (NKJV) And you shall be holy to Me, for I the LORD am holy, and have separated you from the peoples, that you should be Mine.

2 Corinthians 7:1 (ESV) Since we have these promises, beloved, let us cleanse ourselves from every defilement of body and spirit, bringing holiness to completion in the fear of God.

Hebrews 12:14 (NKJV) Pursue peace with all people, and holiness, without which no one will see the Lord.

Romans 6:22 (NKJV) But now having been set free from sin, and having become slaves of God, you have your fruit to holiness, and the end, everlasting life.

A lifestyle of holiness is not just about being separated from the things which displease God. Man has a way of trying to turn everything into a formula where they work hard at trying to overcome this world, as they strive to let go of the things in this world, in order that they feel they are separated from the things which displease God. Many times, man does these things as works because they are doing them in themselves and not through the Holy Spirit. Outside of the Holy Spirit, none are righteous and any works you may do in order to try and ensure your salvation, are merely works without love. God is love and through Him, we manifest that love and because of that love, our desires change and it is NO LONGER works through us that manifest the change. To simplify this, God only desires a people who will love and honor Him. Throughout Scriptures, He says, *"And they will be My people and I will be their God."* However, throughout Scripture, people turned from Him. People turn from God because their response to that statement has always been, *"Yes, I will be His people IF He fixes the problems in my life, IF He blesses me with the riches of this world, IF He heals my body of sickness and disease, etc."*

The question today is, if He will be your God and you His people, is God not enough? Is He enough if there is NOTHING else? The answer throughout the Scriptures by the majority has been, *"No, that is not enough!"* The answer today by the majority and their actions show that this is NOT enough! Yes, through yourselves, it is hard to overcome sin in your life because in reality it is impossible. However, we are called to holiness that can only be obtained through the work of the Holy Spirit in our own lives. Without the Holy Spirit at work in us, we cannot overcome sin! So, it is not enough to just be separated by the things that displease God. Holiness is not a formula or a list where we make ourselves do certain things trying to produce a life that looks holy. Holiness is the manifestation of the hunger and desire to know God intimately and to love Him intimately. God desires a people that love Him and have the desire to know Him. All throughout the Scriptures, He says, *"They shall be my people and I shall be their God!" (Genesis 17:7,8; Exodus 20:2,5,7,19,20; Exodus 29:45; Leviticus 11:45; Leviticus 22:33; Leviticus 25:38; Numbers 15:41; Leviticus 26:12,45; Ezekiel 14:11; Ezekiel 34:24; Hosea 13:4; Joel 2:27; Joel 3:17; Zechariah 8:8, 2 Corinthians 6:16, Jeremiah 32:38, Ezekiel 11:20; Ezekiel 34:31; Ezekiel 37:3, 27, Jeremiah 7:23, Jeremiah 31:1, 33; Revelation 21:3, 7; Exodus 6:7; Jeremiah 11:4; Jeremiah 30:22; Ezekiel 36:28; Psalm 50:7; Psalm 81:10; Isaiah 41:10; Isaiah 41:13; Isaiah 43:3; Zechariah 10:6)*

New Testament:

Hebrews 8:10 (ESV) For this is the covenant that I will make with the house of Israel after those days, declares the Lord: I will put my laws into their minds, and write them on their hearts, and I will be their God, and they shall be my people.

As we are called, we are chosen to be His people and our lifestyles are transformed to be a lifestyle of holiness.

Deuteronomy 14:2 (ESV) For you are a people holy to the LORD your God, and the LORD has chosen you to be a people for his treasured possession, out of all the peoples who are on the face of the earth.

We are called out from all the people of the earth to be set apart for His purpose not living conformed to this world.

2 Corinthians 6:16-18 (ESV) What agreement has the temple of God with idols? For we are the temple of the living God; as God said, "I will make my dwelling among them and walk among them, and I will be their God, and they shall be my people. ¹⁷Therefore go out from their midst, and be separate from them, says the Lord, and touch no unclean thing; then I will welcome you, ¹⁸and I will be a father to you, and you shall be sons and daughters to me, says the Lord Almighty."

Psalm 4:3 (ESV) But know that the LORD has set apart the godly for himself, the LORD hears when I call to him.

2 Corinthians 7:1 (ESV) Since we have these promises, beloved, let us cleanse ourselves from every defilement of body and spirit, bringing holiness to completion in the fear of God.

We are told many things in the Word of God about our eyes and our ears. I have discussed in depth about our eyes and ears throughout this book, as being the openings to our heart. They are the gateway to our soul. These are the two openings for the outside world to enter, and they are also the opening to receive the wisdom and knowledge of the Word of God. For anyone to awaken to the true gospel of Jesus Christ, they must guard those two openings. What is on the inside of us, in our heart, depends on what we choose to read, watch on television, those things we read and listen to on social media, those we associate with as well as those we sit under that share the Bible. The majority somehow think that they can pour as much of this world into them as they desire, as long as they attend a church service from time to time and strive to be considered by the world's standards a good person. However, if you study Scripture you will begin to see that most of what comes from the pulpits in America are not sharing truth which does no good to those in attendance that really need the truth, in order to be set free from sin and death.

Romans 8:2, 5-8 (ESV) For the law of the Spirit of life has set you free in Christ Jesus from the law of sin and death. ⁵For those who live according to the flesh set their minds on the things of the flesh, but those who live according to the Spirit set their minds on the things of the Spirit. ⁶For to set the mind on the flesh is death, but to set the mind on the Spirit is life and peace. ⁷For the mind that is set on the flesh is hostile to God, for it does not submit to God's law; indeed, it cannot. ⁸Those who are in the flesh cannot please God.

If you are lukewarm, living outside of Jesus Christ, you need to read Revelation to see what Jesus had to say about the churches. Jesus speaks of the lukewarm, as well as those churches that strive to be rich. I teach on this from time to time, but if you will look at the seven churches, place the church you attend in one of those categories and see what your outcome will be. Those that Jesus claimed that they see themselves as rich, He sees them as poor. How do churches see themselves as rich? That would be those huge ministries filled with multitudes. After all, in order to be considered rich by this world's standards, you must have a lot of money in the bank. The more you can convince people to give, the more money you will gain. The more your messages line up with what the people want to hear, the more people that will come. The more people, the more money in the bank. However, He also says that those who see themselves as poor, He sees them as rich. That my friend would be a small church that does not have a multitude of people attending or a multitude of money flowing, but some of those continue to strive to teach those attending the true, bold messages that people do not want to hear. Riches to God have nothing to do with our paper money. Our money in this world was created and made by man; one day it will all pass away and be totally worthless.

We struggle many times with being able to walk according to the way Jesus' disciples walked. The reason is because we must train our eyes and our ears to read and listen to those things which are going to bring about a change within our lives, as it pertains to Scripture. An example, we are told to think on those things which are pure. How is that going to work when your thoughts are far from pure? As we strive to live a life with Christ, we put more and more of Him inside of us where more and more of the world that is inside will be pushed out. What is not pure will not remain, as it is replaced with that which is pure.

Philippians 4:8-9 (ESV) ⁸ Finally, brothers, whatever is true, whatever is honorable, whatever is just, whatever is pure, whatever is lovely, whatever is commendable, if there is any excellence, if there is anything worthy of praise, think about these things. ⁹ <u>What you have learned and received and heard and seen in me</u>—practice these things, and the God of peace will be with you.

Notice in verse 9, Paul tells us that what we learn, receive, hear and see in him, we should practice those things. Paul is to be an example to us because in his race to gain eternal life, he was on that narrow pathway. He taught those he ministered to that they should learn from him. We should learn from him. How do we learn from Paul, or how do we learn from anything in the Word of God? We train ourselves to daily spend time pouring into His Word and allowing those things to penetrate within our heart. What we choose to read and listen to is what our heart will be full of. People have no problem spending countless hours pouring into social media which is filling their hearts with so much of the world, it is no wonder that the world is perishing and taking the majority with it. We must awaken that our desires are to be filled with truth.

Paul tells us to imitate him as he imitates Jesus Christ. I remember a pastor years ago telling his congregation to imitate him, as he was imitating Christ. I knew this man very well and basically, he lived like the lukewarm. I remember him telling his leaders that it was okay to tell those they were ministering the same thing. I remember thinking, *"I will not follow anyone on this earth today whose walk does not look like Paul's walk."* Let's face it, there are not a lot of people in this world whose walk looks like Paul's walk. There's not a lot of people in this world whose walk looks like any of Jesus' actual first disciples. I'm not saying there are not those out there that are not walking as Paul walked, but I am saying that we have Paul as an example and that's good enough. Even though, I hear the Lord's voice many times and in my own walk there have been times I walked very closely with the Lord and times I struggled. However, my point is that I would never dare tell anyone to follow me as I follow Christ. I am called to lead others to Christ not to lead them to me, as I follow Him. Was Paul wrong in doing this? Absolutely not, Paul had firsthand knowledge of Jesus Christ and just as John the Baptist, they gave up every single thing in their life to walk in Jesus' footsteps and to die doing so. We have so many great examples in the Word of God that are there to help us see more clearly how to walk out this walk.

Living outside of Jesus Christ is merely living and breathing with no hope for tomorrow. We are all created in His image and there is so much more to life than living in bondage to this world instead of spreading our wings to soar through another realm that brings us up under His wings. Living in bondage will never allow your eyes to truly see nor your ears to truly hear His message for you today.

CHAPTER FOURTEEN
LET HIS CHURCH ARISE

His church one day will arise; however, there will be multitudes that are not lifted up to live in eternity with Jesus Christ, as we know according to Scriptures. There will only be the few that spend their days seeking to know Him greater, studying to have knowledge and understanding, and walking away from the temptations of this life. In this chapter, we will examine our lives in order to understand the design—being body, soul, and spirit. In this we will study the sinful nature and look at true salvation, as well as true repentance. Once we are able to examine these areas, we will have a clearer picture of the true church of Jesus Christ that one day will arise to spend eternity with Him.

Every single person breathing today is made up of a body, soul, and spirit. How do we know this? According to Scripture, we can see that there is an inner self and an outer self. Let's examine these two first to better understand who we are.

2 Corinthians 4:16-18 (NKJV) Therefore we do not lose heart. Even though our outward man is perishing, yet the inward man is being renewed day by day. ^{17}For our light affliction, which is but for a moment, is working for us a far more exceeding and eternal weight of glory, ^{18}while we do not look at the things which are seen, but at the things which are not seen. For the things which are seen are temporary, but the things which are not seen are eternal.

Here we are able to see that we consist of two parts. Our outer self which would be our fleshly bodies that are slowly wasting away day by day which are temporary, compared to the inner self that we cannot see. Our inner self is renewed day by day IF we are doing something to renew it. If you go and read 2 Corinthians, you will see that Paul was speaking to all those who had chosen to follow Jesus Christ, the true Christians. Therefore, as followers of Jesus Christ, their inner self was being renewed day by day because they were seeking Him daily. Notice, it talks about a light momentary affliction that was preparing them for an eternal weight of glory, a glory that was beyond all comparison. The light afflictions are for a moment in time whereas the eternal weight of glory is forever. Trials in this life may seem heavy but weighed against a life of glory forever, they are merely simple tests that are manageable when we walk side by side with our Savior. True Christians, seeking Jesus Christ daily, will come to understand that there are storms we will encounter, but it is those very storms that grow us to know Him greater. Without the storms or afflictions in our lives, we would live day in and day out seeing no need to seek Him. However, we are able to see that because of those afflictions in our lives, they prepare us for eternal glory. This eternal glory will be our lives in heaven one day, as we were faithful allowing what was necessary to keep us intact with the true sheep. Jesus as a good shepherd, will do whatever is needed in order that NOT ONE of His sheep goes astray. We should be thankful for the necessary storms that keep us intact with the other sheep, as He watches over us.

John 10:2-5 (NKJV) "But he who enters by the door is the shepherd of the sheep. ³To him the doorkeeper opens and the sheep hear his voice; and he calls his own sheep by name and leads them out. ⁴And when he brings out his own sheep, he goes before them; and the sheep follow him, for they know his voice. ⁵Yet they will by no means follow a stranger, but will flee from him, for they do not know the voice of strangers."

John 10:11-15 (NKJV) I am the good shepherd. The good shepherd gives His life for the sheep. ¹²But a hireling, he who is not the shepherd, one who does not own the sheep, sees the wolf coming and leaves the sheep and flees; and the wolf catches the sheep and scatters them. ¹³The hireling flees because he is a hireling and does not care about the sheep. ¹⁴I am the good shepherd; and I know My sheep, and am known by My own. ¹⁵As the Father knows Me, even so I know the Father; and I lay down My life for the sheep.

A hireling is merely a hired hand who does not own what he is hired to watch over and therefore, will not care for that which he does not own like that of the owner. In Thessalonians below, Paul is speaking once again to those who are true Christians and here is where the whole design—our makeup of the 3 parts of man, is revealed.

1 Thessalonians 5:23 (NKJV) Now may the God of peace Himself sanctify you completely; and may your whole spirit, soul, and body be preserved blameless at the coming of our Lord Jesus Christ.

We are body, soul, and spirit. Our body, the flesh is just the house that we live in temporary until the day we die and leave our bodies. Your soul is who you are in personality, intellect, emotions, etc. We all have a spirit, as well because the spirit is the very breath of life that was breathed into Adam and into every single person that lives today.

Genesis 2:7 (NKJV) And the LORD God formed man of the dust of the ground, and breathed into his nostrils the breath of life; and the man became a living being.

In Genesis 1, we are told that we were created in the image of God—male and female.

Genesis 1:26a, 27 (NKJV) Then God said, "Let us make man in Our image, according to Our likeness. ²⁷So God created man in His own image; in the image of God He created him; male and female He created them.

In Scripture, we also know that God is 3 parts.

Matthew 28:19 (NKJV) Go therefore and make disciples of all the nations, baptizing them in the name of the Father and of the Son and of the Holy Spirit.

Our makeup is in His image, and we are created in 3 parts as is God. Let's go further, it is easy to agree that our body would be our outward flesh but let's examine the soul. I normally teach this as we are the soul and we live in a body up until our body dies. Dependent upon our salvation will determine if our soul lives on in heaven or hell. The soul is the person according to Scripture as noted below in a few examples.

Ezekiel 18:20a (NKJV) The soul who sins shall die.

1 Peter 3:20 (NKJV) who formerly were disobedient, when once the Divine longsuffering waited in the days of Noah, while the ark was being prepared, in which a few, that is, eight souls, were saved through water.

This would be the person, your inner self. So, our design is our outer self which is the flesh or body and the inner self is our soul. The soul makes up who we really are, as previously stated—our mind, intellect, emotions, etc. and it also determines our will. Our will are the things we choose to do, our choices to either do good or evil. What determines those choices?

Ephesians 3:16-19(ESV) that according to the riches of his glory he may grant you to be strengthened with power through his Spirit in your inner being, [17]so that Christ may dwell in your hearts through faith—that you, being rooted and grounded in love, [18]may have strength to comprehend with all the saints what is the breadth and length and height and depth, [19]and to know the love of Christ that surpasses knowledge, that you may be filled with all the fullness of God.

This is for those who choose to follow Jesus Christ, once again. First, we know that we also have the breath of life within all of us who are breathing today whether you are one of His or one who does NOT know Him. The breath of life which every single person first breathes when they are born physically is NOT the same breath of life needed for eternal life with Jesus Christ in Heaven. If you belong to Him, His Spirit is breathed into your inner being which is your soul. His Spirit, the Holy Spirit bears witness with your own spirit. To bear witness means to show that something exists and is true.

Romans 8:16 (NKJV) The Spirit Himself bears witness with our spirit that we are children of God.

To sum this up, by faith, Christ dwells in our heart but this is NOT the physical heart rather this is our inner being, and this is the Holy Spirit that bears witness with our own spirit. When we talk about hearing His voice or just knowing somewhere inside of us we feel His presence in our lives, this is our inner being which we can refer to as our heart because it is the spiritual heart of man. Just as the physical heart keeps the physical body alive with every beat, your spiritual heart is the lifeline to your spiritual being which also lives and breathes because He lives inside of you, by faith in knowing that He exists. We know this because we feel His presence within our lives daily IF we are following Him. We hear His voice within that spiritual heart, which is the Holy Spirit bearing witness with our own spirit. This is how we know that we know Him! To emphasize, just as the physical heart gives life to the body, the spiritual heart gives life to the soul. As body, soul and spirit, our body has life because of our physical heart and our soul has life because of our spiritual heart. God designed the physical and the spiritual, He breathed life into the physical as well as into the spiritual man. The two coverings which makeup who we are right now are our body for the physical and our soul for the spiritual.

Once we understand the makeup of who man is, it is easier to understand the terms and meanings within Scripture, in order that we can grow daily in His ways instead of the ways of this world. In seeking to find Him, where He abides in our lives, our battles will begin in our inner being. As I have said, we are the soul and live in a body which is sinful. It is only through our spirit bearing witness with His Spirit that we are able to overcome the sinful nature where our heart is pure. Remember, your heart is the life of your inner being and it is inside of you that holds your thoughts, emotions, intellect, etc. When our heart is filled with the wisdom and knowledge of this world, our thoughts that come forth are contrary to the Word of God. In the natural, the heart is merely an organ but a mighty organ at that. In the spiritual, we cannot look at the spiritual heart as being a physical organ because it is so much more! The heart of a man spiritually, is what communicates with God. We have to be able to understand how powerful this is. Our soul is not a body that ages and eventually dies. Your soul is so much more and will live forever. It will either live in hell or heaven. Your heart of your soul is also so much more, it will either connect with evil or good. Your soul is continually at war, as there are two spiritual sides battling for your will and both are also battling with your mind and/or intellect. There is the spiritual forces of darkness and the spiritual forces of light. We either pour into this world and our heart is full of darkness that fills our whole being to include the soul and influence our members, or our heart is filled with light that also will fill our whole being to include our soul and influence our members, where our choices will be to follow in the footsteps of Jesus Christ. Just a quick reminder, your members are your physical body such as your hands, feet, etc. This simply means whatever influences your life will determine your choices in this life—where your feet will take you, what your hands choose to be used for, etc.

Romans 7:22-25 (NKJV) For I delight in the law of God according to the inward man. 23But I see another law in my members, warring against the law of my mind, and bringing me into captivity to the law of sin which is in my members. 24O wretched man that I am! Who will deliver me from this body of death? 25I thank God—through Jesus Christ our Lord! So then, with the mind I myself serve the law of God, but with the flesh the law of sin.

The law of God is the Word of God in its entirety. We cannot follow some of the Bible, for we must follow all of the Bible. It is His laws filled inside of us that trains our members to live a sinless life. Your members are equivalent to your body as I shared above briefly, such as your eyes sin as they choose to watch those things which displease God; your feet take you to places which are sinful; your ears choose to listen to that which is unholy; your hands choose to do those things which bring shame to the Gospels of Jesus Christ, etc. These are your members which are part of your body which is sinful.

Bearing Witness with His Spirit

It is only through Him breathing life into your spirit that your spiritual being overcomes and is strengthened, as you spend time pouring into His wisdom that you can overcome the sinful nature of man. You will never ever be able to overcome in yourselves, only through the Holy Spirit bearing witness with your spirit. In seeking Him diligently, we are warned through Scripture that there are other spirits out there that are not from God, and these spirits are designed to be able to keep you in bondage where you never really know Jesus Christ.

1 John 4:1-6 (ESV) Beloved, do not believe every spirit, but test the spirits to see whether they are from God, for many false prophets have gone out into the world. ²By this you know the Spirit of God: every spirit that confesses that Jesus Christ has come in the flesh is from God, ³and every spirit that does not confess Jesus is not from God. This is the spirit of the antichrist, which you heard was coming and now is in the world already. ⁴Little children, you are from God and have overcome them, for he who is in you is greater than he who is in the world. ⁵They are from the world; therefore they speak from the world, and the world listens to them. ⁶We are from God. Whoever knows God listens to us. By this we know the Spirit of truth and the spirit of error.

There is a lot said here. We can see that not all spirits are from God and that every spirit that is NOT from God is from the antichrist, false prophets. Please, do not get caught up on those who confess Jesus as being from God because satan has no problem in deceiving the many by lies that come forth from those who speak falsely. It is evident that you will know them by their words because the world listens to them, and the world will not listen to those who have the true Spirit of God breathed inside of their lives.

The problem here is that the majority who claim to be Christians, claim that they know God. However, in that day, Jesus will say to the majority, *"Depart from me for I never knew YOU!"* You can claim all you want that you know Him but if He doesn't know you, you will NOT enter heaven. His Spirit must bear witness with our spirit. If His Spirit is NOT living inside of you bearing witness with your spirit, you are not going to heaven. When the Holy Spirit comes to us and we receive Him, our lives will change. Your life will not change overnight, but who you are on the inside will change immediately. What I mean by that is once His Spirit begins to bear witness with our spirit, we will feel Him working in our lives. The biggest problem today is that people think they are saved, but they have never really had this conversion and do not feel His presence in their life. The reason is because His presence is NOT in their life, and His presence will not live inside of a body that is sinful. To clarify, Paul in Romans 7 spoke of a war between his members. Paul declared that he did not do the things he knew he should but rather did the things he hated. This war he spoke of was against the law of his mind, and it made him captive to the law of sin. Paul goes on to state in Romans that he served the law of God with his mind but the law of sin with his flesh. We have to read the chapters before 7 and also the chapter after 7 to understand that those who live by the law will also die by the law. Far too often, people feel that it is not possible to live a sanctified life, AND it is NOT possible except through Jesus Christ. We cannot use certain Scriptures for crutches to continue living in our sin. There is war between those things that we should do and those things that we should not do as Christians. However, if you study Romans, it is very clear that grace does not abound, as a license for us to continue in our sin. We no longer have to be enslaved to sin because our old self is also crucified with Christ, and we are set free from sin. In this, sin should NOT reign in our mortal bodies, and our members should be presented to God as instruments for righteousness. In other words, our eyes, ears, hands, feet, etc. should be used to bring glory to God. In Romans 8, we are told that we walk NOT according to the flesh, but we set our minds on the things of the Spirit. This again, is our spirit bearing witness with His Spirit.

God will not walk with those who have set their mind on living a sinful life. This doesn't mean that we become perfect because we don't as long as we are in these bodies, but there will be a huge transformation in your life. The Bible clearly tells us that we are renewed day by day, as I shared at the beginning of this chapter in 2 Corinthians 4:16. We come to Him a mess but as we spend time in His Word, it changes who we are and there is evidence. Those who are truly His will desire and hunger for more of Him and as they seek to be filled, the world gets pushed out of their inner being as it begins to fill up with more and more of Him. I know this because I have lived and breathed this. There have been times in my life that I allowed the busyness in this world to overtake me, and I would find myself drowning in the cares of this world. At this place, I would have to get on my hands and knees crying out to Jesus to save me from this world. Salvation is a process but we cannot lose sight of Him, and it is only through His Word that we truly find truth that sets us free from this world. If you don't get this, the enemy will keep you so busy in striving to be like this world in everything you do. Even if the things you do are good things compared to this world, living a good life will NOT save you. Our good will never be good enough because we are not perfect beings. It is only as we live a life full of Him that we will be led to that narrow road, where one day we stand before Him as we are welcomed into heaven.

John 3:3-8 (ESV) Jesus answered him, "Truly, truly, I say to you, unless one is born again he cannot see the kingdom of God." ⁴Nicodemus said to him, "How can a man be born when he is old? Can he enter a second time into his mother's womb and be born?" ⁵Jesus answered, "Truly, truly I say to you, unless one is born of water and the Spirit, he cannot enter the kingdom of God. ⁶That which is born of the flesh is flesh, and that which is born of the Spirit is spirit. ⁷Do not marvel that I said to you, 'You must be born again.' ⁸The wind blows where it wishes, and you hear its sound, but you do not know where it comes or where it goes. So it is with everyone who is born of the Spirit."

Being born again has to do with being born of the Spirit. It once again is His Spirit bearing witness with our spirit. Salvation is seeking Him to where the wind or the breath of the Holy Spirit bears witness with your own spirit. In the Greek, which was the first translation of the New Testament, the word spirit is *pneuma* which means to breathe—blow as primarily denoting the wind. Just as in the natural we hear the wind blow but we do not know where it comes from or where it goes, in the spiritual sense, we neither know where the Holy Spirit comes from or where He goes. This signifies to be true with everyone who is born of the Spirit of God. When we truly seek Him, we will find Him. When we truly desire that His Spirit breathes life into us, that wind will come and your life will change as He lives and breathes inside of you. It is the evidence that you are born of God!

John 16:7 (NKJV) Nevertheless I tell you the truth. It is to your advantage that I go away; for if I do not go away, the Helper will not come to you; but if I depart, I will send Him to you.

Matthew 10:28 (NKJV) And do not fear those who kill the body but cannot kill the soul. But rather fear Him who is able to destroy both soul and body in hell.

When we live according to His plan fulfilling our lives as we walk as Christ walked, those in this world can kill our fleshly bodies, but they cannot kill our soul. However, whoa to those who follow the false teachings today. Those whom we become entangled that preach what is false, will blind the eyes and ears from knowing Truth. Without Truth, both the body and the soul will be destroyed in hell.

Romans 12:1-2 (ESV) I appeal to you therefore, brothers, by the mercies of God, to present your bodies as a living sacrifice, holy and acceptable to God, which is your spiritual worship. ²Do not be conformed to this world, but be transformed by the renewal of your mind, that by testing you may discern what is the will of God, what is good and acceptable and perfect.

Romans 8:9 (NKJV) But you are not in the flesh but in the Spirit, if indeed the Spirit of God dwells in you. Now if anyone does not have the Spirit of Christ, he is not His.

Romans 2:15-16 (ESV) They show that the work of the law is written on their hearts, while their conscience also bears witness, and their conflicting thoughts accuse or even excuse them ¹⁶on that day when, according to my gospel, God judges the secrets of men by Christ Jesus.

If His law is written on our hearts, our actions and words would proclaim a life that walked by faith and a life full of His Words. However, works of the law may appear to show those as being Christians, but their thoughts are far from that which is Truth. When we seek Him diligently, we fill our hearts, our inner being with His Words—His laws and it pushes out the world because we become so full of Him.

1 Corinthians 3:16 (NKJV) Do you not know that you are the temple of God and that the Spirit of God dwells in you?

1 Corinthians 2:11-16 (ESV) For who knows a person's thoughts except the spirit of that person, which is in him? So also no one comprehends the thoughts of God except the Spirit of God. ¹²Now we have received not the spirit of the world, but the Spirit who is from God, that we might understand the things freely given us by God. ¹³And we impart this in words not taught by human wisdom but taught by the Spirit, interpreting spiritual truths to those who are spiritual. ¹⁴The natural person does not accept the things of the Spirit of God, for they are folly to him, and he is not able to understand them because they are spiritually discerned. ¹⁵The spiritual person judges all things, but is himself to be judged by no one. ¹⁶"For who has understood the mind of the Lord so as to instruct him?" But we have the mind of Christ.

Listen to what it says here, our own spirits know our thoughts. This is NOT the Spirit of God but our own spirit. He is showing us that NO ONE knows the thoughts of God except the Spirit of God just like no one knows our own thoughts except our own spirit. However, God knows everyone's thoughts because He is God, yet not everyone knows His thoughts. This is really powerful. The reason it is powerful is because we are to have the mind of Christ to run this race. We are to understand His wisdom and gain His knowledge in order to overcome, but how can we do this if we do NOT know God's thoughts? Simple—it is because our spirit, as I have stated bears witness with His Spirit when Jesus Christ through faith abides in our heart or inner being. If His Spirit, the Holy Spirit, bears witness with our own spirit, we are taught by His Spirit and are able to interpret spiritual truths and therefore we are able to judge all things. If His Spirit lives inside of us, we understand the mind of Christ. We are able to read Scripture and understand. We are able to overcome this world including sin in our lives. This is why a true Christian will study and receive the true wisdom of God in order that they have Him living inside of them and NOTHING is impossible! Do you hear that? Nothing is impossible for the true believer because they can accomplish everything God has called them to do, including overcoming this world and the temptations in this world because greater is HE that lives in them than he that lives in this world!

1 John 4:4 (NKJV) You are of God, little children, and have overcome them, because He who is in you is greater than he who is in the world.

Galatians 5: 16-17 (ESV) But I say, walk by the Spirit, and you will not gratify the desires of the flesh. ^{17}For the desires of the flesh are against the Spirit, and the desires of the Spirit are against the flesh, for these are opposed to each other, to keep you from doing the things you want to do.

Romans 8:12-17 (NKJV) Therefore, brethren, we are debtors—not to the flesh, to live according to the flesh. ^{13}For if you live according to the flesh you will die; but if by the Spirit you put to death the deeds of the body, you will live. ^{14}For as many as are led by the Spirit of God, these are sons of God. ^{15}For you did not receive the spirit of bondage again to fear, but you received the Spirit of adoption by whom we cry out, "Abba, Father." ^{16}The Spirit Himself bears witness with our spirit that we are children of God, ^{17}and if children, then heirs—heirs of God and joint heirs with Christ, if indeed we suffer with Him, that we may also be glorified together.

Here is the thing, we owe this body nothing and it is this very body that will lead you straight to hell. Within each person there is a battle and especially with those who have been called by Jesus Christ. In order that we rise up to be the heirs with Christ, we must die to the sinful nature in order to live as children of God. Many believe that this cannot be done, yet Jesus left us with the Holy Spirit who is there for those who truly have the inner desire to live for Christ. Living for Christ is glorifying God in every single thing we do. In order to rise above this world and be in like mind with Jesus Christ, it takes submitting and seeking and believing and crucifying our own flesh that we are one with the Father, Son, and Holy Spirit. If this is NOT the life you want, you might as well STOP playing church because in the end, your life will be one who Jesus tells to depart from Him because He never knew you. If you desire to live in submission to the Holy Spirit, then know that you can crucify the flesh through His strength and His power and His might!

Colossians 3:5 (ESV) Put to death therefore what is earthly in you: sexual immorality, impurity, passion, evil desire, and covetousness, which is idolatry.

Called to Suffer

What are we called to? We are called to a life that is the same as Our Savior's. If Jesus Christ suffered, and He did, we too shall suffer alike with Him. We should be able to see that all those who claim to be followers of Jesus Christ, yet their lives have been blessed with the riches and fame of this world, are NOT suffering as He did. If, we are to be called His children, we too shall suffer as the first disciples did and as Jesus Christ did. Are you willing to suffer for your Savior? Every single person will suffer at some point, either in this life or the life after. Your choice is which life would you rather suffer and who would you rather suffer for?

1 Peter 2:19-21 (ESV) For this is a gracious thing, when, mindful of God, one endures sorrows while suffering unjustly. [20]For what credit is it if, when you sin and are beaten for it, you endure? But if when you do good and suffer for it you endure, this is a gracious thing in the sight of God. [21]For to this you have been called, because Christ also suffered for you, leaving you an example, so that you might follow in his steps.

1 Peter 4:1-2 (ESV) Since therefore Christ suffered in the flesh, arm yourselves with the same way of thinking, for whoever has suffered in the flesh has ceased from sin, [2]so as to live for the rest of the time in the flesh no longer for human passions but for the will of God.

Where are your passions today? We seem to have passion for many things in this world. If your passions are not for the Kingdom of Heaven, you my friend will perish with all of your earthly possessions. We must have the mindset that living and suffering for Jesus Christ is the only passion that should fill our whole being that we walk forth daily as a sacrifice for the gospels of Our Savior.

1 John 3:6-10 (ESV) No one who abides in him keeps on sinning; no one who keeps on sinning has either seen him or known him. [7]Little children, let no one deceive you. Whoever practices righteousness is righteous, as he is righteous. [8]Whoever makes a practice of sinning is of the devil, for the devil has been sinning from the beginning. The reason the Son of God appeared was to destroy the works of the devil. [9]No one born of God makes a practice of sinning, for God's seed abides in him; and he cannot keep on sinning, because he has been born of God. [10]By this it is evident who are the children of God, and who are the children of the devil: whoever does not practice righteousness is not of God, nor is the one who does not love his brother.

The question is, who are you following today and have you really thought about everything that you have placed value on and whether it is really worth it?

Romans 6:1-2 (NKJV) What shall we say then? Shall we continue in sin that grace may abound? [2]Certainly not! How shall we who died to sin live any longer in it?

I've discussed true salvation throughout this book and true repentance in chapter 12; however, you cannot have salvation without a true repentance. When there is true repentance, there is a complete turning around from that sin and walking away from the darkness into HIS marvelous light!

1 Peter 2:9 (NKJV) But you are a chosen generation, a royal priesthood, a holy nation, His own special people, that you may proclaim the praises of Him who called you out of darkness into His marvelous light.

As His children, we hear that calling, and we either choose to walk out of the darkness into His light or we choose to remain in the darkness. I know there are times that you may feel that you cannot do this walk because it is a hard walk. I have been there and felt the same thing, but you only feel this way because you are trying to do this walk in yourself. We were NEVER called to walk this alone! It is when we submit to His will that this walk becomes a walk that is just LIFE for the Christian. Meaning it is YOUR LIFE! It is just what you do, just as you have routines where you brush your teeth every morning and night, you eat when you are hungry and drink when you are thirsty. You don't really give it much thought to the things you are naturally programmed to do. When you submit to His will, it becomes what is natural to you at some point. You get up in the mornings and immediately, your thoughts will drift to Him as you begin your day communicating with Him. You will think about Him often throughout your day. It becomes normal to you daily to seek Him through His Word, through communication, through studying, etc. As you fill your life with Him, He becomes what is normal in your life and outside of Him feels uncomfortable. Daily, you hear His voice in every single activity, He is there! It is an awesome feeling to know when you are going through the times of suffering and the storms of this life, that you feel His presence through it all. He has NOT forsaken you through every single aspect of your life when you submit to Him and put Him first.

Saved by Grace

True salvation is by faith alone not by works. This is where we are saved by grace. It doesn't matter who you are or what you have done, but it does matter how you see this. Grace saves you, but it will never be your license to sin. We will never be perfect as long as we are in these bodies, but faith in Jesus Christ is what does the work in us to bring us to that place of true repentance and the place where we begin to turn and turn and turn. What I mean by that is salvation is a process of where He continually pours into us that we change daily. Our changing is the result of Him filling our lives with more of true Christianity and less of this world. As we change, those things that once held us in bondage have no power over us. The Word of God is powerful and mighty to working out your salvation through Jesus Christ. Paul tells us that it is a race. Paul tells us that he even had to continue on a daily basis through discipline running that race as an athlete would run. Otherwise, Paul would have been disqualified. Following Jesus Christ is not something we put on one day and take off the next. If that is how you run this race, you will NOT make it to the finish line.

1 Corinthians 9:25-27 (ESV) Every athlete exercises self-control in all things. They do it to receive a perishable wreath, but we an imperishable. ^{26}So I do not run aimlessly; I do not box as one beating the air. ^{27}But I discipline my body and keep it under control, lest after preaching to others I myself should be disqualified.

True Christianity will only work for those who run after Jesus, so that He pours into them in order to know Him greater and greater. Through this process of chasing after His anointing, we come to know Him intimately. Our hearts become filled with truth, as this world is pushed out of us by the determination to seek Him daily and constantly. We make those choices to what we will fill our heart with by what we choose to read and listen to. Those changes and discipline have huge consequences in our lives. It will be the willingness to let go of this world and allow the Holy Spirit access into our lives. As we are filled with the presence of God, the cleanup process begins and our desires will continually change where we have His heart, His mind, etc. These changes are the evidence of the fruit in our lives. As such, our lives will be separated and holy unto Him.

Ephesians 2:8 (NKJV) For by grace you have been saved through faith, and that not of yourselves; it is the gift of God

As I have said, we are saved by grace but grace does not give us a license to sin.

2 Timothy 1:9 (NKJV) who has saved us and called us with a holy calling, not according to our works, but according to His own purpose and grace which was given to us in Christ Jesus before time began.

So, what exactly is grace? In the Greek, grace in the New Testament is *Charis*, which focuses on the provision of salvation. It is only because of God's love, that His provision was to send His Son to die on the Cross in order that we could be reconciled to Him and one day receive heaven.

2 Corinthians 5:21 (NKJV) For He made Him who knew no sin to be sin for us, that we might become the righteousness of God in Him.

Jesus paid the price for us, so that through Him, we can be saved.

Romans 3:22-25 (NKJV) even the righteousness of God, through faith in Jesus Christ, to all and on all who believe. For there is no difference; 23for all have sinned and fall short of the glory of God, 24being justified freely by His grace through the redemption that is in Christ Jesus, 25whom God set forth as a propitiation by His blood, through faith, to demonstrate His righteousness, because in His forbearance God had passed over the sins that were previously committed.

Ephesians 1:7 (NKJV) In Him we have redemption through His blood, the forgiveness of sins, according to the riches of His grace.

Salvation has always been by God's grace and only through faith, even during Old Testament times. Abraham was saved by grace but through faith. In Hebrews 11, it teaches us about all those in Old Testament times who lived by faith, this was prior to Jesus being born for our salvation. However, it explains how these men of God were saved starting in verse 13.

Hebrews 11:13-16 (NKJV) These all died in faith, not having received the promises, but having seen them afar off were assured of them, embraced them and confessed that they were strangers and pilgrims on the earth. ¹⁴For those who say such things declare plainly that they seek a homeland. ¹⁵And truly if they had called to mind that country from which they had come out, they would have had opportunity to return. ¹⁶But now they desire a better, that is, a heavenly country. Therefore God is not ashamed to be called their God, for He has prepared a city for them.

If you read all of Hebrews 11, it speaks of Abel, Enoch, Noah, Abraham, Isaac, Jacob, Sarah, Esau, Joseph, Moses, Rahab, Gideon, Barak, Samson, Jephthah, David, Samuel, etc. These all died in faith prior to the promise of the Messiah. These had eyes to see and ears to hear, and they acknowledged that they were strangers of the earth. In other words, they lived out their lives not of this world but of the world to come. They lived holy because they were separated from this world. Their desires were not for the things in this world because they dreamed of a better country, which was a heavenly home.

Today, we have the Holy Spirit that came to walk with us and bear witness with our own spirit, in order that we can have the mind of Christ and overcome sin in our lives. We have His Spirit that transforms our lives day by day but only for those who seek Him diligently. God is NOT a supplement that you swallow down once a day by reading a few lines of Scripture. He is our life! We embrace Him through the Holy Spirit only by seeking Him. If we do not have that desire to live and breathe His Words continually, we do not have the mind of

Christ. The only reason people cannot overcome their sin is because they are filled with this world. The Holy Spirit is God's presence in our lives and yes, Jesus paid the price for our sin, but our lives must be holy.

In Old Testament times, those who loved God, it was the same Spirit that walked with them in those days, and those who truly loved Him, poured their lives into seeking Him so that they were filled with His presence, even then. For instance, Noah heard the Lord's voice all those years that he spent building the arc. These men of God from Old Testament times lifestyles were for the world to come. Their desires were for the next life not this life on earth. They desired to live eternally with God and it showed in their walk daily. They lived unashamed of God! However, their salvation was due to their faith. Faith is believing that God is who He is and when you have faith that moves mountains in your life, it will be evident in your walk.

Romans 4:1-5, 16 (ESV) What then shall we say was gained by Abraham, our forefather according to the flesh? ²For if Abraham was justified by works, he has something to boast about, but not before God. ³For what does the Scripture say? "Abraham believed God, and it was counted to him as righteousness." ⁴Now to the one who works, his wages are not counted as a gift but as his due. ⁵And to the one who does not work but believes in him who justifies the ungodly, his faith is counted as righteousness. ¹⁶That is why it depends on faith, in order that the promise may rest on grace and be guaranteed to all his offspring – not only to the adherent of the law but also to the one who shares the faith of Abraham, who is the father of us all.

Faith is not just a word that is thrown around lightly. Faith is accompanied by works because it is only through your faith that you will be able to do that which is impossible. It is only through your faith that you can live out a lifestyle of holiness. We are all sinners but through genuine faith, we can overcome sin and live a lifestyle of holiness. If you are not living this lifestyle, you do NOT have faith.

James 2:19-23 (NKJV) You believe that there is one God. You do well. Even the demons believe—and tremble! [20]But do you want to know, O foolish man, that faith without works is dead? [21]Was not Abraham our father justified by works when he offered Isaac his son on the altar? [22]Do you see that faith was working together with his works, and by works faith was made perfect? [23]And the Scripture was fulfilled which says, "Abraham believed God, and it was accounted to him for righteousness." And he was called the friend of God.

Without faith it is impossible to please God and without faith, you are NOT counted as righteousness unto God.

Hebrews 11:6 (NKJV) But without faith it is impossible to please Him, for he who comes to God must believe that He is, and that He is a rewarder of those who diligently seek Him.

Like I said, you cannot lightly throw that word around. For one, if you are NOT seeking Him, there is NO faith! In order to draw near to Him, we must diligently seek Him.

1 Peter 1:10-12 (ESV) Concerning this salvation, the prophets who prophesied about the grace that was to be yours searched and inquired carefully, [11]inquiring what person or time the Spirit of Christ in them was indicating when he predicted the sufferings of Christ and the subsequent glories. [12]It was revealed to them that they were serving not themselves but you, in the things that have now been announced to you through those who preached the good news to you by the Holy Spirit sent from heaven, things into which angels long to look.

The prophets longed for the time of grace, and it was God's Spirit within them that produced this desire within, in advance of Jesus Christ being born of man into this world. Even in those days, God's Spirit bore witness with their spirit which produced the prophetic messages at that time. The core of the prophetic messages in those days led others to this lifestyle prior to the New Testament, where their faith was justified as righteousness. The *"gospel themed"* messages were concerning the coming and suffering of a Savior which was the Messiah.

Luke 24:25-27 (NKJV) Then He said to them, "O foolish ones, and slow of heart to believe in all that the prophets have spoken! 26Ought not the Christ to have suffered these things and to enter into His glory?" 27And beginning at Moses and all the Prophets, He expounded to them in all the Scriptures the things concerning Himself.

Luke 24:44 (NKJV) Then He said to them, "These are the words which I spoke to you while I was still with you, that all things must be fulfilled which were written in the Law of Moses and the Prophets and the Psalms concerning Me."

Acts 3:18 (NKJV) But those things which God foretold by the mouth of all His prophets, that the Christ would suffer, He has thus fulfilled.

In Old Testament times, the great men and women of God who were justified because of their faith unto salvation, also yearned and waited for the day which had been told to them of the Savior, Jesus Christ.

All those before were saved by grace through their faith and their sins were also forgiven on that Cross at Calvary. In Ephesians 2, we are told that we are saved by grace, through faith and will be raised up and seated with Jesus Christ in heavenly places. Jesus Christ paid the ultimate sacrifice to cover our sins but our salvation only comes by grace and through our faith.

A Chosen Generation

1 Peter 2:9-12 (NKJV) But you are a chosen generation, a royal priesthood, a holy nation, His own special people, that you may proclaim the praises of Him who called you out of darkness into His marvelous light; [10]who once were not a people but are now the people of God, who had not obtained mercy but now have obtained mercy. [11]Beloved, I beg you as sojourners and pilgrims, abstain from fleshly lusts which war against the soul, [12]having your conduct honorable among the Gentiles, that when they speak against you as evildoers, they may, by your good works which they observe, glorify God in the day of visitation.

According to Scripture, many are called but not all are chosen. *(Matthew 22:14)* If you are chosen, God will continue to allow the necessary storms infiltrate your life to awaken you. He will chase after you and you can bet, until you get it right, you will feel the pressures upon your life. As chosen people, we are a royal priesthood and a holy nation. We are called out of darkness and into light. We are urged to abstain from the passions, desires, and lusts of the flesh which are at war against our soul. Our conduct should be one that is honorable accompanied with good deeds. It is when we carry ourselves in this manner that we glorify God in every single thing we do. This is royalty. God is the highest royalty. The royalty of this world will all pass away because it is frugal compared to who God is! How do we carry ourselves in this world as a chosen people in the manner of royalty? I believe it is hard for those who are truly following Jesus Christ to look upon themselves, as we are seen through His eyes. However, Jesus came as a man born from a woman. There are Scriptures that refer to Jesus as the Son of man and Scriptures that refer to Him as the Son of God. Jesus was both. Jesus was born of Mary and had her blood which goes all the way back to Adam; therefore, He was the Son of Man.

1 Corinthians 15:21-22, 45-47 (NKJV) For since by man came death, by Man also came the resurrection of the dead. [22]For as in Adam all die, even so in Christ all shall be made alive.

⁴⁵And so it is written, "The first man Adam became a living being." The last Adam became a life-giving spirit. ⁴⁶However, the spiritual is not first, but the natural, and afterward the spiritual. ⁴⁷The first man was of the earth, made of dust; the second Man is the Lord from heaven.

Jesus being conceived and born by Mary, a virgin, through the power of the Holy Spirit, from God the Father—was the Son of God. Therefore, Mary being His mother, Jesus was the Son of Man and also the Son of God. When a baby is born, that child has his mother's blood as well as his father's. Jesus' Father was God and His mother was Mary. Man came into existence through the first Adam; therefore, Scripture uses the illustration of the first Adam and the second Adam. In reality, Jesus was considered the second Adam because there are two blood lines. There is the natural blood line and the spiritual blood line. Since Jesus came from heaven but had the same blood as man, He paved the way to make it possible for us to have the right to be as royalty. In other words, if your mother was considered the lowly of this earth and your father was of royal blood, you could very well be raised as your father's child and gain everything that one of royal blood was entitled to.

There was a story that I came across and it is even a movie today. This was a true story which happened in the 1700s in the British West Indies. There was a baby born, a little girl, whose name was Dido Elizabeth Belle. She was born into slavery as her mother was Maria Belle, an enslaved African woman, but her father was Sir John Lindsay, a British career naval officer who was later knighted and promoted to admiral. Lindsay took Belle with him after her mother had died when he returned to England in 1765, entrusting her to be raised by his uncle, William Murray who was the 1st Earl of Mansfield and his wife, Elizabeth Murray, Countess of Mansfield. Murray was also the Lord Chief Justice in England during this time. The Murrays educated Belle, bringing her up as a free gentlewoman at their Kenwood House. She lived there for 30 years in which Lord Mansfield confirmed her freedom in his will and provided her an outright sum and an annuity to her, which made her an heiress. This is a very fascinating story and one which reflects who we are in Jesus Christ, as Christians. If you would like to read the full story on Dido Elizabeth Belle, you can google her name as there are many articles written.

In the 1700s, it was unheard of for anyone of African blood to have freedoms, much less be raised by a British nobleman who was also the head of the judiciary of England and Wales and the president of the courts. We can parallel this story to our own lives if we are Christians. God made a way for us to have royal blood. Belle had the blood of her mother who was a slave and she had the blood of a nobleman. Jesus, His mother being Mary, she had the blood of Adam which is the same blood that we all have. We are all related at some point with Adam being the beginning of all man-kind. Jesus having Adam's blood as well, makes all of us blood relations to Jesus through the first man, Adam. As the Scriptures declare, He wished that none should perish, even though we know that only few will turn from their sin and follow the pathway to heaven. However, we are all given the choice to choose a life with the second Adam, Christ. It is because of the two blood lines that we can choose to live as Christ rather than as Adam. It is our choice as to who we follow. It is our choice to who we run after. It is our choice what blood line we choose.

The Last Days

In the last days which we are living, His church will rise up, the true church of Jesus Christ. This is NOT a building but every single person whose lifestyle emanates the presence of God through holiness. Is it impossible to live this kind of life? Absolutely not! It is NOT possible through ourselves but nothing is impossible through Him. However, it will never be about striving to program each day to do the things that a true Christian should be doing. You will only live this lifestyle because of Him living and working in your life. With that said, I want to reflect on what this may look like compared to what I showed back in chapter 11 on those who claim to be Christians but their walk looked no different than that of this world. Please, do not take this literal, as I will explain at the end of this scenario below.

For a true Christian, your week may go something like this, 49 hours to sleep, which comes to 7 hours a night instead of 8. However, there are some people who may need more sleep but I have found when you begin to follow Him, it is not uncommon to be awakened very early in the morning. I will also say this number can be less than 7, as well. Like I said, when you begin lining up your life with His purpose, there will be times that He awakens you early. Myself, most mornings, He awakens me very early to get up and pray. I have learned to just be obedient, even when my flesh does NOT feel like getting up. As for praying, according to Scripture, we should pray without ceasing.

1 Thessalonians 5:16-18 (NKJV) Rejoice always, [17]pray without ceasing, [18]in everything give thanks; for this is the will of God in Christ Jesus for you.

You may say, *"How can you pray without ceasing?"* The word ceasing means to stop, end, halt, finish, etc. We are never to stop or finish what we began. To pray means to address a request or expression of thanks to a deity or object of worship. Praying is to wish or hope strongly for an outcome or situation. So, let's break this down. Praying to our Lord does not mean you have to be down on your hands and knees continually crying out to Him. Praying has to do with where we are in a spiritual sense. When His Spirit bears witness with our spirit, we have the mind of Christ which means that we know His heart as He knows our heart. If you are right with God, your inner being, your heart and soul are continually in communion with Him. You know how you talk to yourself inside without even saying words? When we are right with God, that communication goes on verbally and silently all the time because His Spirit is always communicating with our spirit in every single thing we do and say. Yes, there are times you may be on your knees crying out to Him and there will be times that you are just talking to Him, but the point is, you feel Him with you always and always to the ends of this age. *(Matthew 28:20)* I cannot put an actual number in this part because this number goes on and on, even in your sleep. Many times, there are dreams and visions with perhaps a song in your heart, as He awakens you to rise early. You will find yourself meditating on Him as you are awakened, what do you do? You grow to learn that He has a reason for you to rise up early, and you gain strength through Him to overcome the flesh and allow the Spirit to live and reign over your mortal body. Awaken, do not slumber, for who reigns? Your flesh or your spirit? You will find much delight in arising early to spend quiet times with the Lord, as He will pour into you.

I'm not going to get into this, but the 4th watch of the night is normally the timeframe that He will awaken you. Be obedient and you will gain much! You see, if we were living this day in and out, we would hear His voice all the time and be in communication with Him during the time we sleep, the time at our job, the time driving down the streets, the time fellowshipping with our family and friends. You are giving Him worship and praise, as you go about your day. You are maybe voicing requests to be heard and even in silence. Your lifestyle is one of thankfulness, as you have a song in your heart and praise on your lips. Throughout your day, thoughts will enter your mind continually that are God thoughts— example, there are times that someone particular will pop into my thoughts. This has happened many, many times. I may have not spoken to that person in a long time and sometimes it has even been years. As they pop into my mind, my thoughts are, *"Maybe, I should call them today."* What has been strange many times is that before I can call them, my phone begins to ring and it is that person. I just had this happen several times lately, but one of those times, I had not spoken to this person for probably 4 years. I had tried to call her one time and the number did not work. This person lives overseas much of the time, but we have been very close friends for almost 20 years. When I saw her number calling me, I was ecstatic because of her popping into my mind that morning upon awakening. You see, God operates exactly like that when you are always in tune to Him. There may be times that He is leading you to someone because our life is to be filled with sharing our personal Christian walk with others out there. It is not necessarily about going into the streets and ministering; although, it can be. However, if we are in tune with Him always, He will lead others to us. Your lifestyle becomes one of worship, as you give Him the glory for every single thing you encounter whether it is good times or times of storms. He will be part of everything you do 24 hours a day!

To continue with what your week may look like, you may spend up to 6 hours in the actual church building or place you choose to fellowship maybe two times a week, where you are also socializing to share what is in your heart. If you are spending a lot of time seeking Jesus Christ through your week, there should NOT be much of the world inside of you to spend hours each week sharing the foolishness of this world. Of course, you may not spend the 6 hours in a church building because we are the church. So, those 6 hours can be included with coming together with other true believers to share and minister to each other. I cannot say just because someone sits in a building, that they are really doing church. Yes, that seems to be the place to meet with other believers, but if you were to spend time on the streets sharing Jesus, that is the same thing too. I cannot tell you where you need to be, when the Scriptures merely teach that we are not to forsake the coming together with other believers. *(Hebrews 10:25)*

Let's keep the good works at 2 hours a week, even though your whole Christian walk should be about doing good throughout your day. You may be in the supermarket like I have been many times, to observe someone elderly struggling to carry their groceries. All the while, you notice many of the younger generation that work in these places watch but never seem to assist. If it is NOT in their job description, they tend to look away because parents have failed to teach their children that it is okay to help people, even though they are NOT getting paid for it. This is an example, but our lifestyles, if Jesus is inside of us, we will hear His voice constantly telling us to be courteous, let others go before us, give money, be the hands and the feet, etc. Most of your rewards in heaven are going to be for those things that you did and received NOTHING in return. It is going to be for those things you did and no one saw you; therefore, you received no recognition. Stop in traffic and let someone go before you, even if it means you are going to be late for an appointment. Who are we representing? Jesus or this world?

We will say 40 hours a week working at your job, but like I said earlier, if you have poured Jesus into you each day, the world is pushed out and you will be sharing what is in your heart with those you come in contact with during this 40-hour work week. I pray every morning that He sends those across my path to share Jesus. It is amazing that someone will cross my path and you know it was God. As a true Christian, those in the workplace should know what you stand for because your walk should be different than those who do not profess Jesus Christ. If we are spending time seeking Him instead of this world as in the first scenario, our lives would always be prayed up ready in season and out of season for those who cross our path for answers. Those you work with will come to you when they need real answers. I can remember at one time where everyone in my office lived as the world and were cold, except there was one who did believe and attended church each week with his family. However, he seldom spoke of anything to do with the Bible. Yet, one day, when there was no one around but me and him, he came to me in confidence because he had a question about the Bible and knew that I was a believer. I was able to give him his answer. You will have these encounters with those truly seeking IF you are pouring into His Word.

Let's study the Word, 1 hour a day which comes to 7 hours a week, this includes reading Scriptures and researching, there's no excuse. If we really love Him, we should be at a place where we love studying and reading. The Bible is our love letter from Him. It should awaken us where we hunger for more. Also, another 7 hours a week listening to messages or reading a Christian book to gain other perspectives which is a vital part of growing. I love gaining knowledge and I love hearing what others have gained. If I don't agree with what I read or listen to, then I have the Bible to go back and study myself. This is important to growing. We were called to be joined with other believers but not all believers live in your community. We are blessed to have access through the internet, but the internet unfortunately controls most people which will lead to a spiritual death. We can control the internet where our choices are to use it to our benefit in seeking and reading those things which produce life not death.

We also need to add in hours it takes to take care of your responsibilities such as laundry, cooking, bathing, dressing, etc. If your lifestyle is one of simplicity, these things should NOT take you more than 14 hours a week and probably less, but we will go with 14. If your responsibilities go beyond that number, you need to start simplifying your life because God has not called us to acquire so much in our lives that it takes away from Him, which brings me to your family. The second most important aspect of a Christian's life, with first being to spend time with Our Lord, is our family. You may be single or married and you may have children. To break this down, you have a responsibility to your spouse first if you are married and your children second if you have children. Other family members are also important, as well as friends and social contacts. Let me say for those mothers out there that have chosen to homeschool their children, what a privilege it is to be in a place where you can do so. The public schools are so far away from God, it is a great downfall to America. I won't get into that, but if you homeschool your children, it is the same as having a job. You are pouring into them for that 40-hour work week just as your husband is working bringing home the finances, in order for you to do so. Many couples have chosen to sacrifice in order that the wife can stay home. Once again, such a blessing if it is possible but I am sure that most families do not have that privilege.

Adding up everything to this point comes to 125 hours and we also have to put time in for eating. For eating, we will continue with the 14 hours as in chapter 11. However, by all means those 14 hours can and should be combined with family and others as much as possible. If you go back to the pioneer days and prior to the television, most families joined together for meals and this was the time to communicate. We should be using every single moment we can to impart Jesus to those whom we are close. We have a responsibility to our loved ones here on this earth. Our spouse and our children are of utmost importance. This now totals 139 hours and we have 29 hours remaining. Those 29 hours should be filled with your time involved with those you love and those God sends across your path. You may even have a ministry on the side, but use it wisely that your second priority is not pushed back somewhere in the line, where those you love are not being given your time. With 29 hours remaining, this is enough time to spend 3 hours each day during the work week with your children and with your spouse; and you still have 14 hours left for Saturday and Sunday or whatever days that you have off of work. I do understand that many may have to put in overtime at work and that has to be accounted for. Just know that working overtime is not always God's will for your life but that will be something between you and Him. You may at this point be wondering where there is time for your phone and television. I deliberately did not put those in there because you will be answering your phone or maybe calling someone but it falls into the time above. Our time spent on the phone, if it does NOT have to do with our job, should be used wisely and should be used to glorify God. As for the television, there may be times that you want to watch something that will give you wisdom and/or programs that you can watch as a family but if our desire and our love is towards Jesus Christ, our time does NOT need to be wasted on something worldly. As I have noted, I watched the movie Belle. It was done very clean and it was very educational. Even though, the movie itself had nothing to do with the Bible, I was able to get perspective from it to share something Biblical. I am NOT your God and cannot tell you what is right or wrong. Many times, God will lead us to watch something for that perspective to give us insight. What you watch is completely between you and Him but judge wisely.

The point of this is, that this is merely a list of rules, and we should never be following rules, but instead we should be following Jesus Christ. We should be following what is written in the Word of God. My point in writing this is to show those who feel that they cannot live this lifestyle that they are wrong! This can be lived but it is NOT about writing down a list where you strive to follow certain conditions each week spending 6 hours doing this and 10 hours doing that. This is about having a heart for Jesus Christ and understanding that satan desires that we live according to the list, as written in chapter 11, instead of this list which looks more like the true walk of a Christian following in the steps of Jesus Christ which leads to holiness! This list is to merely show what a true Christian's walk may look like but each week, it will be different. A true Christian's walk will be one that seeks Him first above all else and if you are really hearing His voice, He will continually be showing you where you are to be and who you are to be pouring into. Jesus will let you know when you are not giving enough time to your spouse or children. He will let you know when there is someone you are supposed to be ministering to, or He will just send them across your path. There may be times that those He sends across your path take away from your family. However, being a man or woman of God has nothing to do with the amount of time you spend with someone, rather it is the quality of time. You can spend 2 hours with your children watching something on television and never even speak to them, or you could spend 30 minutes in a deep conversation that is filled with insight of walking a life with Jesus Christ. This principle is the same with any person you spend time with. It is either quality time or quantity time. Also, there may be times that you hear His voice that He wants a weekend with just you! Yes, there may be times that He desires you leave all for a weekend and go someplace secluded, where all of your time is spent with Him—a vacation with Jesus Christ! He desires that we know Him first and in knowing Him, we can be who He created us to be where our time is NOT wasted on this world but on the spiritual aspects of touching lives beginning with our family, and it flows out to others in this world from there.

Different from the World

Coming to the close of this chapter, Jesus created the church to be different than the world, and His church will rise up to be what He called it to be. What we see today among the many buildings all throughout our country are many churches of man not Jesus Christ. Any time man gets a hold of something, it normally becomes civilized as in the terms of this world. Man's finished product is always conformed to this world, instead of transformed by the Word of God. Once this happens, there is no longer any wilderness left and once conformed, the many move in because they can believe in what they can see.

As Christians striving to find truth in a world that has so much false perceptions, it is our duty to proclaim these truths at every opportunity because there are many seeking but they are seeking in the wrong places. There was a song many years ago called, *Looking for Love in all the Wrong Places*[1], and it was talking about going into the bars, nightclubs, etc., in order to find that person you desire to spend the rest of your life with. There are probably many of us who met and married people who we found in darkness. Many of those marriages did not work out. Our wisdom has never been His wisdom and true love can only be found, as we seek for Him first. God is Love! He is the definition and all other love is counterfeit to

His love. As the song says, we look for love in all the wrong places because it begins with true love that can only be found in and through Him and has nothing to do with nightclubs because all love outside of finding Him first is found in darkness.

To take this a step farther, when the majority are seeking to find Jesus but they are seeking to find Him in church buildings that preach false messages, this is the wrong place and He won't be found. Yes, the Word of God tells us that if we seek, we will find; however, if we are being taught falsely, are the teachings even clarifying what that means? Let me clarify, if the majority of people within the American churches today really desired a deep heartfelt relationship with God, they would not continue going week after week through the motions, if they really wanted more. The reason is because at some point, if you desire more of Jesus, you will step out to seek Him deeper and by doing so, you will find truth. In finding truth, you will walk away to where the teachings are Biblical. However, in the same sense, if you are being taught the Scriptures falsely and have come to the place where you believe what you are being taught as truth, then what you have is all you will ever have unless you do something different. The dangers of the man-made religions today are that there are none teaching those following that they need to study themselves. There is NO man telling them that when they die, they are going to hell if they are NOT seeking Him. When we believe in a man-made religion, we see no need to put forth much effort into studying for truth because we believe we are all good, and we believe that we are all going to heaven, as one huge church where the majority evidently get into heaven, even though this is NOT what the Scriptures teach us.

In the majority of the churches today, the people are taught that they must find Jesus by coming to their churches. They are taught that by attending with a group of *"so-called"* believers, that this is the right place to develop that relationship with Jesus Christ, in order to find Jesus. Again, we won't find true love by seeking for it in all the wrong places. Finding Jesus Christ is not about being in the right church building. If you think about it, that is foolishness. Even in the right church building, it is a building! We need to stop putting God in a box. He is much bigger than a building, and He is everywhere not just in a building. Again, it is NOT about being connected with the right people, they are merely men and women who are sinful just as we all are. This again, is putting God in a box. We find Him alone! No one can hold your hand all the way to the gates of heaven. When you stand before your Creator, you will be standing there alone. You will NOT have your church family standing there with you. Your relationship is ONE ON ONE! However, finding Jesus is all about being in the right place but this is NOT a physical place!

We have to stop thinking like this world because we are told that our ways are NOT His ways and our thoughts are NOT His thoughts! *(Isaiah 55:8-9)* By following others, we are following the ways and the thoughts of mere men. It is not about following what we perceive to be light because to man, all churches would be considered the light and nightclubs would be considered darkness. However, true light is what is pleasing to God. If the majority of the churches today are NOT preaching truth, then those churches are full of darkness just like the nightclubs. We cannot separate sin. To God, sin is sin, even though the churches today seem to be doing a lot of good works, our good works do not ensure we make heaven. To find Jesus Christ takes true perception and true hope. To truly find Jesus Christ will take a people who are willing to sacrifice their time by pouring into His Word until their thoughts line up with His thoughts.

Philippians 4:8 (ESV) ⁸ Finally, brothers, whatever is true, whatever is honorable, whatever is just, whatever is pure, whatever is lovely, whatever is commendable, if there is any excellence, if there is anything worthy of praise, <u>think about these things</u>.

As the true church, we should think about these things. If our thoughts are not his thoughts, then to change our thoughts would be to think on that which is true, that which is honorable and just, that which is pure, lovely, commendable and excellent, and that which is worthy of praise. We do not find God through a man but through the Holy Spirit. He came to teach us, to reveal to us, to remind us, and to convict us. If we are looking for that love in all the right places, that alone takes seeking Him through the Holy Spirit and not through a building, denomination, or even a man or woman of God. Finding Him will be a one on one asking, seeking, and knocking. Yes, we are to be connected with other true believers in order that we can edify, encourage, and grow together as one body because we are ONE, if we are joined to Jesus Christ.

Many of us in the natural, sold out for a relationship as we found our spouses by looking in all the wrong places, instead of allowing Jesus Christ to bring that person into our lives. In the end, many wound up with a relationship that was a false perception and gave us false hope. These relationships can be changed for good when we allow God to clean up our own lives because He can save marriages. However, in the end, when we come to the final stage of life and stand before Our Creator, the only thing that is going to matter is if we sold out for what we thought was Christianity and it was a false perception of who God is!

God is calling His people today. He is calling them out of darkness into the true light. *(1 Peter 2:9)* Are you being called today? His people will come out of darkness and seek for that which is light. His people will never be satisfied with that which is false. His people desire a Savior, one that will save them from themselves. He will chase after those who are His. Are you hearing His voice today? Are you seeking Him today? As the true church, do you really know Him? In 1 John below, this is merely a test that shows if you really are a true disciple of Jesus Christ—if you really know Him.

*1 John 2:3-11 (ESV) ³And by this we know that we have come to know him, **if** we keep his commandments. ⁴Whoever says, "I know him" but does not keep his commandments is a liar, and the truth is not in him, ⁵but whoever keeps his word, in him truly the love of God is perfected. By this we may know that we are in him: ⁶whoever says he abides in him ought to **walk** in the same way in which he walked. ⁷Beloved, I am writing you no new commandment, but an old commandment that you had from the beginning. The old commandment is the word that you have heard. ⁸At the same time, it is a new commandment that I am writing to you, which is true in him and in you, because the darkness is passing away, and the true light is already shining. ⁹Whoever says he is in the light and hates his brother is still in darkness. ¹⁰Whoever loves his brother abides in the light, and in him there is no cause for stumbling. ¹¹But whoever hates his brother is in darkness and walks in the darkness, and does not know where he is going, because the darkness has blinded his eyes.*

CHAPTER FIFTEEN
THE REFLECTION OF YOUR LIFE

This chapter will focus on the life of a true Christian and the reflection of your lifestyle in this world. The wonderful thing about the word reflection, is that it simplifies what our walk should look like when we walk in His Truth!

John 14:6 (NKJV) Jesus said to him, "I am the way, the truth, and the life. No one comes to the Father except through Me.

The word reflection means the throwing back by a body of light, heat, and sound, without absorbing it. We will look at all three of these aspects. As true Christians, we are disciples of Jesus Christ. A disciple of Christ is anyone who has the desire to seek and follow Him on a daily basis. As you seek Him, you will grow and His life will be reflected in your life, and you will reflect Him to others as well.

Matthew 16:24-25 (NKJV) Then Jesus said to His disciples, "If anyone desires to come after Me, let him deny himself, and take up his cross, and follow Me. ²⁵For whoever desires to save his life will lose it, but whoever loses his life for My sake will find it.

A true disciple of Jesus Christ will lay down his own life and choose to follow Him. Following Him is letting go of the things in this world that separate us from God. Those things which displease God will be the very things that hold you in bondage where your lifestyle will be a struggle. As you seek Him, the Holy Spirit will begin the super natural clean up in your life, where your walk will eventually become one of a true disciple. At this place, you will bear fruit, His fruit within.

John 15:4 (NKJV) Abide in Me, and I in you. As the branch cannot bear fruit of itself, unless it abides in the vine, neither can you, unless you abide in Me.

True disciples were chosen, as He knows those that belong to Him. The good news is that if you have read this far in this book, more than likely He is calling you. It takes letting go and just allowing the Holy Spirit to begin the transformation.

John 15:16a (NKJV) You did not choose Me, but I chose you and appointed you that you should go and bear fruit, and that your fruit should remain.

John 15:19 (NKJV) If you were of the world, the world would love its own. Yet because you are not of the world, but I chose you out of the world, therefore the world hates you.

Let Your Light Shine

We will begin with the light. As you begin to be filled with His Spirit, you are being filled with the true light. His light reflects in you and your lifestyle begins to be as one who walks daily with the Lord.

You remember the song that is taught in many Sunday school classes for children, *"This Little Light of Mine?"* The song was originally written in 1920 by Harry Dixon Loes who was a well-known Christian hymn writer. Yes, it is that light which illuminates your Christian walk. Let's revisit the song.

> *This little light of mine, I'm gonna let it shine*
> *Let it shine, Let it shine, Let it shine*
> *Everywhere I go, I'm gonna let it shine*
> *Let it shine, Let is shine, Let it shine*
> *All up in my house, I'm gonna let it shine*
> *Let it shine, Let it shine, Let it shine*
> *Out there in the dark, I'm gonna let it shine*
> *Let it shine, Let it shine, Let it shine*

This was the actual words to the original song, but there was always room to add other lyrics, as I have done below. This verse was one in which our church many years ago included.

Hide it under a table, NO! I'm gonna let it shine
Let it shine, Let it shine, Let it shine

The point is, that His light is reflected in us, as true followers of Jesus Christ and light should not be hidden but seen.

Several years ago, I had my granddaughter go into a small room of the house with me. We closed the door and turned out the light where it was complete darkness. At that point, I lit a candle which was just a very tiny light among the darkness. I was able to show her that all it takes is one little bitty light reflected in the darkness where your eyes are able to see. With that one small light, everything in that room was reflected. As true disciples, we are called out of darkness into His marvelous light, but that does NOT mean we do not walk in darkness every single day because it surrounds this world. The majority are living in darkness, but all it takes is that one little bitty light to shine among the darkness where others are able to see. The world is blinded by false perceptions taught by man. As disciples, we should never hide our light when walking among darkness. We should illuminate the true pathway, and that can only be done when we walk forth daily unashamed of who we are in Jesus Christ. Our light should shine at work, in the market place, among strangers, and especially within our own homes.

Be on Fire for the Lord

As true disciples of Jesus Christ, our reflection to others should reflect the light of Christ, but it should also reflect heat and sound. These go hand in hand, as your heat refers to your walk as being hot. We are not to be cold nor lukewarm, but we are to be hot. Your lifestyle should be one that is on fire for the Lord Jesus Christ. If you have Him living inside of you, you will have truth of the gospels pouring into you. I cannot gain His wisdom and knowledge and not go forth sharing what He has shown me. Of course, everyone may not want to hear what you have to say, but if you are truly seeking and pouring into Him, He will lead those across your path that are ready. We cannot force Jesus on anyone, but just as His walk portrayed those seeking Him, He will also send those who are seeking across our path because they are ripe for the harvest.

John 4:34-35 (NLT) Then Jesus explained: "My nourishment comes from doing the will of God, who sent me, and from finishing his work. [35]You know the saying, 'Four months between planting and harvest.' But I say, wake up and look around. The fields are already ripe for harvest.

The reflection of heat and sound go together as I said. Your heat will be evident when you have so much of Him in you. As you pour into Him, He fills you. As you gain His wisdom and knowledge, it fills you and pours out of you. Simplified, His Word is filled in your spirit which comes alive because the Word is life to those who find it.

Proverbs 4:20-22 (NKJV) My son, give attention of my words; Incline your ear to my sayings. [21]Do not let them depart from your eyes; Keep them in the midst of your heart; [22]For they are life to those who find them, And health to all their flesh.

Let Your Voice Be Heard

As it fills you, the world is pushed out and His Words come out of you which is your sound. The reflection of your life will line up with the walk of Jesus Christ. You will not be able to keep His wisdom and knowledge inside of you, it will come out. It will come out, as He sends those across your path. This is reflecting your life onto others that cross your path—His light, His fire, and His Word. True Christians will go forth with an urgency to share His truth to a dying generation. His fire burning in their heart is what leads them daily to do what they do for His Kingdom.

The last part of the definition of reflection is that which reflects does NOT absorb what it is reflecting upon. Let me clarify, light reflects upon darkness but it does not absorb the darkness. This can be two-fold. We reflect as true Christians, but we do not absorb any of that darkness back into our lives. This is very important because many who come to the Lord came from a background where there were many strongholds. There must be a time of growth in many before He will actually send them into those places of darkness which were strongholds in their lives. To emphasize, Jesus does not need us walking into nightclubs or bars to try and save lost souls. This is not to say that He hasn't called some to do just that, but normally, it will not be someone who struggled with drugs and alcohol. Yes, those who struggled with drugs and alcohol will be called to minister to others that are in that place, but it will be them coming to their turf not the other way around. The day will come when those who had struggles overcome totally, but it does not mean we willingly go into darkness unless you know that God called you to do so.

Many years ago, there was a small-time preacher named David Wilkerson. I briefly mentioned Wilkerson in Chapter 9, but he is pretty well-known among the Christian community today, even though, he passed away in 2011. Wilkerson was raised in a spiritual home his whole life and began preaching at age 14. He became a minister in the early 50s, and began *Teen Challenge* in the late 50s. Wilkerson during the late 50s and early 60s felt moved by the Holy Spirit to go to New York City to preach to the street gangs. He had never lived in the dark places of drugs, alcohol, etc. With compassion, he felt the Lord lead him to a specific gang to share the love of Jesus. His presence with the Lord, radically changed the leader of the gang, Nicky Cruz as well as many other members of two gangs, as they found the love they had never known through Jesus Christ. Later, Hollywood produced a movie called, *Cross and the Switchblade* to depict the events that took place. If you have never read the book or watched the movie, I encourage you to do so. It was amazing what God did through this man, and God still to this day is doing the same things when His people rise up to be the feet, the hands, and the mouth. However, God will not send someone who has not walked with Him for a substantial amount of time, into those dark places. In this story, Wilkerson, brought many gang members to Jesus, as well as Nicky. Nicky Cruz was the Warlord of the street gang, the Mau Maus. Cruz' life was drastically changed because he had an encounter with Jesus Christ. Cruz went on to go through years of being separated from the streets of New York and spent that timeframe in a Bible college to learn of Jesus and heal from his past. It was much later, God called Cruz back into the streets. Today, Cruz continues traveling and sharing the love of Jesus along with his own testimony of how his life was radically changed.

The other aspect of not absorbing the darkness is the flipside. The majority of churches today have done a great injustice to those who may have truly been seeking Jesus Christ. The modern-day church's intentions have been to grow man's ministry instead of the church of Jesus Christ. In this day and time, churches believe that people belong to them. It sickens me that there are so many who even declare that you must become a member to belong to their church. No one belongs to a church building or body of believers, they either belong to Jesus Christ or they are lost souls. We do not go forth to reflect our light upon the lost only to claim them as our own. This is merely darkness absorbing these souls instead of imparting truth to them, so that they can receive the light of Jesus Christ and be transformed into who He has called them to be. They are to be His sheep, following only Him and not a ministry. Yet, the churches today reflect their own beliefs, rules, and laws upon them in order to manipulate the people to be conformed to fit into a particular denomination. It should be His laws that are burnt upon our heart.

Hebrews 8:10-11 (NKJV) For this is the covenant that I will make with the house of Israel after those days, says the LORD: I will put My laws in their mind and write them on their hearts; and I will be their God, and they shall be My people.

¹¹None of them shall teach his neighbor, and none his brother, saying, 'Know the LORD,' for all shall know Me, from the least of them to the greatest of them.

God, through His Spirit bearing witness with our own spirit will be the One who puts His laws into our minds and writes them on our hearts, where there is NO need that we are taught by men. If we were meant to be taught by man, there was no need that the Holy Spirit be given to everyone that desired to know Him. If we were meant to be taught by man, His Spirit only needed to be given to those who were called to be teachers and apostles. However, that's not the case, we are all called to be His disciples and as such, we are all given His Spirit that will lead our lives and transform our lives to be who He called us to be—not a man-made ministry. Jesus says the time would come when there would be those who believe they are serving God when in fact, they neither know God nor Him. That day is here when there are many ministries out there that are using man's methods instead of seeking to truly find Jesus Christ.

John 16:1-3 (NKJV) "These things I have spoken to you, that you should not be made to stumble. ²They will put you out of the synagogues; yes, the time is coming that whoever kills you will think that he offers God service. ³And these things they will do to you because they have not known the Father nor Me."

To clarify, there are teachers that teach the true Word of God, but a true teacher will only teach to lead His people to the truth where they find Jesus Christ through the Holy Spirit. A true teacher does NOT lead them to a ministry where they camp out the remainder of their days doing good works, in order to believe that they have had a conversion and are saved. We are NOT called to buildings and definitely not called to increase a man-made ministry, for we are only called to Jesus Christ. It will never be about a man or a building but about the Lord Jesus Christ. Yes, we should be joined together and if you find a group that meets and teaches truth, by all means you should be joined with that kind of ministry, but your individual ministry will never be behind those walls. We are called to go into this world and make disciples. The true messengers of the gospels will be ready in season and out of season to share Jesus with every single person that He sends across their path. satan has so many false prophets and teachers going forth today to blasphemy the Holy Spirit, and God is calling those who truly seek Him to go forth as well to spread the true gospel of Jesus Christ.

To enlighten this further, the word absorb means to take up the attention of someone as in their interests. The modern-day churches have become parasites that prey on those who are seeking answers. We do not own people, we only impart Jesus and allow Him to radically change their lives where they grow to be what He called them to be, not what we want them to be. Jesus will never call you to increase a ministry that increases a man. Absorb also means serious thought or consideration, study, ponder, meditate, contemplate. Think about this, when we absorb something, we have done our homework and spent a considerable amount of time in serious thought and meditation, studying, considering, etc., to understand how exactly that looks. We are to absorb the Word of God but we are NOT to absorb others that we lead to Jesus. However, the modern-day churches spend much time with their own individual plan of how their church should look to the world, in order that they gain the multitudes which increases that man to be lifted up for the world to take notice. Those churches plan their entire services around their philosophies and their own agendas. They strive to bring in more and more to increase their flock by imparting their own rituals to others, where those coming in absorb their beliefs and are blinded by God's Word. This is exactly what the Word teaches us about a wolf.

Matthew 7:15 (NKJV) "Beware of false prophets, who come to you in sheep's clothing, but inwardly are ravenous wolves.

Jeremiah 23:16 (NKJV) Thus says the LORD of hosts: "Do not listen to the words of the prophets who prophesy to you. They make you worthless; They speak a vision of their own heart, Not from the mouth of the LORD.

Matthew 24:24 (NKJV) For false christs and false prophets will rise and show great signs and wonders to deceive, if possible, even the elect.

2 Timothy 4:3-4 (ESV) For the time is coming when people will not endure sound teaching, but having itching ears they will accumulate for themselves teachers to suit their own passions, [4]and will turn away from listening to the truth and wander off into myths.

Acts 20:28-30 (ESV) Pay careful attention to yourselves and to all the flock, in which the Holy Spirit has made you overseers, to care for the church of God, which he obtained with his own blood. [29]I know that after my departure fierce wolves will come in among you, not sparing the flock; [30]and from among your own selves will arise men speaking twisted things, to draw away the disciples after them.

Jesus was speaking to those whom He had called to be overseers of the church. You cannot be called if you are not a follower of Christ. There are churches out there today that preach truth and we should be connected to those; however, there are more false ministries today than those truly teaching the true gospels. It is imperative that we know Him intimately. I believe when I was among the ministries that were false, the majority of Christians believed that the false prophets were people that were very radical and it was easy to recognize them. However, we can see according to Acts that these false prophets and teachers began almost immediately after the resurrection of Jesus Christ. These false teachers are among us in multitudes these days, and those who are teaching truth are few. This is why we must seek Him one on one, in order that we know the truth and are not seduced by lying spirits.

Yes, we are to be joined together with other believers of like mind, but there should be NO man that we follow and no ministry that we follow, other than the Bible. Jesus should be who imparts to each of us individually, as He has given us gifts and talents that were designed for our own personality. None of us are created the same but all are uniquely designed by Him.

Psalm 139:13-15 (ESV) For you formed my inward parts; you knitted me together in my mother's womb. [14]I praise you, for I am wonderfully made. Wonderful are your works; my soul knows it very well. [15]My frame was not hidden from you, when I was being made in secret, intricately woven in the depths of the earth.

David spoke of how God had formed him beginning in his mother's womb. God not only formed his soul but also the outward frame. We are not all made in the image of David but uniquely, we are made in God's image just as our children are made in the image of their mother and father. There are characteristics of both parents that are visual but also there are inherited traits and desires that have been rooted deep inside every person.

1 Corinthians 11:8-11 (NKJV) For to one is given the word of wisdom through the Spirit, to another the word of knowledge through the same Spirit, [9]to another faith by the same Spirit, to another gifts of healings by the same Spirit, [10]to another the working of miracles, to another prophesy, to another discerning of spirits, to another different kinds of tongues, to another the interpretation of tongues. [11]But one and the same Spirit works all these things, distributing to each one individually as He wills.

We are all given our gifts and talents as He wills. He divides and allocates appropriately to those that He chooses which should set each one of us on a course to learn of Him, so that we can grow to be all that He called each of us to be. The reflection of your life is like none other as you are unique. We grow as we draw close to Him and begin to see who we really are on the inside and what we are capable of achieving, only through Him.

CONCLUSION

To conclude this book, I would have to refer my readers to the Word of God which is the ultimate of all books. Writing can be inspired by God or inspired by Truth which is one and the same, or writing may have nothing at all to do with truth. Gifts are given accordingly, as God looks upon His creation and makes each person unique in His own way. My writings have always been inspired, but I have not always known where that inspiration came from. Only time spent with our Lord and Savior can begin to open the eyes to our own soul that we are able to see Truth, His Truth for our own lives and for the gifts that He has bestowed upon us.

There have been many writers who were unique in their words whether credit was given to God or given to themselves, as being great. However, with the creation of man by God, He still has made those gifts within all mankind whether the credit was given or not. As I spend much time in studying the Word of God and researching other aspects of the divine spoken words, I have come to the conclusion and sadness to know that not everyone has the ears to hear nor the eyes to see. Jane Austen, an English novelist in the 18th century and the daughter of a clergyman from that era, noted in her works of *Northanger Abbey*, *"It's not so much a question of what we read but how we read. We must exercise our own judgement after all, and our mistake fantasy for reality. You may agree that the art of art lies in its power to deceive but that is a dangerous course. Art is as different from reality as water is from air, and if you mistake water for air then you drown. Of course, if you are a fish, then the danger lies in the air."*

Austen was a great writer for her time and I must agree that it is not as much of what we read but how we read. To come to conclusions on what is reality and what is fantasy, we must study both and do so with open eyes and ears that can only be opened by our Savior.

I suppose you could take the remark, *"our own judgement, our mistake fantasy for reality"* in different ways; however, I believe that most of us perhaps even unaware would choose life in a fantasy land where everything was planned just as we would have wanted, but the reality is that life doesn't work that way. On the other hand, being caught up in the world we cannot see where there is evil battling against good, it can seem like a fairy-tale of sorts but as you come to know Jesus Christ through the Holy Spirit, these things are no longer impossible to believe. However, the Bible is by no means a fantasy but a reality to those who have diligently set out on the course to find the Narrow Pathway that leads to the gates of heaven. Yet, even those who walk close with the Lord must always be on guard, as the creation of mankind by God alone is the ultimate of all art and we must never let our guard down to only capture that which is artificial art, merely superficial and doesn't take much effort to perceive.

However, the Bible, the oldest and most unique form of art to mankind has withstood the test over the years, as it has sold more copies than any book ever written in history. In the Greek, the word workmanship means a product, fabric, or a thing that is made. The word is used in the Bible one time in the New Testament, where we are told that *"Man is God's workmanship."* Everything about man is God's workmanship; we are His art! He gives us gifts which are uniquely made, and we go forth using those gifts to create and make things—clothes, paintings, poetry, writings, and I could go on and on. My point is that God was and is the ultimate creator of magnificent beauty and form, but He instills in every single person the gift to create—all forms of art.

Real art is deep within and can only be seen with the interpretation of the Living Word of God as He opens your eyes to see both, the outer perimeters as merely artificial and the hidden gem which is deep within the heart—which is the soul to our existence. Yes, the outer areas of art have the power to deceive, where most will never find the hidden pearl. Art is different from reality in this world and as we are told, we are not of this world. So then, are the very lives we walk as we are hand in hand with our Creator on this earth, a life of reality or fantasy? For those who have truly found the hidden gem, their walk with the Lord is genuine and true reality, but for those who are blind live in the fantasy, as they only see the out-layer of the art at hand and its power has deceived the many.

Once we understand how powerful art is, we can understand its importance. Over the past centuries, there were many artist who spent years painting Biblical pictures, writing poems and plays to depict Scripture, all in forms of art, such as Rembrandt, Van Gogh, Salvador Dali, Michelangelo Buonarroti, Leonardo da Vinci, Hieronymus Bosch, Moroder Lusenberg, Albrecht Altdorfer, Jean-Francois Millet, Vittore Carpaccio, Luis Juarez, Gerard van Honthorst, Velazquez, El Greco, Caravaggio, Raphael, Bertram of Minden, Eugene Delacroix, Cima da Conegliano, Giovanni Lanfranco, Jan Vermeer, Carl Bloch, Pietro Perugino, Joos van Wassenhove, Hans Holbein the Elder, Paul Gauguin, Piero della Francesca, Konrad Witz, Vittore Carpaccio, Jacques Louis David, and more artist continue to display the beauty of the Scriptures on canvas, statues, poems, plays, books, movies, etc. It is art that becomes a means of understanding, interpreting, and experiencing Scripture. If you study some of the lives of these great artists of history and others as well, you will also discover most of their relationships were very much devoted to our Lord and Savior.

Yes, the Word of God is real art which is God breathed and inspired to His creation. After-all, the Creator uses His Word to inspire His creation to create.

REFERENCES

Chapter Two
The Wilderness Road

1. Columbus to Dona Juana de la Torre, Raccolta di documenti e stud pubblicati della R. Commissione Colombiana, pt. 1, vol. ii; /Scriti di Cristoforo Colombo, ed. Cesare de Lollis (Rome: 1894), p. 82.

2. Hawkins, K. (March 20, 2019). Gracious Ramblings (Blog Post). Retrieved from
https://graciousramblings.home.blog/2019/03/20/4-9-out-of-5-stars/

Chapter Three
The Voice Less Followed

1. LifeWay Research: Americans Are Fond of the Bible, Don't Actually Read It, Bob Smietanan (April 25, 2017)
https://lifewayresearch.com/2017/04/25/lifeway-research-americans-are-fond-of-the-bible-dont-actually-read-it/

2. Juicy Ecumenism, Institute on Religion & Democracy, Vicari, C. (April 27, 2017). Survey: Americans Say Bible is Helpful, but Don't Read It
https://juicyecumenism.com/2017/04/27/survey-americans-say-bible-helpful-dont-read/

Chapter Four
The Voice of Evil

1. The Orthosphere
Peter Drucker's Role in the Corruption of Evangelism, by Alan Roebuck (December 13, 2012)
https://orthosphere.wordpress.com/2012/12/13/peter-druckers-key-role-in-the-corruption-of-evangelism

2. Church of Tares: Purpose Driven, Seeker-Sensitive, Church Growth & New World Order, Holy Bible Prophecy, by Elliott Nesch (November 19, 2012)
https://www.holybibleprophecy.org/2012/11/19/church-of-tares-new-documentary-film-coming-soon/?doing_wp_cron=1562262556.3753969669342041015625

3. How Do You Keep the Team's Passion for Ministry from Deflating?
Vision Leaks, by Andy Stanley
https://scholar.google.com/scholar?client=ms-android-att-us-revc&v=8.23.9.21.arm&hl=en-US&biw=411&bih=731&dpr=1.75&oe=utf-8&gcc=us&ctzn=America/Chicago&ctf=0&fheit=0&ntyp=15&ram_mb=1817&wf=pp1&padt=200&padb=732&um=1&ie=UTF-8&lr&q=related:wA5xyJNecMdTXM:scholar.google.com/#d=gs_qabs&u=%23p%3DwA5xyJNecMcJ

4. The Seattle Times
The Rise and Fall of Mars Hill Church, by Craig Welch (September 13, 2014)
https://www.seattletimes.com/seattle-news/the-rise-and-fall-of-mars-hill-church/

5. The Beardsley Ministry
Robert Schuller General Teachings/Activities
http://jbeard.users.rapidnet.com/bdm/exposes/schuller/general.htm

6. The Purpose Driven Church, by Rick Warren, Chapter 8 Applying Your Purpose, Ten Ways to be Purpose Driven

Chapter Five
Visionary Leaders

1. Live Science
1st-Century Roots of 'Little Red Riding Hood' Found

By Megan Gannon, News Editor
https://www.livescieence.com/41206-evolution-of-little-red-riding-hood-mapped.html

Chapter Six
The Con-Artist

1. Church of Tares: Purpose Driven, Seeker-Sensitive, Church Growth & New World Order, by Elliott Nesch
https://www.holybibleprophecy.org/2012/11/19/church-of-tares-new-documentary-film-coming-soon/?doing_wp_cron=1562262556.3753969669342041015625

2. Purpose Driven Church, by Rick Warren, Chapter 11 Developing Your Strategy; Chapter 12 How Jesus Attracted Crowds, Getting People's Attention

3. Ladies' Home Journal, March 2005,
Learn to Love Yourself: You can be priceless without perfection, by Rick Warren, page 36

4. The Purpose Driven Life, by Rick Warren
Day 1, It All Starts with God

Chapter Seven
Gatekeepers

1. Answers in Genesis
How Long Did It Take for Noah to Build the Ark?
By Bodie Hodge (June 1, 2010; last featured May 23, 2018)
https://aswersingenesis.org/bible-timeline/how-long-did-it-take-for-noah-to-build-the-ark/

Chapter Nine
Cold ~ Lukewarm ~ Hot

1. Christianity.com

What Do I Need to Know about the Anglican Church?
By Barton Gingerich
https://www.christianity.com/church/denominations/the-anglican-church.html

2. My Way or the Highway (CMG Song# 162657) – Relient K
Writer: Matt Thiessen; Producer: Mark Lee Townsend
CMG Control: 100.00%
Copyright © 2011 Universal Music – Brentwood Benson Songs (BMI) (adm. at CapitolCMGPublishing.com) All rights reserved. Used by permission.

Chapter Thirteen
Living Outside of Christ

1. Commentary on the New Testament
Commentary on Luke 12
By C.H. Spurgeon

Chapter Fourteen
Let His Church Arise

1. Looking for Love in All the Wrong Places – Johnny Lee
Composers and publishers: Wanda Mallette, Wanda Mallette Music; Bob Morrison, Southern Days Music; Patti Ryan, Patti Ryan Music

Other Books by Jolene Harris

The Long Journey... The Search Within

Sustaining in Battle...
Breaking Through the Storms Vol. 1

Sustaining in Battle...
Breaking Through the Storms Vol. 2

I Will Stand & Not Be Moved

I Can't Make You Love Him

Let Us Have A Good Day
Covid-19

www.ingramcontent.com/pod-product-compliance
Lightning Source LLC
Chambersburg PA
CBHW071953110526
44592CB00012B/1073